# CORNELL JOURNAL OF ARCHITECTURE

# CORNELL JOURNAL OF ARCHITECTURE

ISSUE
11

# FEAR

# FEAR-LESS

After what seemed like an eternal hiatus, the *Cornell Journal of Architecture 8: RE* arrived on the scene with enormous optimism, imagining a relational future contextualized by a transitional past. Rapidly followed by volumes nine and ten, *Mathematics* and *Spirits*, this eleventh issue of the *Cornell Journal of Architecture* lays down *Fear*—both adjective and noun—as its thematic construct. This begs the questions, who is afraid, and of what, or whom, are they afraid?

Given today's political atmosphere, architects are often asked to respond to growing fears of immigration, rooted in a *fear of the other*, or a fear of the unknown. Many of the essays that follow both respond to fear by asking how architecture might (can it?) edge us toward a more equitable, fearless, resilient world that recognizes the strength there is in difference. Some of the authors address the destruction of our world's cultural heritages through war, displacement, and natural and unnatural disasters. They face the fear that architecture—in both its physical and cultural solidity or permanence—is in fact fragile and fleeting. With the increasing abilities of software and automation, are we as architects also becoming less necessary? This issue of the *Journal* represents a finite selection of the many fears that have become real in our contemporary world: *glossophobia*—fear of public speaking (p.010), *phasmophobia*—fear of ghosts (p. 024),

ANDREA SIMITCH

Stephen H. Weiss Presidential Fellow; Chair, Department of Architecture

*sciophobia*—fear of shadows (p. 106), *mnemophobia*—fear of memories (p. 162), *anthropophobia*—fear of people (p. 196), and *chronophobia*—fear of time (p. 294). As architects dissect how these real, named fears relate to our practice of design, the authors in this collection speculate on how we might respond.

Junichiro Tanizaki's essay *In Praise of Shadows*,* aptly argues that beauty resides not in the thing itself, but in the shadows cast. In other words: "were it not for shadows, there would be no beauty." The shadow confirms the presence of light.

Architects must be *fear-less* in the shadows. Stepping into the light, we must push back on our increasingly marginalized roles in informing not only the future of our cities, but also the habitability of our built and natural environments, the provenance of our materials, our processes of construction, and the preservation of layers of our cultural heritages—*this is our discipline's collective responsibility*.

We must be deeply committed to the construction of a more nimble and resilient world that is not threatened but rather is reinforced by diversity. We open our discipline to the possibility that emerges when we borrow and share, or recycle and reuse. In so doing we refuse to fear imagination and reimagination of our resources and tools. Architecture must be an agent in stabilizing, even mending, and healing, in building a world with light and shadow, fear-lessly.

# A FEARFUL PREFACE

Anthropologists tell us that fear is an innate trait among most primate species, a principal aspect of learning-to-survive. Still, most of us primates are equally adept at learning new fears, fears that are irrational and non-productive, and frequently enflamed by others among our own species.

Architecture is as often programmed by fear as it is called upon to promulgate fear. Fear has had an historically deeply-rooted grasp on architecture, from fortifications to castles, Guarini domes to gated communities, zoning regulations to building codes. Monumental architectures of glorification, memorialization, and nationalism are as often as not likely to be architectures of subjugation, admonition, and intimidation. Today, we find palpable fear present in everything from embassies to airports, border crossings to big-box stores.

This is probably because fear—as diversion, as mission, and as byproduct—has become the principal leitmotif of modern politics, with inevitable repercussions on the production of architectural form. The fears we once had *for* the other (the tightrope walker, the freezing homeless) have been largely supplanted by fears *of* the other. And the paradoxically exhilarating fears we've found in rollercoasters and thrillers—what Poe called "the fierceness of the delight of its horrors"—

VAL WARKE

Editor-in-Chief
(B.Arch 1977)

have become increasingly popular as means of escaping our fears of perceived realities.

We have been conditioned by films and literature, theories and philosophies, hearsay and experience to presume a dystopian undercurrent to every utopia, to sense an uncanniness in all familiarity, and to amass impressive anthologies of newly-minted phobias. Our increasing dependence on technology has brought on intensifying distrusts, awareness of the erosion of our public and private realms, knowledge that representations can never be transparent, and a fear that our livelihoods will be pilfered by automatons. And there is that fundamental, underlying fear of architecture itself, of its proclaimed abilities, of its compulsion for originality, of its urge to devour nature even while being itself devoured by nature, and of its threats to evolve beyond the safety of nostalgia toward something possibly even *im*possible.

Oddly, despite our theme, this may prove to be the most optimistic *Journal* of all. An awareness of fear has been known to inspire invention, imagination, and substantial change. Is the opposite of fearful—fearlessness, perhaps?—a form of belligerence or ignorance, or is it found in determination or courage?—or is it perhaps a type of calm?—or of knowledge?

Herein are attempts at dispelling some of these fears.

# LEARNING FROM FEAR

This eleventh installation of the *Cornell Journal* calls upon architecture to act as an agent of betterment for the discipline. FEAR confronts our present discourse to learn from contemporary issues and their origins, often questioning the truth of what we consume. As these issues filter through the realm of architecture, fear translates into a desire to rationalize phobias into tangible solutions. These pieces call upon the empathy in each of us to ask why or how before giving in to fear and fatalism.

Anthony Vidler, in *The Architectural Uncanny* captures the apprehension we feel towards the present when discussing the "uncanny habit of history to repeat itself…[through] this anxiety of time as expressed in intellectual attempts to imagine impossible futures or return to equally impossible pasts." One could argue that architecture is particularly culpable for igniting feelings of unease, but this eeriness often comes from associated memories born from the spaces we inhabit, or imagine. While architecture embraces the ambiguity of memory, it is hardly the harbinger of fear.

As architects, we fear stagnation in a field of creativity (Ochshorn, p. 074); obsolescence by surrendering to nature (O'Donnell, p. 284); deceit by imagery (Young, p. 146); forgetting the monumental lessons

AYA
MEARS

(B.Arch 2018)

of history (Boutros, p. 122); failing oneself or others. This *Journal* hopes to address some of these concerns, but by no means has a solution for reconciling the ghosts in our work (Rosa, p. 086), managing self-destructive tendencies (Santa Lucia, p. 300), or understanding the origin of ignorant fears (Pellegrino, p. 212). The pieces in this eleventh volume tackle these irrationalities head-on to renounce fear in favor of humanity.

THE
& EDITORS

# CONTENTS

## Anthropophobia, Fear of People



## Chronophobia, Fear of Time



LETTERS



CREDITS

It's about I don't want to talk

able an

even

about it

THOM
MAYNE

# GLOSSOPHOBIA

012

FEARING THE QUESTION

*The following conversation, between Thom Mayne* [TM] *and Val Warke* [VW], *took place in the Cornell AAP New York facility on August 14, 2018. It was preceded by a number of phone conversations regarding the theme of "fear." It has been edited with several hours of digressions removed, and many of VW's questions eliminated when the content is obvious in the transcript.*

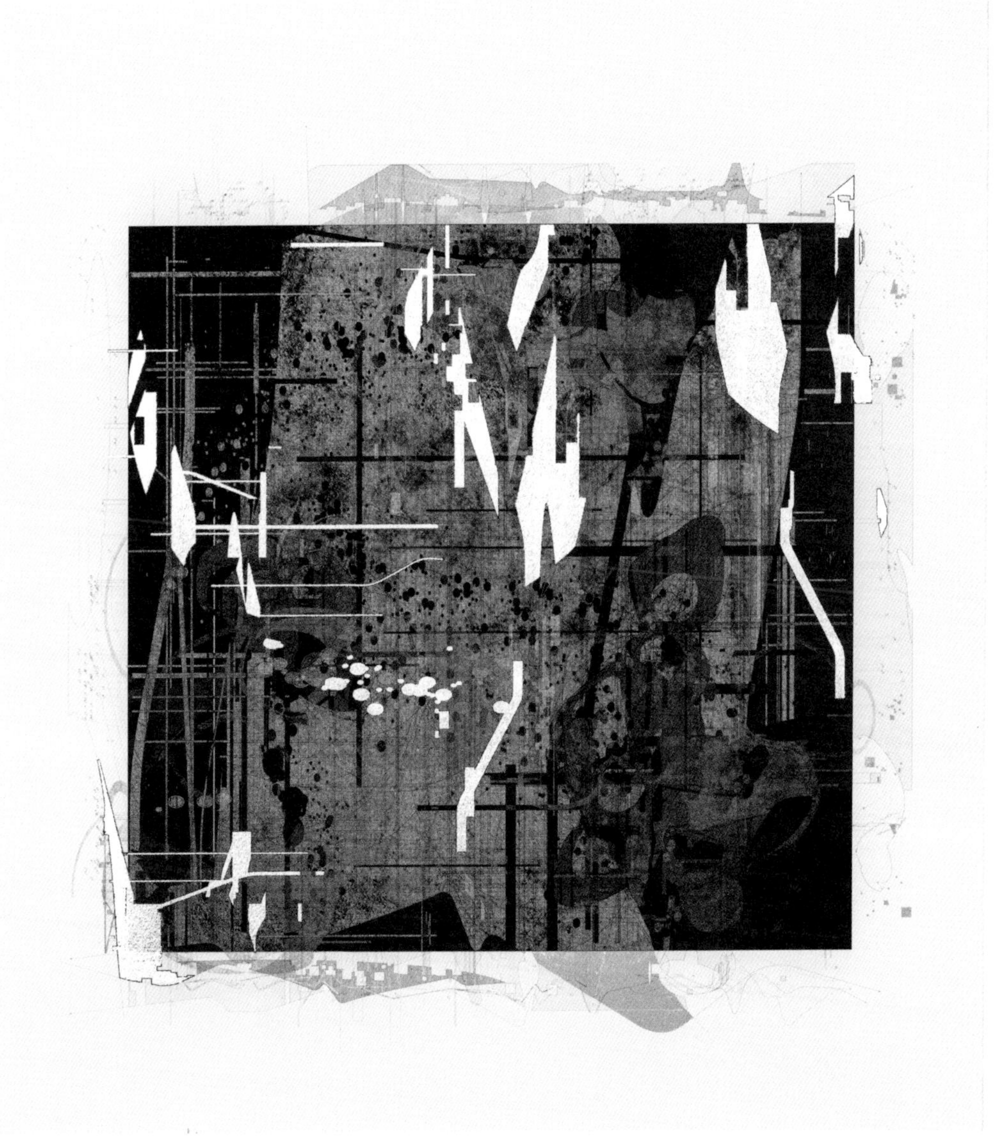

**TM** The notion of fear has often been associated with me as a practicing architect. And it was something I became aware of when my practice was quite young. I'd been told that my buildings frightened children. I find it kind of curious today that I was often getting such strong responses to my buildings; responses that were something like absolute fear.

First of all, for an architect, the public's response to your work can take a number of forms, at different times, and I think it's necessary to separate the discourse and the conversation from the work itself. Because these days the discourse—especially that leading up to the design—is going to have to do with something much more complicated: the architect's personality, the nature of how one operates socially, and so on. Personally, I'm not particularly gifted at this level of conversation. Ultimately, I want what I want, and the conversation that gets me what I want is just not going to be very interesting. It's more like a bludgeoning: I'll do what I have to do to get it built, and I'm not interested in doing the "friend" thing.

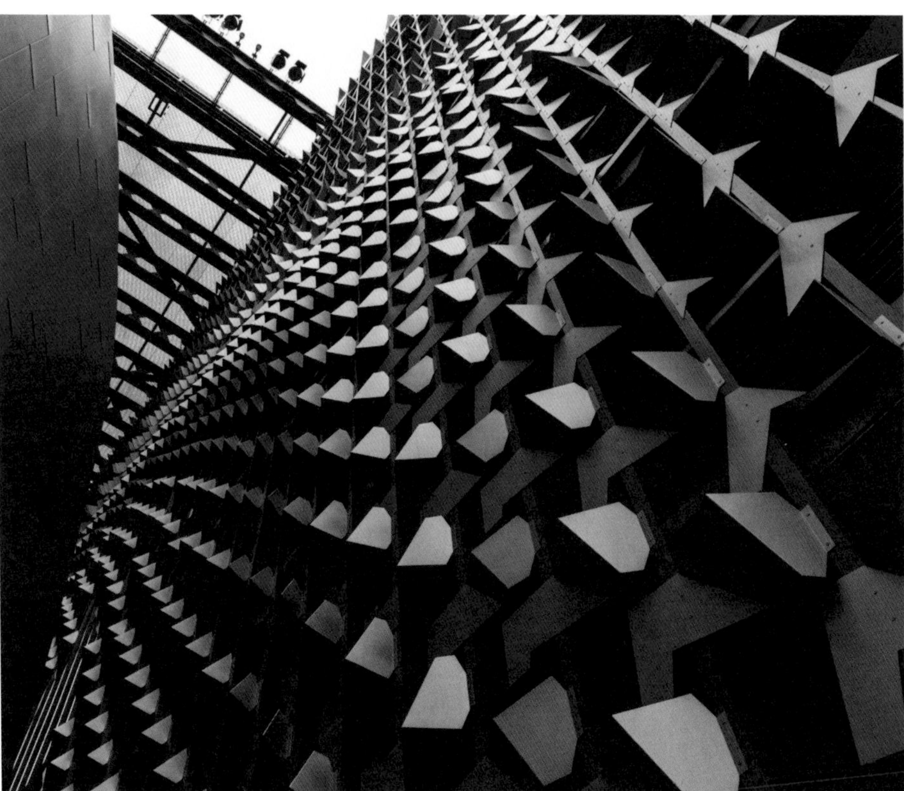

Previous: Thom Mayne, *Combinatory Form, Composite 02*, 2014, lithograph/serigraph. This page: Morphosis, *Emerson College Student Union*, Los Angeles, 2014. Photo by Jasmine Park.

I find that the same people who might dislike you during the process often become the ones who love you when the work eventually turns out okay. Everything before the work means nothing. I learned that years ago.

But what's interesting, what's motivated me throughout my life, and what's actually had a huge effect on my career—on the work that I get or don't get—is the nature of the work. It starts with my interest in architecture. And my interests have a lot to do with the relationships of disturbances, uncertainties, and chance. It's quite demonstrably a critical architecture in that it, by nature, challenges anything habitual or status quo. From the get-go, I'm challenging any permanent notion of belief.

There was a great, hilarious piece in *The Guardian* the other day, about "fake news" and the era of "post-truth." It included an excerpt of Yuval Noah Harari's *21 Lessons for the 21st Century*: "When a thousand people believe some made-up story for one month, that's fake news. When a billion people believe it for a thousand years, that's a religion."[1] And I thought: right, in our discourse involving our work so far, the goal of the thinking is to propagate an overt notion of uncertainty and an absolute questioning of any singular belief.

And I think, by its nature, another goal is to disturb people. As a result, it produces a kind of fear that's palpable. And I'm talking about forty-five years of work.

And so, when you look at the work, it's clear that the work revises our accepted notions of "part" and "whole." Talking with Peter Eisenman recently, he said that I inverted this notion of "part/whole." The part is no longer a subset of whole, but part becomes a dominant feature. Nevertheless, I've never abandoned the connectivity between the two. So I can't connect it to any classical idea, because the part becomes somewhat dominant. You can say the work becomes a collection of parts that still have connective tissue, but the connective tissue is weaker. This is the opposite in someone like Palladio: you can say the connective tissue is still dominant and the parts are subservient. Because I make the parts dominant and the connective tissue subservient, you get a network of radically different meanings, and I can connect seemingly autonomous elements together, thereby overtly challenging any singularity—because the whole thing is about attacking singularity. I've never been interested in—or at least I'm ambivalent about—classical notions of proportions, beauty, or any belief in the physiognomic.

And as an aspect of that reversal, the work's clearly process-driven. It results from a process throughout which I'm somewhat relaxed about whatever the final thing will be. Where I will look at it, thinking, "Hmm. That's an odd one."

For example, when I brought [a group from a very prestigious museum of modern art] to the Cooper Union building, they were speechless. Either they were terrified by the thing, or they were just speechless because they wanted onyx or rare marble, and they wanted everything to meet and connect. But in our studio, the first thing that happens is that, because there are these systems, each with their own expressions, they always do this [hand gesture something like a butterfly], and they never align; they have their own autonomy and their own power, and yet it's totally legible. And I look at it and think: so, it just turned out this way. It's always kind of strange, and it often could be clumsy. Because I'm also interested in the imperfect, I'm evaluating it in very different terms that have nothing, of course, to do with any standard notion of the habitual. I'm totally comfortable with that. And then the fact that I'm comfortable with that even heightens the problem [laughs].

In other words, I look at a thing and I think, "Well, yeah. It's kind of odd. It is odd. I can explain where it came from." For me, it's more like producing a psychoanalytical explanation of an architecture's production—again, talking about willfulness and chance—an explanation that demonstrates the results of how one investigates certain problems. It comes from an emotional and very complicated social context in terms of the people you're working with, the kinds of conversations taking place, and all the while you're making a series of discretionary decisions as you move through the process. These are decisions that are very happenstantial and that you can never replicate, since they have to do with a very particular time and place. The psychological investment at a particular time is never repeatable. And if it happened a day later, and in a different place, it would be totally different.

Even then, given all that, when people ask me to explain a building—and this may be why I've had a challenging relationship with critics—they'll ask me to explain the building, and I'll say, "Well, why would you want me to do that? I wouldn't believe anything I said. The last person I'd ask is me. And, by the way, if you asked me tomorrow, I'd maybe give you a very plausible, positive answer whereas today I'm struggling. How did I ever do this thing? It's abominable and I don't even want to talk about it. But next week

I'll have a different feeling about it. That's who I am." Or possibly, "What part of it would you like to talk about? Let's be more specific." It's an incredibly fluid conversation.

At the same time, we're intrinsically habitual characters. So, if one wants to challenge a convention, you find yourself reaching a fairly deep level of thought that, with an average person, has to do with very firmly held beliefs—beliefs that address the core of the stasis and stability of things—and I'm clearly interested in destabilizing.

Or, I can see it as a language, of sorts. I'm looking out the window and just recording the world I see. And for me, it might be like the language of Joyce.[2] There's no invention, actually. You're just observing the window, and what you see out the window is a series of very disparate pieces. It's a world made up of conflicting elements. Yet those conflicts, and their diversity, can make a new coherence.

And I've been totally fascinated with working with these ideas. In our recent work, I'm interested in using both the chance occurrences and this huge diversity of seemingly conflictual information that can be made into something coherent. And I think it's legible. And often that scares those people who find comfort in the stasis and stability of the habitual.

People want the same things again and again. Even when they think they're expanding their views, in museums they want [a well-known architect of museums]; they want architects who have smooth verbal deliveries, practiced spiels that make people feel comfortable. But I make them feel uncomfortable. It doesn't come out of anger. I'm actually a pretty liked architect. I think I'm a normal, friendly guy. But in working, I'm going to say what I want to say and I have no problem objecting to somebody, and in having works objected to. If anything, it's the objections that tend to excite me—but you know that. The worst reaction would be if a work's just seen as benign. You either love it or hate it. They're both okay with me. But I'm interested in a work that actually shapes behavior in some way, whether at a personal level or a social level—a work that actually has some impact.

**VW** Werner Seligmann always had a prescription for speaking with clients: never talk about architecture, talk about performance, function. That's where people feel comfortable. In the end, though, even with the fragmentation, de-stabilization, and the unfamiliar, there is still the fact that most constructions, especially buildings in cities, are *things*. They're contained. Once you go inside, it's a world. You can leave it, and it's effectively not there anymore, although in the best of worlds, there may be some lingering influence. There's inevitably a beginning and an end. There is a containment, even if it's made of parts—even if the parts tend to dominate, because somehow there's a "canvas" or whatever it is.

**TM** Well, the parts are unfinished. I always leave elements moving outward because I want the reading of something in process, as unfinished. But that's also what's unsettling. Because people want a sense of a finished containment—a finality—and I refuse to have any finality.

**VW** And that's possibly why that large "O" or "0" over the road in the dormitory in Toronto drove some people crazy.

**TM** Yes. But someone asked me about that a while ago, commenting, "Well, you're purposely provoking; you're interested in novelty." I'm never interested in novelty. It's just the stuff that emerges from the way we [at Morphosis] think. This is why I have a hard time talking about the work. I just do stuff. It seems totally obvious at the time. And the thinking is always very direct, in terms of the things we develop and the order in which we develop them. To me, it just seems totally normal. But it's normal under the organizational premises we're working with.

**VW** But it's not really a process per se, is it? Since the processes themselves seem to shift from day to day, though there are consistent treatments of the elements.

**TM** There are continuities. I've called them six points of departure: continuities I see in the work over the past forty years. It starts with problem formation, and then organizational ideas—starting with something like collage and then moving toward a more combinatory strategy, and then willfulness and chance, and specificity of material, and so on.

There are continuities in the kinds of questions we ask. There are also continuities in the formal language, I suppose, though I don't see it as much as other people. I've been told you can spot a Morphosis building, though I can't see it. I'm so focused on making them different from each other. They're apparently not as different as I think.

Morphosis, *Emerson College Student Union*, Los Angeles, 2014. Photo by Jasmine Park.

**VW** Well, one can tell they're not Siza buildings, for instance.

**TM** Well, yeah. Our buildings started out as being always complex. We were hammered for being fetishists, because of this complexity.

I had to wait to get projects that had the need for my interest in complexity. That took a while. But, back to the subject, I think the world is quite simple in terms of its demands of architecture. I suspect that if you go back to the roots of fear in architecture, you need to go back to the role of convention in history. It wouldn't have happened in the fifties in LA. It was a time when newness was kind of hip and a part of that culture during that decade or two. And now we're in a period where it's much more difficult, and you can see it in the profession and you can certainly see it in U.S. architecture, where there seems to be a very large constituency with a type of conservativism that's fully dominant and that doesn't allow for the kind of exploration we're interested in. If you're asking too many questions and if you're too persistent, if you constantly challenge the status quo, that's already a metric of fear. At least it engenders an annoyance: "Why are you asking those questions? We already know the answers."

**VW** Do you think you're finding answers?

**TM** I don't think there are any answers, just interesting questions. The answers are all provisional. But I think all knowledge is provisional and I'm totally comfortable with that, too. And so I think I know nothing, and as I get older I think I have even fewer certainties, other than the fact that I'm more comfortable today with the dynamism of "truth" or the dynamism of what we think is knowledge. But...whether it's age and DNA or something, I realize that I'm somehow comfortable with things that terrify a vast portion of the world, starting with the instability of knowledge, truth, and meaning. And we're all determined to believe we have a definite meaning on earth. The alternative is considered paralyzing. Oftentimes, these beliefs become confused with fact. I don't understand this position: why do people think it's necessary to be fixed, static? I find that I'm more fascinated by the idea that everything is moving, changing. Of course, we all live by belief systems, but you live very differently if you find those belief systems to be provisional and they're still useful. And they're useful in terms of social continuity, in terms of enabling dialogues that allow us to navigate various communities, ethical behavior. It's like what

Joseph Campbell pointed out years ago, articulating the commonalities of various religious beliefs. But in architecture, it's absolutely vital that you don't believe in a single, "correct" architecture, because you need that openness and fluidity in order to move freely. You need to think beyond something in order to make it worth getting up the next day.

And with that should come a sense of humor. You've just got to laugh, "Well, today I'm going to move something. I may not be moving it forward, I have no idea where it's going. It's just moving." (I'm not going to claim any notion of progress, because that's a whole other philosophical question.) If you're comfortable just thinking and exploring, that's enough.

But as an architect, you do concretize, monumentalize, and conclude, to some degree, your thinking. There is a building. And that's another thing that's interesting about being an architect: now you have to live with this solidified speculation that's become a part of reality. But there aren't too many people who are going to share that outlook.

**VW** But also, even within architecture, there's an unwillingness to understand some of these points. Years ago we had a conversation about the notion that architects themselves had a fear of form; that form had become a really bad thing. And that architecture instead represented a fundamental, functional iteration of social operations.

**TM** I went through that argument early in my career, with Rudofsky, *Architecture without Architects*, and actually in our first campus project we attempted to develop an autonomous architecture, looking at the LA gas stations. [Ed] Ruscha had just put out his work on that—or was it perhaps just the neutralizing forces of Miesian modernism?—but very quickly we realized that form was impossible to escape. Because, once it takes a physical existence, it's a matter of the nature of the form, and the notion of "neutral" is already an absolutely subjective notion and already a question mark; and it's ultimately a cultural phenomenon that something minimal and Cartesian is free of form. It's a very inadequate notion.

Should we divide flora and fauna—an amoeba versus a skunk versus a zebra—by the nature of visual simplicity versus visual complexity? It's absurd. They're constructed of similar molecular structures but they respond to radically different forces and hugely different levels of complexity. I just found that conversation to be a total waste of time. But architects easily get wrapped up in conversations of minimalism and maximalism. The description of the final thing should involve a response to the forces being presented and the problems they set, and not in terms of naming a superficial form.

In the formation of a problem, the location of form and how it's discussed has shifted radically in the last decade or so. We see, for example, in the case of a recent automobile [the Tesla], that the first discussion actually frames a very large aspiration, pertaining to environment, energy, and then only eventually to the issues of individual design, such as the number and type of moving parts.

But architecture isn't dealing with these larger issues. We have hundreds of thousands of shapes. We have four to six billion Starbucks cups a year. That's one square kilometer of cups with a 500-year shelf life. I find that problem to be more compelling. This consideration should move the question of form beyond the current discussion. Architecture itself can't afford to operate autonomously. It's a social, environmental, and urban infrastructural activity that has huge consequences beyond our individual work.

It doesn't mean you have to give up at all. I'm not going to stop being a visual person. You can fight for some of architecture's manifest autonomies, but we have to understand its autonomies in the context of its relatedness, especially as works have a larger constituency. With the larger works, you have to move in that direction, because we're working in areas where we have dialogues, and the fear thing goes away. It's not about the object anymore, within conceptual, formal terms. It's making a case for the building; people can have arguments, yet the disagreements will be political. For example, in San Francisco, at the opening of the Federal Building, [a well-known local politician] hated the building, wanting something Victorian. I told her it's difficult to do a fifteen-story building that's Victorian, but you may be interested in the fact that it's the first tall building in the United States with no air conditioning, and it actually powers 600 homes. And ten of these would contain a community of 25,000 people, pre-energy, and we provided an unprogrammed public piazza, and gave space to the Ninth Court of Appeals, and we changed the hierarchies of the workforce, with the management inside and the staff outside. She still didn't like the way it looked, but she liked what it does. It's like not liking my shirt, but thinking I'm okay.

It goes back to fear, actually. With certain types of work, you realize that you broaden an agenda and you find alignments and agreements at a political level, and I think it's inescapable that as a work gets larger you have to do that. But then, what's interesting is that you can sneak in and—maybe this is a way of alleviating some of the fear that's happened—you stop talking about design. "Yeah, it looks kind of funny. But it does all these things."

We can go to Heidegger and the hammer thing.[3] You don't realize the disruption in these funny-looking works, and yet it's still useful. It forces you to rethink what architecture is, perhaps with a little more intelligence and perceptivity, even if it's annoying. This rethinking may be helpful.

Otherwise, they look out the window and disappear. They lose any voice. Of course, it gets more interesting in a culture where the relation of the self to authority is built into the structure of the culture; and a simplistic notion of identity conflicts with our skepticism of authority. It definitely affects architects. The inertia in the profession—the fear of challenging—is very powerful.

1 Yuval Noah Harari, "Yuval Noah Harari extract: 'Humans are a post-truth species,'" *The Guardian*, August 5, 2018.

2 Windows, for example, seem to be a prominent element in *Dubliners*, often as membranes separating a more-or-less controllable domestic interior world from a largely mysterious urban exterior.

3 This refers to Martin Heidegger's characterization of the working hammer as "ready-to-hand." The less we just stare at the hammer-thing, and the more we seize hold of it and use it, the more primordial does our relationship to it become, and the more unwieldy is it encountered as that which it is—as equipment. The hammering itself uncovers the specific "manipulability" of the hammer. The kind of Being which equipment possesses—in which it manifests itself in its own right—we call "readiness-to-hand." From *Being and Time*, 1927.

I am dis

into this

# appearing inch by inch house

# NEITHER HERE NOR THERE

026

MARK
MORRIS

PHASMOPHOBIA

Lucy: Or maybe you have pantophobia. Do you think you have pantophobia?
Charlie Brown: What's pantophobia?
Lucy: The fear of everything!
Charlie Brown: THAT'S IT!

—Charles M. Schulz, *A Charlie Brown Christmas*, 1965.

I am a claustrophobe. I need air, space, light, a view. I crave the big windows, skylights, open plan living, open…everything. Once achieved, this perfect expansive space, I find that I do not want to leave it, cannot leave. No other place will do, I must stay here. I am an agoraphobe, house proud and homesick. But it would seem unlikely, if not impossible, to suffer from claustrophobia and agoraphobia at the same time.

In *Warped Space: Art, Architecture, and Anxiety in Modern Culture* (MIT 2000), Anthony Vidler introduces agoraphobia and claustrophobia as nineteenth-century inventions—nail-biting children of psychoanalysis and urban planning. Claustrophobia, Vidler insists, is almost coincident—and more or less equal and opposite—to agoraphobia. It is a response to being hemmed in, bound by architecture, interiorized. In mid-nineteenth-century Vienna, plazas of a previously unseen scale fronting vast governmental and cultural buildings along the new Ringstrasse generate a "fashionable" dread of open public spaces. Agoraphobia is Platzschwindel (plaza dizziness) or Platzangst. Sigmund Freud may have taken his daily walks along the Ringstrasse, but it was Carl Friedrich Otto Westphal who popularized the term agoraphobia in 1871 in response to patients being fearful of going out into wide streets and squares. He observed his patients' overwhelming concern for being seen by others. Westphal notes this as "a fear of fear," a by-product of the phobia itself.[1] Benjamin Ball names claustrophobia in 1879 after working with a soldier frightened at the thought of being stuck in an ever-narrowing passage or corridor. In this case, anxiety is linked to perspective and suffocation.[2]

In a book review of *Warped Space*, Jesse LeCavalier recalls a skit broadcast on the Fox comedy sketch show, *The Edge* from 1993:

> Throughout *Warped Space*, one particular short piece called "What the Agoraphobic-Claustrophobic is Doing Right This Minute" kept coming to mind. It opens with a shot of a quiet suburban bungalow from which comes a scream followed by a woman running outside. Once outside, she pauses, looks around nervously, screams and runs back inside, pauses, screams, runs back outside, pauses, screams…the cycle repeats once and then fades to commercial.[3]

Previous: Frank Lloyd Wright, *Living Room, Fallingwater*, Mill Run, Pennsylvania, 1936-39. Photo by Jack E. Boucher.

It is funny to pair the two. The absurdity of suffering from both phobias at the same time begs the question: should these pathologies really ever have been conceived of as separate conditions? Would it not be more useful to consider them as two parts to a whole condition, and could combining them be useful to analysing architecture?

If we take a couple of obvious examples, the interplay of agoraphobia and claustrophobia might offer fresh readings of well-known projects. Perhaps played out best at Fallingwater, but present in many of his works, Frank Lloyd Wright's strategy with sequencing spaces was to alternate between cramped and relatively dark, small vestibule-like zones, and bright, voluminous primary rooms. Critics don't hesitate to label the smaller spaces accordingly:

> Architectural historians note that Wright was famous for subtle sleights of hand, and I looked forward to being conned by these. For instance, he often obscured his entryways to force visitors to closely examine his houses before entering. He also cleverly manipulated interior spaces, making a room seem larger, for example, by obliging people to enter through a claustrophobic hallway.[4]

But what might be more interesting is to extend the hunt for claustrophobic versus agoraphobic moments within any given room of Fallingwater. The living room was as open a plan as any American house of 1935 could be. It bends around, ebbs and flows, has no clear boundary. Yet, despite its generous square footage, even this grand space is curiously compressive. The stone floors, piers, and hearth deny any light and airy atmosphere. Indeed these elements are only steps away from evoking a medieval fortress or primeval cave. Wright wanted the residence to feel rooted to rock, growing from it, and so it does. The ceiling with its coffered panelled lighting does not help. It is the continuous band of windows that lends a sense of openness, and their preponderance seems to offset the heaviness of the rest of the room.

Subsidiary rooms at Fallingwater likewise combine claustrophobic and agoraphobic moves. The master bedroom features a desk straddling two worlds, spatially speaking. To its right is a fireplace composed of tiered flat stone with larger slabs cantilevered out as shelves echoing the design of the overall house. The depth of the firebox is balanced by a niche above, a rare spot to receive decoration. The desktop notches into a break in the hearth's mortar, implicating the desk as another part of the miniature restatement or model of Fallingwater. To its left is almost nothing but space and view. Glass sets in a hidden channel chiselled in the stone and pulls outward to turn a corner and encase the left-hand side of the desk in more window. As if to balance this opening out, the ceiling folds down and lowers.

Another desk, this one in a dressing room, gets the opposite treatment. It scrunches in a corner of stonework, the unevenness of which is exaggerated by bookshelves wedged into it. To simultaneously offset and underscore this dark corner, windows break to either side of the desk. To the right are narrow casement, almost lancet, windows, and to the left another folded glass maneuver. A quarter circle is cut into the desktop to permit the window to swing open into it. The corner window can also be opened, the drama of that move always an apex

This page: Frank Lloyd Wright, *Bedroom*, *Fallingwater*, Mill Run, Pennsylvania, 1936-39. Photo by Jack E. Boucher. Opposite: Le Corbusier, *Living Room*, *Villa Savoye*, Poissy, France, 1928-31. Photo by Val Warke.

of the guided tour. In the opening of the corner the architectural tourist is meant to appreciate Wright's dedication to space, to vista, to airiness and the engineering afoot to make this little but telling move possible. But even this moment of breaking the corner is countered by the mullions of the corner panels of glass and the folding of the window back into the massive wall/desk alcove.

If Fallingwater was understood to be Frank Lloyd Wright's response to European modernist architecture, we might assume the game here was appropriating elements from Walter Gropius or Mies van der Rohe, and putting them to his own use in relation to his "organic architecture." Yet its embrace of modernist space is half-hearted. Every move toward openness is held in check by a countervailing burrowing move. One could read Fallingwater as an agoraphobic's response to a modernist brief. For all its innovation and sweeping views, integration with landscape and daredevil structure, Fallingwater is more at the agoraphobic end of an agora-claustrophobic continuum. His "claustrophobic hallway" is an agoraphobic response to the seemingly boundless living room.

Boundaries are a key to understanding the nuances of agoraphobia. It is not just that a space is big, but without apparent borders, unframed. To take a second example in Le Corbusier's Villa Savoye (completed four years before Fallingwater in 1931), we have a house that Wright was at pains to say did not influence Fallingwater—except it obviously did. Villa Savoye is about maximum openness, light, visual depth; in effect, a place that could never cause claustrophobia. You have to go nosing around the servants' quarters or one of the lesser lavatories to find any remotely constrained space, and even these get sunlight. The principle bathroom is as open as any architect would dare design, with skylight and tiled lounger connecting occupant to passing clouds. The more you linger at Villa Savoye, the more you take in its obsessive spaciousness. In contrast to the living room at Fallingwater, Le Corbusier's is a clearly bound rectangular box. Its ebbing and flowing is not found in plan but in the interior elevations, revealing full-height windows to the terrace and ribbon windows elsewhere. Its hearth is reduced to just the firebox and flue; the complete opposite of Wright's mountainside approach. There are no niches, no corner-loving hermit desks. The Villa Savoye is a house conceived to thwart claustrophobia at every turn. One might reread Le Corbusier's Five Points as a straightforward list of a claustrophobic architect's coping mechanisms.

If we imagine Wright transformed the Villa Savoye into Fallingwater—in a process of agoraphobizing the claustrophobic precedent—as a strange kind of reverse engineering, we can appreciate Fallingwater as the more complex of the two houses. It is a doubly phobic project, it uses tightly compressive versus open expansive spaces to heighten contrast, to play on our sense of dread and relief in both directions, not so differently from *The Edge* skit.

In this vein, the completely open glass box of Mies van der Rohe's Farnsworth House is all about claustrophobia, whereas Philip Johnson's Glass House is more like Fallingwater. They are not so alike, after all. Johnson brings the hovering Farnsworth down to the earth. His glass box gets the hearth-concealing-bathroom brick cylinder. This seeming aberration makes the utterly naked openness of the rest of the house bearable to anyone with a tinge of agoraphobia. One can marvel at the pastoral view, what Johnson referred to as his "expensive wallpaper," and then glance over to the hefty, shadowy mass of the looming cylinder. The bathroom of the Glass House conceals a shower marked out merely by a circular swell of tile on the floor and a corresponding shower curtain rail at the ceiling—a cylinder within a cylinder, one spinning into the other—burrowing again. Spatial theorist Steven Connor introduces two terms to describe these spaces: spatiopetal, that which is contained by the glass walls, and spatiofugal, that which is contained by the cylinder.

> Gaston Bachelard evokes in his *The Poetics of Space* the qualities of the burrow, the nest and the shell, that primary form of abode made by the simple rotation of a body in its own space. The snugness and comfort of the burrow derive from the fact that is formed from the body's own shape and the track of its movements. This is space scooped or spun out from the inside outwards. Most buildings are not formed in this way. Rather than burrowing out space, they lasso it, by an act of projection (the model, the plan), followed by encapsulation of air.[5]

The clautrophobe prefers spatiopetal architecture, the agoraphobe spatiofugal. The hearth-bathroom permits the rest of the house be, well, next to nothing. Like Wright, Johnson offers both the expanse and the cave. Like Le Corbusier, Mies van der Rohe has no need of caves to allay agoraphobic fears.

Philip Johnson, *Interior, Glass House*, New Canaan, Connecticut, 1948-49. Photo by Jack E. Boucher.

When fear is the objective, say with gothic or horror genre literature, agoraphobia and claustrophobia are useful to the cause. Looking to what many critics consider the finest haunted-house book ever written,[6] *The Haunting of Hill House* (1959) by Shirley Jackson is notable for its total lack of blood and gore or even visible ghosts. Instead, it focuses on the characters' inner turmoil and backstories. A pervading sense of dread and terror is established and maintained almost exclusively through architecture. For Jackson, the haunted house was not merely a setting for narrative, but a foreground, equal to any character. To accomplish this, the author drew detailed floorplans and consulted photographs of real "haunted" houses in and around San Francisco to guide her writing. Her favourite of these was a house she only later realised was designed by her great-great-grandfather. From its opening lines, the house's centrality is established:

> Hill House, not sane, stood by itself against its hills, holding darkness within; it had stood so for eighty years and might stand for eighty more. Within, walls continued upright, bricks met neatly, floors were firm, and doors were sensibly shut; silence lay steadily against the wood and stone of Hill House, and whatever walked there, walked alone.[7]

Hill House confounds its occupants through mischievous design and triggers for claustrophobes. Dr. Montague, the researcher responsible for bringing a ragtag group of visitors to Hill House, explains why its design causes doors to spookily swing shut and the stairs to cause dizziness: "...every angle is slightly wrong. Hugh Crain must have detested other people and their sensible squared-away houses, because he made his house to suit his mind. Angles which you assume are the right angles you are accustomed to, and have every right to expect are true, are actually a fraction of a degree off in one direction or another."[8] But the real scare is had in getting lost in the house and feeling hemmed in. The Victorian house plan is to blame, according to Dr. Montague, "Some of these rooms are entirely inside rooms...No windows, no access to the outdoors at all. However, a series of enclosed rooms is not altogether surprising in a house of this period, particularly when you recall that what windows they did have were heavily shrouded with hangings and draperies."[9] The plan, these nested claustrophobic rooms, starts to drive them all mad. The most disturbed character, Eleanor, constantly dreams of leaving the house for a picnic, but fears she is fusing with the house, "I am disappearing inch by inch into this house," perhaps the ultimate fear of the claustrophobe.

Previous: Sam Jacob, *Inverted Glass House*, 2012, mixed media. This page: Denise Nestor, *Portrait of Shirley Jackson for the Atlantic*, 2016, graphite on paper.

*The Haunting of Hill House* was Jackson's fifth and most famous novel. By the time she was writing it her health was faltering. Obese and chain-smoking, she suffered from acute anxiety and agoraphobia. The book was therapeutic to the extent that she could use her suffering—the inability to leave her own home—to inspire the plot of her story. Making her haunted house crushingly claustrophobic was both a counter to her agoraphobia and an indication that, alongside agoraphobia, she was also becoming claustrophobic and frustrated by the self-induced confinement causing her to disappear "inch by inch" into her own house and away from public life. Jackson's last novel was, appropriately, all about agoraphobia. *We Have Always Lived in the Castle* (1962) was lauded by critics; an exceptionally strong swansong. The story, technically a murder mystery, involves two sisters—Kat and Constance Blackwood—living apart from their community in an old house that had always belonged to their family. The murders have already taken place at the start of the book. All the other members of the Blackwood clan, save for an invalid uncle, have died from a poisoned dessert—arsenic substituted for sugar on blackberries—served at the family meal. The three live a reclusive but comfortable life behind garden gates and thick doors. Only Kat ventures out weekly for groceries and library books, taking all sorts of abuse from the townspeople certain that Constance, who cleaned the sugar bowl before the police arrived, was behind the murders.

Bit by bit the reader comes to understand that Constance is agoraphobic and increasingly unable to even venture into her own garden. Her world is one of ritual cooking and cleaning, caring for her uncle and wayward sister, who is the real murderer. The word agoraphobia is never used, but Constance's condition is central to the plot. Kat is Constance's co-dependent and helps protect her sister and the family home with many magical hidden safeguards: "All our land was enriched with my treasures buried in it, thickly inhabited just below the surface with my marbles and my teeth and my colored stones, all perhaps turned to jewels by now, held together under the ground in a powerful taut web which never loosened, but held fast to guard us."[10] The arrival of scheming cousin Charles intent on sussing out where the safe full of valuables is hidden in the house, ingratiates himself with Constance and starts to upend the peace and autonomy of the Blackwood home. Frustrated that her magic charms have not kept Charles away, Kat angrily tips his still smoking pipe into a wastepaper basket only to set the whole house alight. The fire destroys half the house, leaving them to make do in a ruin, which they come to see as an improvement: "Our house was a castle, turreted and open to the sky."[11] Constance laughs until she cries looking at the ruined stairway and the gap in the roof. "I am so happy," she admits. Constance is thus released from the oppression of the old house without having to leave sacred home turf. Her happiness is not about beating agoraphobia, but, rather, its resultant or associated claustrophobia; the twinned conditions each getting something out of the architectural changes brought by the fire. Agoraphobia triumphs in the novel, claustrophobia is conquered.

If, as Vidler outlines, agoraphobia and claustrophobia are invented terms for over-sensitivity to space, either too open or closed, can we assume that such sensitivity, in lesser register, is an abiding quality of any architect? Are not all architects at least mildly agoraclaustrophobic? Would not acute awareness of space—its shaping, framing, sequencing, visual and emotional perception—be one of the things that compels architects to be architects? Benjamin Ball resisted the idea of combining all morbid fears related to space under the blanket term topophobia, wanting to keep agoraphobia and claustrophobia distinct. Topophobia may be too broad a term, like pantophobia, to be useful, but it acknowledges the clear relationship between agoraphobia and claustrophobia and suggests a spatial sensitivity spectrum across which we might place any architect, or any architectural project. When Johnson defines architecture as "the art of how to waste space," he at least offers that architecture is bound up in making spaces beyond reasons of functionality. Wastefulness in this context might be attributable to aesthetic aspiration, but it could also be down to fear and navigating (or playing with) topophobic anxieties. In vivo exposure, facing up to your fears, is a treatment common to both agoraphobia and claustrophobia. Stepping out into a wide street, or taking an elevator up and down, are pathways to alleviating these conditions. It is recommended that one take a friend along as part of the therapy. The presence of a sympathetic companion has as much to do with handling the situation as anything else, and no one could be more sympathetic, in either case, than an architect.

1 Vidler, Anthony, *Warped Space: Art, Architecture, and Anxiety in Modern Culture* (Cambridge: MIT Press, 2000), p. 27.

2 Ibid., p. 32.

3 LeCavalier, Jesse, Book Review, *Loud Paper*, "Transit," vol. 4, iss. 1 (2001).

4 Curtis, Wayne, "Sitting Down with Frank Lloyd Wright," *New York Times*, December 9, 2001.

5 Connor, Steven, "Building Breathing Space," Public lecture, The Bartlett School of Architecture (London: 3 March 2004), transcription accessed on December 1, 2018 at http://stevenconnor.com/bbs.html.

6 As reviewed in King, Stephen, *Danse Macabre* (New York: Gallery Books, 1981), p. 310.

7 Jackson, Shirley, *The Haunting of Hill House* (New York: Viking Penguin, 1959), pp. 3.16.

8 Ibid., pp. 105-106.

9 Ibid., p. 64.

10 Jackson, Shirley, *We have Always Lived in the Castle* (New York: Viking Press, 1962), p. 41.

11 Ibid., pp. 144-145.

# THE ART OF THE IMPOSSIBLE

042

STEPHEN
DUNCOMBE

PHASMOPHOBIA

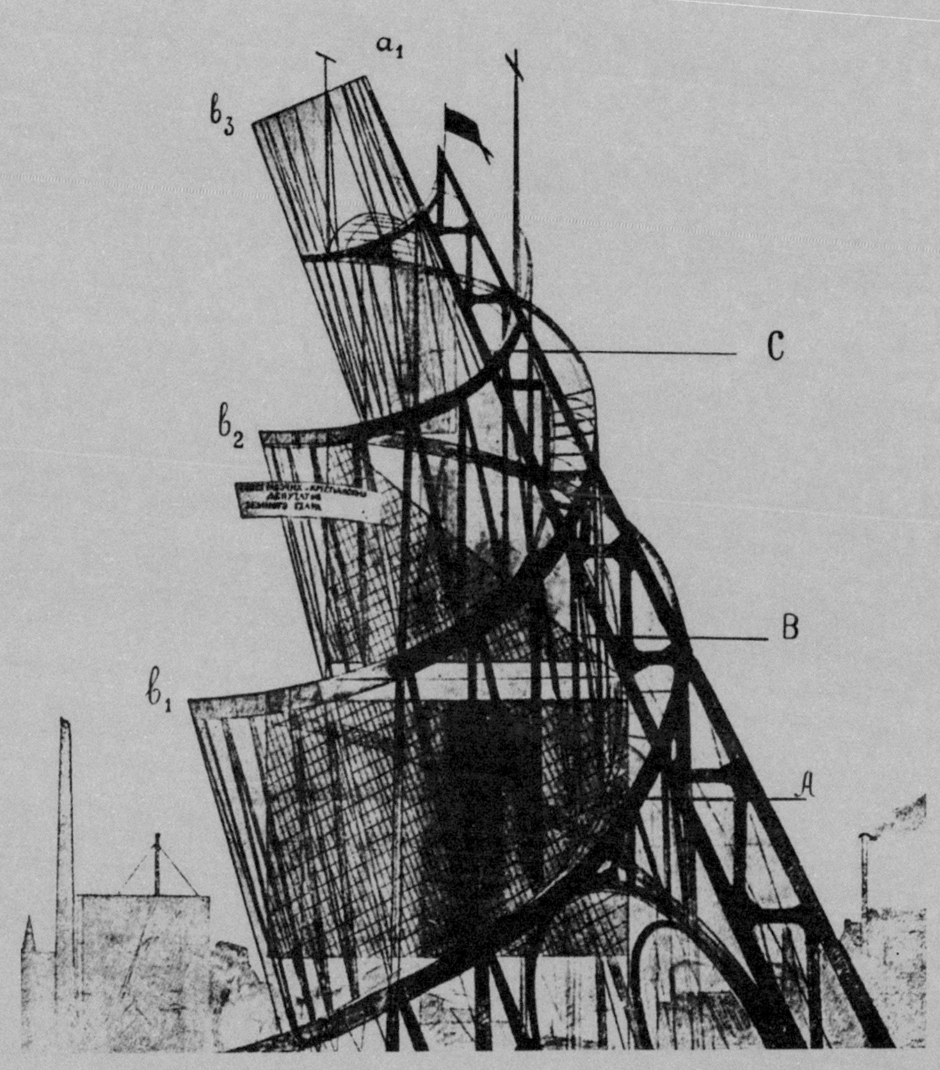
$a_1$
$b_3$
C
$b_2$
B
$b_1$
A

## FIRING THE IMAGINATION

> I could name at least ten ideas I would have found intolerable or incomprehensible and frightening, except as they came after dreams and poems.

With these words, the poet Audre Lorde teaches us two important lessons. First, fear is the prison warden of the imagination. What is unfamiliar, uncommon, or unimaginable is deeply frightening; it upsets our expectations of how the world is supposed to operate, including the limits of possibility. Lorde's second lesson, however, is equally important: art—and by extension architecture—can free us from this prison of the possible. How, then, might we think about an art of the impossible? Vladimir Tatlin's Monument to the Third International serves as a case study and appropriate point of departure.

Previous: Vladimir Tatlin, *Plan for Tatlin's Tower*. For *Pamiatnik III Internatsionala (Monument to the Third International)*.1920. This page: Vladimir Tatlin, *Tatlin's Tower in situ*, 1919-1920, photomontage.

Commissioned soon after the Russian Revolution, in 1919, by The Department of Artistic Work of the People's Commissariat for Enlightenment, Tatlin's Tower was to stand 400 meters tall, almost 25 percent higher than the Eiffel Tower, and straddle the Neva river in central Petrograd. Tilting at the same angle as the Earth (23.5 degrees) and taking the idea of "revolution" quite literally, the tower was constructed of three internal revolving levels. At the bottom, a massive glass and steel cube housing the Soviet legislative assemblies rotated once per year. In the middle, a pyramidal structure serving as assembly spaces for executive committees revolved once per month. Above that, a cylinder containing information and propaganda services completed a single rotation daily. Complementing this cylinder, a giant screen equipped with massive loudspeakers would broadcast the latest revolutionary news. Perched atop this political edifice, Tatlin proposed a hemisphere housing radio equipment capable of transmitting propaganda world-wide and a projector with the ability to cast images on the clouds.

Needless to say, the Monument to the Third International was never built.[1] Excluding prohibitive material constraints, the Tower's structural feasibility remains contested. The closest realization of Tatlin's dream monument manifested as a five-meter model built of wood, tin, paper, nails, and glue (and a smaller, cruder one photographed being dragged around on a float as part of a Mayday parade in Petrograd in 1920).

The monument's infeasibility was recognized and criticized at the time by Tatlin's cultural and political comrades. Though generally supportive of the early Soviet avant-garde, Anatoly Lunacharsky, the Soviet Union's first Commissar of Enlightenment and commissioner of the Monument to the Third International, openly critiqued the constructivists with whom Tatlin affiliated, accusing them of "…play[ing] at being engineers, but [not knowing] as much of the essence of machinery as a savage." Writing about Tatlin in particular, Lunacharsky leveled a related review: "Tatlin mimics the machine…[but] this is a machine on which it is impossible to work."[2] Other revolutionaries were no less critical. Leon Trotsky, reflecting upon the monument in his book *Literature and Revolution*, wrote, "I remember seeing once, when a child, a wooden temple built in a beer bottle. This fired my imagination, but I did not ask myself at that time what it was for…" Now, regarding Tatlin's monument, he writes: "I cannot refrain from the question: What is it for?"[3]

Trotsky, of course, unknowingly answered his own question regarding the function of Tatlin's monument. What is it for? *To fire the imagination!* Later in his life, Lunacharsky came to understand and appreciate this imaginative function of design. Writing about Vladimir Mayakovsky's poems in 1931, a year before Socialist Realism was to become state practice and two years before his death, he bravely defended the revolutionary function of the patently impossible:

ДА ЗДРАВСТВУЕТ

> …though [Mayakovsky's] works are not in themselves utilitarian, they should provide the stimuli or methods or instructions for producing these utilitarian things. All this will bring about a change in environment and, therefore, a change in society itself.[4]

Tatlin himself, as much as he wrapped himself in the utilitarian rhetoric of the revolutionary Russian avant-garde, clearly believed that design could have another function.[5] The ideal of "uniting purely artistic forms with purely utilitarian aims," Tatlin writes in his proclamation "Art into Technology," is to create "models which stimulate inventions in the business of creating a new world."[6]

Impossible designs require this revolutionary mindset as fire for the imagination and stimuli for new methods of thinking and inventing—this is hardly a novel idea. Designers and architects design objects for utilitarian use as well as what educator Seymour Papert termed "objects-to-think-with."[7] What I want to do is neither praise nor bury this latter ideal of design, but instead deepen our understanding of what this entails and its embodied politics by presenting a radical way of *thinking about objects to think with*.

## UTOPIA

To unpack these thoughts, I want to go back 400 years before Tatlin's Tower, to Thomas More's *Utopia*—the original impossible design. As depicted by Raphael Hythloday—the traveler who "discovers" the island and describes it to More—it lives up to its name. The utopic island operates without money, private property, or privately held wealth; there is a democratically elected government and priesthood, and women can attain positions of power; living and labor are rationally planned for the good of all and there is a public health and education; Utopians are guaranteed the freedom of speech and religion; the island provides foreign aid to other countries, targeted toward their poor; and, perhaps most utopian of all, there are no lawyers.

*Utopia*, in brief, is everything More's sixteenth-century Europe is not. One of the few anecdotes in this book successfully illustrates this dichotomy with a group of foreign ambassadors who come to Utopia and, seeking to impress the Utopians, bedeck themselves in gold, silver, and gems. The citizens, however, are not impressed; in fact, quite the opposite. For the Utopians such finery has a different signification: jewels are children's playthings

Vladimir Tatlin. *Tatlin's Tower Model*. In *Tatlin (Protiv kubizma)* [*Татлин (Против кубизма)*]. By Nikolai Punin. Gosizdat, Petrograd, 1921.

and gold and silver are reserved for, among other things, chamber pots. ("O magnificent scorn for gold!" the marginalia in the book reads at this point.) *Utopia* is the world inverted.

When More wrote *Utopia* in 1515 and 1516, literary representations of far-away lands frequently abided by radically different principles: philosophical imaginings like Plato's *Republic*, fanciful travelogues like those of Sir John Mandeville, and—most important—the alternative worlds set forth in *The Bible* (promised lands of milk and honey and visions of heavens where the lion lay down with the lamb), were familiar models. More's *Utopia* literally names the practice, but as the seminal text to define a now commonplace term, it is an exceedingly curious book. *Utopia* is full of contradictions, riddles and paradoxes, yet the grandest irony remains the title itself. Utopia, a made-up word composed by More from the Greek *ou*, meaning "not," and *topos*, meaning "place," literally translates into "no place." In addition, the storyteller of this magic land, Raphael Hythloday, stems from the Hythlodaeus (from the original Latin in which the book was written) and the Greek word Huthlos, meaning *nonsense*. We are told a story of a place named out of existence, by a narrator named equally as unreliable. Thus begins the debate: Is the entirety of More's *Utopia* a satire, an exercise demonstrating the absurdity of social alternatives? Or is it an earnest effort to suggest and promote such radical ideals?

Evidence suggests and even encourages a sincere interpretation of *Utopia*. More was a devout Christian who once contemplated the priesthood and would later give his life for his beliefs. He held the community of common property of Christ's disciples as an ideal and one can argue that this communal model provided the ideological basis for More's utopian society. Indeed, Hythloday tells us that the Utopians, while holding fast to their religious plurality, naturally take to Christianity because it espouses ideals so close to their own. In sum: it strains credulity to believe that More would satirize the community of Christ. In addition, *Utopia*'s description in painstaking detail of the island, the cities, the people and their institutions, as well as facsimiles of maps and alphabets, intend to convince the reader that such a place exists. In one of the letters that accompanied the original 1516–1518 printings of *Utopia*, More worries that he may have recorded the span of a certain bridge incorrectly and begs his friend Peter Giles to ask Raphael Hythloday for the exact measurement when he sees him next. Such a public concern with veracity suggests that More wanted his *Utopia* to be taken seriously.

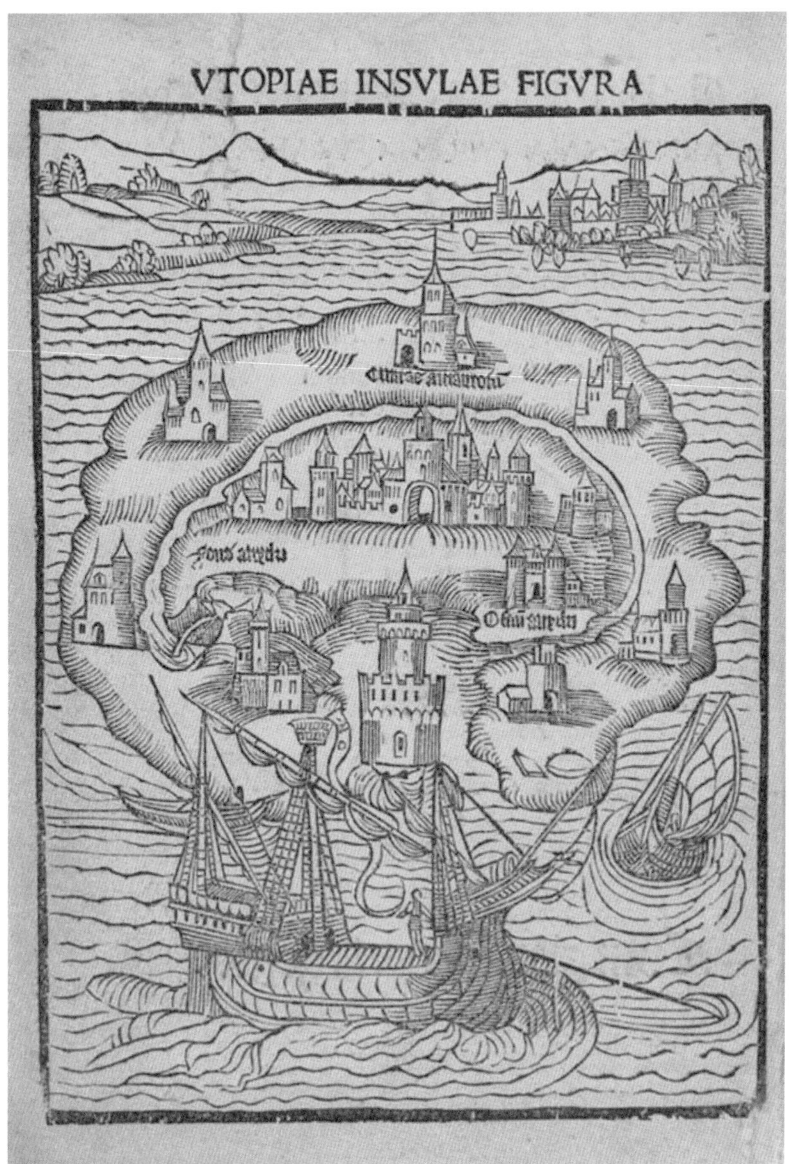


*Map of Utopia*. In *Utopia*. By Thomas More. 1516.

On the other hand, much suggests that More meant for *Utopia* to be read as a satire. In addition to the names given to the place and the narrator, More, in his description of the island of Utopia, makes attractive certain aspects (like female equality, an elected priesthood and government, the banishment of lawyers, and lack of private property) that he, in his *real* personal, economic, political, and religious life (as a man, lawyer, property holder, future

King's councilor, Lord Chancellor, and dogmatic defender of the faith) would presumably be dead set against. He then places these radical political imaginaries within a society that also uses silver and gold chamber pots. As such, one might argue, he effectively ridicules all these possibilities. One might imagine the argument: Communal property and elected priests? That's as absurd as taking a crap in a gold and silver chamber pot!

Ironies aside, the book and the ancillary letters that accompanied initial printings also suggest that *Utopia* is not to be taken seriously. For an example, we need to turn no further than the one introduced above: More's concern over the specific span of a bridge and his request to his friend to ask Hythloday for the genuine measure. Instead of being understood as a gesture of concern on More's part with the overall veracity of the account of *Utopia*, it might be better interpreted as a joke: More will not be corrected in his facts regarding a bridge on a far-off isle because Hythloday, his fact-checker, quite simply, does not exist.

## NOT *OR*, BUT *AND*

Sincere or satiric, earnest or absurd, these are the two sides, each staked out and defended by scholars of *Utopia* for ages.[8] I believe, however, that this orthodox debate obfuscates rather than clarifies, and actually misses the genius of More's book. *Utopia* is both. Written in the tradition of *serio ludere*, or "serious play" that More admired so much in classic authors, the story presents itself as both sincere and satirical, earnest and absurd, fact and fiction. Utopia is someplace and no-place.

More takes pains to convince the reader that Utopia is a real place, and it is through the veracity of the description that they imagine a someplace radically different than their present world. Like an architect's model or a designer's prototype, we are presented with a world wholly formed. We experience a sense of radical alterity as we step inside and try it on for size. What is foreign becomes familiar and what is unnatural, naturalized. Rather than told that an alternative model for structuring society could be possible, we are shown that it is possible. More provides us with a vision of another, better world…and then destabilizes it. This destabilization is the key. More imagines an alternative to his sixteenth-century Europe that he then reveals to be a work of imagination. (It is, after all, no-place.) But the reader becomes infected the moment another option is revealed. They cannot safely return to the assurances of their own present with the naturalness of their world disrupted. The opening lines of a brief poem attached to the first printings of *Utopia* read:

> Will thou know what wonders strange be,
> in the land that late was found?
> Will thou learn thy life to lead,
> by divers ways that godly be?[9]

Or, as the old American WWI song went: "How 'ya gonna keep 'em down on the farm after they've seen Paree?"

Once an alternative—"divers ways that godly be"—has been imagined, to stay stagnant or to try something else becomes a question demanding attention and a choice, yet the choice More offers is not an easy one. By destabilizing his own design of an ideal society, he keeps us from short-circuiting this imaginative moment into a fixed imaginary: a realizable future. We cannot simply swap ready-made Plan A for ready-made Plan B. We must generate our own plans because Plan B is untenable, unrealizable.[10]

The problem with many imaginaries lies in them positing themselves as realizable possibility. Their designers imagine either a future or an alternative and present it as *the* future or *the* alternative. If made manifest, this leads to a number of, not mutually exclusive, results:

1. Brutalizing the present to bring it into line with the imagined future. (Urban "renewal.")

2. Disenchantment as the future never arrives, and the alternative is never realized. (The loss of faith in ambitious urban planning after the 1960s.)

3. A vain search for a new imaginary when the promised one does not appear. (The endless cycle of cosmetic re-designs.)

4. Living a lie. (Pretending "as if" The People prefer eight-foot ceilings)

5. Rejecting possibility altogether. (Dismissing—with a heartfelt conservative distrust or an ironic liberal wink—any alternative as a naïve impossibility.)

But what if impossibility is incorporated into the design in the first place? This is exactly what More does. By positioning his imaginary someplace as no-place, he escapes the problems which typically haunt imaginaries. Yes, the alternatives he describes are sometimes absurd (gold and silver chamber pots? A place called no-place?), but this conscious absurdity keeps *Utopia* from being a singular and authoritative narrative. Rather than force a closed act of imagination to be either accepted or rejected, one's understanding of it must be modified. The presentation of Utopia as no-place and its narrator as nonsense opens up a space for the reader's imagination to wonder what their vision of an alternative someplace might be.

*Utopia* is neither a serious plan nor a prank, but a prompt for further imagination on the part of the reader/spectator: stimuli for new thinking, fire for the imagination. The book, moving metaphors from one medium to another, functions as a sort of source code, providing the core of what can, and must, be modified by us to create a functioning utopian program, for as a program itself, it repeatedly crashes.

This code functions as a utilitarian design for what my friend and colleague, Stevphen Shukaitis, calls an imaginal machine.[11] Utopia is No-Place, and therefore left up to us to imagine it.

Abraham Ortelius (creator of the modern atlas), *Map of Utopia*, 1595.

Designing the impossible seems to be in vogue once again. In 2006, when writing about the 1960 avant-garde architecture group Archigram, science fiction author Bruce Sterling coined the term "architectural fiction."[12] In 2009 the artist-designer Julian Bleecker published his influential essay *Design Fiction*, arguing for the importance of "design provocations," defined as "objects meant to produce new ways of thinking about the near future, optimistic futures, and critical interrogative perspectives."[13] In 2010, MIT Press released *NONOBJECT*, a book based on Branko Lukic's imaginative designs of products that cannot, or should not, be built, but are meant as an "epistemological probe, a means of surveying the bounds of the believable and pressing against the perimeter of the possible."[14] In early 2011, the Art Center College of Design outside of Los Angeles, launched an exhibit entitled "Made Up: Design's Fictions," defined as,

> ...speculative practices [that] invite the use of fiction to produce as much as to provoke...creating critical or philosophical objects, and designing for future scenarios or technological capabilities [that] acknowledge the increasingly uncanny correspondence of the real and the imaginary.[15]

Architecture and design fiction may be moving into the mainstream of the art, architecture, and design world in the United States, but in the margins and on the streets, projects pushing the boundaries of fictional design by consciously, purposefully, and transparently proclaiming their impossibility emerge.[16] After Hurricane Katrina devastated New Orleans, a group calling itself The Hypothetical Development Organization, imagined fanciful uses for abandoned properties in the storm-ravaged city: snooze towers for naps, a narcissistic museum of the self, a sanctioned loitering area. Once imagined, the HDO then displays these phantasmagoric visions on the building sites with the sort of illustrated billboards usually reserved by corporations to showcase future development. The goal of the HDO is not to convince the passerby that such an imaginary building will come into being, but to encourage imagining an alternative to the bleak polarity of devastation left by Hurricane Katrina and the future being promised by commercial developers. Their plans are silly, but that's the point: the very absurdity keeps the imaginative process open. "Unlike a traditional, reality-based developer," they write in their "about" statement, "our organization is not bound by rules relating to commercial potential, practical materials, or physics. In our view," they conclude, "plausibility is a creative dead end." They call out usual images of buildings and public spaces rendered by development corporations as "architecture fiction," but fictions which lay claim to future reality (one already planned) and offer no role for the person-on-the-street other than a consumer. The HDO openly embraces their own fictionality—"a new form of urban storytelling," they call it—and in so doing encourage others to compose their own stories of the future they'd like to see.[17]

This page: Mark Clayton, *No Loitering, Hypothetical Development Organization*, 2010, digital. Opposite: Packard Jennings, Steve Lambert, *Future Wildlife Refuge*, 2007, digital.

## ART OF THE IMPOSSIBLE

In 2008, artists Packard Jennings and Steve Lambert were hired by the San Francisco Arts Commission to produce a set of street posters for large, city-street kiosks. As the posters were meant to display urban design scenarios for the future, the artists tackled the prompt with fervor. They interviewed urban planners, architects, and traffic engineers to record designs for how to make a better city. Then, in the words of the artists, these plans were "perhaps mildly exaggerated."[18] This exaggeration makes these artists' imaginings so politically interesting. Movable skyscrapers. A martial arts studio on a BART train. Public transit by elephant back. Commuting by zip line. Transforming San Francisco into wildlife refuge. Turning a football stadium into a farm (and linebackers into human plows).

The visions of our future offered up by Jennings and Lambert inspire with their honest, transparent impossibility. A city could become more "green" with additional public parks and community gardens, but transforming San Francisco into a nature preserve where office workers take their lunch break next to a mountain gorilla family? Not going to happen—and that's the point. There is no duplicity, only the offering of a dream. These impossible dreams open up spaces to imagine new possibilities. Many professionals find their imaginations already too constrained by the tyranny of the possible to "think outside the box" and imagine new solutions. By visualizing impossibilities, Jennings and Lambert create an opportunity to ask "*what if?*"....without immediately closing down this free space by seriously answering "*this is what.*"

Standing in front of one of their posters on a street corner produces a smile at the absurd idea of practicing Tae Kwon Do on the train ride home. But one may also begin to question why public transportation is so uni-functional, and then ask why public transport *shouldn't* cater to other public desires? This could set off a train of thought wondering why the government is so often in the business of controlling instead of facilitating desires, and then one might start to envision what a truly desirable state would look like. Jennings and Lambert's impossible designs—like More's Utopia, like Tatlin's Monument to the Third International—are means to imagine new ones.

"Politics is the art of the possible." With this phrase Germany's "Iron Chancellor" Otto von Bismarck articulated the core philosophy of the hard-headed, hard-hearted *Realpolitik* he was famous for; a politics that ignores ideals in favor of what's possible given the real conditions of the times. In our times, another sort of politics is called for, defined by Las Vegas style spectacle and "Reality TV" entertainment. With a President of the United States who is a product of both, where the imaginary is an integral part of reality, perhaps it makes more sense to embrace what we might call *Dreampolitik*...and a liberatory gesture that could be called "the art of the impossible."

**1** Contemporary artists are attempting—albeit in a very conceptual way—to build Tatlin's monument today: http://www.tatlinstowerandtheworld.net/. In addition, Wolf Prix, along with students at the Institute of Architecture of the Vienna University of Applied Arts, are investigating the very possibility of building Tatlin's monument in their forthcoming book *Unbuildable Tatlin*, Springer Vienna Architecture, 2012.

**2** Cited in Christina Lodden, *Russian Constructivism*, New Haven: Yale University Press, 1983, p. 239, n.165; original source: Teatr RSFSR, Pechat'l revolyutsiya no. 7, 1922.

**3** Leon Trotsky, *Literature and Revolution*, NY: Russell and Russell, 1957, pp. 247-248, emphasis mine. Trotsky does, however, preface his critique of Tatlin by saying that while the first needs of the revolution are to repair the infrastructure and take care of necessities, once these needs are met and there is a surplus, there will be time to experiment.

**4** Anatoly Lunacharsky, *On Literature and Art*, Moscow: Progress Publishers, 1931/1973; http://www.marxists.org/archive/lunachar/1931/mayakovsky.htm, no page; emphasis mine.

**5** Aleksander Rodchenko, a leader of the Constructivists, was, at his time, calling for art as engineering. From Rodchenko's "Who We Are: The Manifesto of the Constructivist Group" written in 1922:
*We are not dreamers from art who build in the imagination:*
*Aeroradiostations*
*Elevators and Flaming cities*
*WE – ARE THE BEGINNING*
*OUR WORK IS TODAY:*
*A mug*
*A floor brush*
*Boots*
*A catalogue*

One can only guess if Rodchenko was reacting to his comrade Tatlin's monument when criticizing "Aeroradiostations." Rodchenko went on to design eminently utilitarian items like candy wrappers and airplane advertisements.

**6** Cited in Christina Lodden, *Russian Constructivism*, New Haven: Yale University Press, 1983, p. 65.

**7** Seymour Papert, *Mindstorms*, New York, Basic Books, 1980.

**8** The sincerity of More is the general assumption of the canonical *Utopia* scholars Edward Surtz and J.H. Hexter, who together edited the standard modern translation of *Utopia* in *The Complete Works of St. Thomas More*, vol. 4 (New Haven: Yale University Press, 1965). Separately see, for instance, Hexter's *More's Utopia: The Biography of an Idea* (Princeton: Princeton University Press, 1952) in which he, while acknowledging More's sense of humor, demands a singular, and sincere, reading of *Utopia*: "The one point of unanimous agreement about *Utopia* is that it is a work of social comment; and while ambiguity may enhance the value of certain special kinds of poetry, it does not enhance the value of social comment" [p. 11] I would argue quite the opposite: it is exactly the ambiguity that creates the value of social comment. Edward Surtz, in the introduction to his classic (and Catholic) edition of *Utopia* (New Haven: Yale, 1964) also makes the case for the general sincerity of More's vision: "The hope for far better things, sustained by the view (so typically Renaissance) that man may shape and mold himself in any chosen form, is embodied in an apocalyptic vision of the best state possible—Utopia" [p. viii]. The sincere More is also generally promoted by Logan and Adams in Thomas More, *Utopia*, Revised Edition, George M. Logan and Robert M. Adams, eds., Cambridge: Cambridge University Press. The revisionist, satirical position is argued most forcefully by Alistair Fox in his *Utopia: An Illusive Vision* (NY: Twayne/Macmillan, 1993). Fox claims that in writing *Utopia* "More experienced a loss of faith in his utopian vision" [p. 32] and ended up making an argument against any such feasibility of the idea of Utopia, while poking fun at the very idea of human perfectibility. Some of his assertions are a bit far-fetched, but at least Fox understands that what is being presented is more complicated than a simple assertion and defense of an ideal society. Fox's mistake is to believe that it has to be either sincere or satirical, for or against. Ultimately I agree with Fox's frame: the ambiguous text, but not with his assessment that More had lost faith in his utopian project. Quite the opposite: the tension between belief and disbelief allows a place for readers to complete the political project.

**9** "Cornelius Graphey to the Reader" in *The Utopia of Sir Thomas More*, Ralph Robinson, trans., J.H. Lupton, ed. Oxford: Claredon Press, 1895, p. 322; Middle-English modernized.

**10** As Richard Sennett pointed out at the Making/Crafting/Designing conference at the Akademie Schloss Solitude, Sigmund Freud, in "Mourning and Melancholia," theorizes that the degradation of the loved (and lost) object by the grieving subject is necessary in order to release the subject to live and love again. The same, Sennett suggests, might be argued of *Utopia*: that it must fail, and that failure must be experienced, in order to free the reader to imagine another Utopia. *The Complete Works of Sigmund Freud*, vol. 14, London: Hogarth Press/Institute of Psychoanalysis, 1953–1974, pp. 243-258.

**11** Stevphen Shukaitis, *Imaginal Machines: Autonomy and Self-Organization in the Revolutions of Everyday Life*, London/New York/Port Watson: Minor Compositions/Autonomedia, 2009, p. 12.

**12** Bruce Sterling, "Science Fiction and Architecture Fiction," Walker Art Center blog, posted March 20, 2006, https://walkerart.org/magazine/science-fiction-and-architecture-fiction.

**13** *Design Fiction*, Near Futures Laboratory, March 2009, http://www.nearfuturelaboratory.com/2009/03/17/, p. 7.

**14** Branko Lukic and Barry M. Katz, *NONOBJECT*, Cambridge, MA: MIT Press, 2010, p. xxv.

**15** Art Center College of Design, "Made Up: Design's Fictions," January 29-March 20, 2011, Pasadena, CA. http://www.artcenter.edu/mdp/madeup/whatis_madeup.html.

**16** Albert Speer's plans for a Volkshalle to hold 180,000 people, no matter how phantasmagorical, was presented as a plausibility to be completed by 1950.

**17** "About," The Hypothetical Development Organization, http://hypotheticaldevelopment.com, accessed on September 30, 2010. The HDO is the creative brainchild of marketing critic Rob Walker.

**18** Packard Jennings and Steve Lambert, Catalog for *Wish You Were Here! Postcards from our Awesome Future*, San Francisco Arts Commission, April 2008.

# THE NEUTRALIZING VESSEL

058

DANNY
SALAMOUN

PHASMOPHOBIA

M. Arch. Thesis
Advisors: Val Warke &
Jim Williamson

Ryan: And Beirut, doctor? Here you're keeping an eye on another virus?

(...)

Doctor: ...Not a physical virus, but a psychological one even more dangerous than smallpox...We need to know how we can manipulate their emotions, how we can twist the news and trigger off their aggressive drives, how we can play on their religious feelings or political ideals.

—J.G. Ballard, *War Fever*, 1990.

The war-torn structures of Beirut, Lebanon remain caught between a repressed narrative and a symbolic presence within the city. In the years following the Lebanese Civil War of 1975–1990, Beirut found itself saturated in multiple conflicting narratives resulting in a convoluted reading of its recent past. During this period, the *conspiracy theory* emerged as a repressed social text while the *rifle* represented a populous war object. Both dangerous and imbued with contradictory meanings, the conspiracy theory and the rifle shifted between the symbolic and the real. While a conspiracy theory represents both a theory and a fictional story, a rifle symbolizes a neutral order and a deadly disorder. Associations such as *fear* and *control* further alter the definition of a rifle and a conspiracy theory. The rifle, in its holistic form, evokes fear, but its meaning dissipates once disassembled. Conversely, a conspiracy theory gains control of reality by extracting semiotic codes for fictitious texts and alternative meanings.

During the Civil War, the distribution of warfare weapons and their ease of retrieval from foreign political alliances reshaped the city. The building became more than the sum of its architectural elements by serving as a corroborative witness to the conspiracy, an accessory to the rifle, and an active antagonist in the city. The post-war city integrates the fear of latent violence into its development, leading to a reconstruction blanketed under the guise of neutrality. By neutralizing war texts and objects, however, new meanings surface for the ruins to re-engage the people as social actors in the city. Architecture, like text and object, occupies an uncertain disjunction linking meaning and structure;[1] it defies fear as *the neutralizing vessel* to mediate the dialectic gap between fiction and reality.

## CONSPIRACY RHETORIC

J. G. Ballard's *War Fever*, published in 1990, captures an Eastern conspiracy theory through a Western lens. Set against the backdrop of the Lebanese Civil War, the dystopian science fiction story transforms a violent reality into an even darker fiction. In the short story, the U.N. stationed in Beirut poses as a peacekeeper, but in a Ballardian plot-twist, it is revealed to be a distribution center and war laboratory for propaganda and weapons. The city monitors the mutation of two psychological viruses: fear and violence. In a translation between Eastern and Western depictions, a historic Lebanese narrative is mystified. The Lebanese commonly perceive the militia factions as proxies or chess pawns manipulated by international political powers driven by capitalistic agendas. Elaborate plots drawn and imagined by Israelis, Syrians, Americans, or Soviets disrupt Lebanon's political and moral social order.[2] The conspiracy, actuated or not, is captured in the Lebanese colloquial term for the Civil War, *al-ahdath*, loosely translated into English as "the incidents." Although the violence and destruction resulting from these incidents was tangible and conclusive, the correlations between the series of incidents remains contested. The all-encompassing term pacifies the violence, almost excusing it through language. Challenging the definitive nature and historical account of "the incidents" allows for creative speculation. Elucidating an unmuted post-war reconstruction process, the conspiracy rhetoric mines a fearless projection.

The social fiction of the conspiracy theory alternates between intent and coincidence. French philosopher Bruno Latour identifies the dangerous shift through linguistics from an excessive trust in ideologies taken as facts, into an excessive distrust of facts taken as ideologies.[3] The conspiracy theory plaguing Beirut's history finds parallels in this inverted relationship. However, as a zeitgeist of our time, conspiracy theories run the danger of being superfluously misread as truth. In analyzing the term "conspiracy theory" through techniques of language and framing, "conspiracy" is defined as "people," "power," or "secret" with an action of intentionality,[4] while theory is defined as an "explanation" or an "incident." The term shifts between a neutral categorization warranting empirical examination to "a rhetoric for exclusion deeming evidence superfluous or inappropriate."[5] The lack of stability within the term speculates a socially-constructed view on reality, allowing conspiracy texts to act as rhetorical figures that shift between "the fictional quality of reality and the real quality of fiction."[6] The elements of truth embedded in the fiction of a conspiracy theory become an opportunity for examining its material consequences.

Contemporary artist Walid Raad's quasi-fictional archive surrounding the Lebanese Civil War, *The Atlas Group*, reconstructs one's perception of truth through the friction between reality and constructed narrative. In considering the multiple readings of the Lebanese Civil War, Raad challenges the accepted chronology of events by associating otherwise uncorrelated discourses with abstracted data.[7] His use of multiple vantage points for data collection stitches disparate information into an imaginative construct,

M 16
B7 RPG
AK 47
The Lebanese Army
BULGARIA
ROMANIA
WEST GERMANY
BELGIUM
ISRAEL
SNIPER
Other Christian
Al Kataeb
Guardians of the Cedar
Al Marada
Freedom Tigers
NLP National Liberation Party
Lebanese Forces
The Christian Militia
PRIME MINISTER
sunni
JORDAN
The Palestinian Militias
1967
1989
alawits
(SLA)
South Lebanon
PRESIDENT
The Muslim Militia
Al Mourabitoun
The Druze Militia
The socialist Progressist Party
LIBYA
SAUDI ARABIA
IRAQ
PARLIMENT SPEAKER
Amal Movement
The Hezbollah
M1
B7 RPG
M4

transforming the viewer from questioning the validity of facts to questioning if the truth really matters. This displaced reality, hovering between physical and metaphysical memory of conflict, can be mined by architecture within the city. The Ballardian depiction of Beirut, a quasi-real perception of history, reveals material consequences, modifying how people behave and interact with the city.

Revisiting the colloquial term of "the incidents," with inherent associations of fear and control, the term can be redefined as "the spectacles" to implement Ballard's fiction believed by the city. Fear of the "other," whether an outside power or an opposing political party, can be quantified through surveillance in the city. As an ambiguous interpretation of either the opposing political party or the fictional U.N. propaganda laboratory, the presence (or absence) of "the other" unifies a city fragmented by disparate ideologies into one of autonomous operation under constant surveillance. As a city brought together by conspiracy, yet distended with informal surveillance, Beirut acts as an automated instrument through displacement maneuvers,[8] revealed through weapon distribution patterns within neighborhoods. The accessibility and affordability of warfare weapons from foreign political alliances reshaped the city. These patterns gave rise to "the spectacles" and echo French philosopher Guy Debord's situationist definition of "the spectacle" as an unrealism of the real society.[9] In *The Society of the Spectacle* (1967), Debord discloses the implications of objects in the city, projecting artificial desires onto its inhabitants. He unveils the city as an object-oriented instrument fostering apathy and a narrowed world view.

While the city became overwhelmingly saturated with instruments of war during the conflict, these instruments of warfare provided an objective metric to decipher the incidents that occured. To understand the accounts and different factions of a contested history, the logging of military weapons and the forensic science surrounding them acts as a neutral method for warfare data collection. An example of this method is demonstrated by Samer Kassis in his book *30 Years of Military Vehicles in Lebanon* (2006), where Kassis takes photographs and collects newspaper images to log data on the military equipment found in Lebanon and their respective political associations.[10] When looking at texts alone it is this universal relationship with the instrument that allows for an accurate account of the events otherwise contested.

Previous: Tracking the origin of firearms and their types to local militia factions and different neighborhood districts in Lebanon

The extended duration of the Civil War (1975–1990) inconspicuously but radically transformed the relationship between people and their urbanity. A casual type of surveillance and observation became a characteristic mode of inhabiting a city under the siege of long-term urban warfare. Heightened awareness and fear manifested into overwhelming desensitization within everyday rituals. Buildings served as mediators between body and city to take on new characteristics in urban warfare and mirror the interchange between gun and gunman. Latour defines these interchanges as "scripts" in social theory. A script, according to Latour, is the force that guides the roles of actors within a story.[11] The gun establishes a new mode for the understanding of spatial projections through a restructuring of human observation and by anticipating instrument ballistics; the gun disassembles, assembles, and calibrates impact. Thus, a building can also mediate the relationships between bodies and space through unprecedented scripts guiding component disassemblies and assemblies.

The AK-47 automatic firearm was commonplace during the Beirut Civil War. The hybrid term "firearm" combines natural element "fire" and a measure of the body, "arm." The rifle empowers yet disassociates the body from the act of interchange between object and space. Throughout "the incidents," the rifle was an agent that unfaithfully transcended divisive political alliances. The rifle detaches and desensitizes the killer from the killed, paradoxically uniting the city through its idiosyncratic and collective use in conflict. The connotations of fear and denotations of control embedded within the rifle's assembly weaponize diverse ideologies while disembodying the body unilaterally.

Since its initial production in 1947,[12] the AK-47 has become a symbol of the Communist Era and an actor in urban warfare, guerrilla warfare, and terrorism. A social and spectacular agent in present-day terror attacks, it contributes to numerous crimes committed in public spaces and captures the attention of the world through the propagation of fear.[13] According to Latour, the interchange between the gun (object) and the gunman (subject) is bidirectional. He defines the symmetrical modification between the artifact and the man as technical mediation. "You are different with a gun in hand; the gun is different with you holding it… The gun is no longer the gun-in-the-armory or the gun-in-the-drawer or the gun-in-the-pocket, but the gun-in-your-hand, aimed at someone who is screaming. Neither subject nor object (nor their goals) is fixed."[14] The active disassembly of the rifle changes its meaning through a process involving time and control, physical coordination, and visual observation.

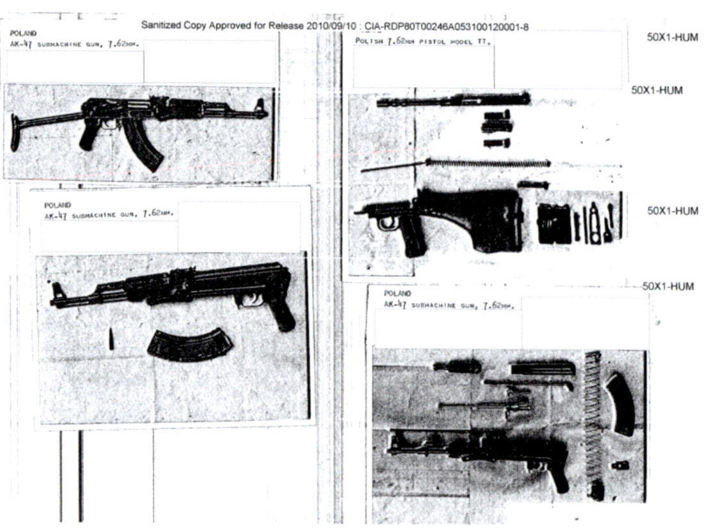


This page: *Component assembly photograph of an AK-47 Submachine Gun and TT Pistol.* In *Information Report*. By Central Intelligence Agency (CIA). Poland, March 31, 1960.
Opposite: The Beirut City Center war ruin was originally designed by architect Joseph Phillippe Karam in 1965 and located on the Green Line in Beirut. The theater shell and column structure below are disassembled in an axonometric projection as one would disassemble an AK-47 rifle.

Latour illustrates the dichotomy of the gun through two opposing slogans; "guns kill people" and "people kill people, not guns." Within technical mediation, design and manufacturing are trapped between material and sociological intent. A materialist and sociological position are presented: in the materialist position, the components of the gun have an autonomous destiny that no human can master, extraneous to the social construct of the gunman; the sociological position presents the gun as a neutral tool under complete human control.[15] He argues that "it is neither people nor guns that kill." Mediation, according to Latour, is when the responsibility for action is shared among the various actors. In revisiting the AK-47 rifle, Mikhail T. Kalashnikov, a Russian inventor, credited for the rifle's development in 1947, acts as an "absent actant" in the scripts involving the rifle. Kalashnikov designed and assembled this weapon to become the standard rifle of all communist grounds and inadvertently empowered alternative ideologies to threaten public space. Control, as a political and design consideration for the neutralization of rifles, is debated through the use of texts, images, and scripts to support opposing ideologies. These methods exploiting fear and control through text, object, and script transform the social and political fabric of the city.

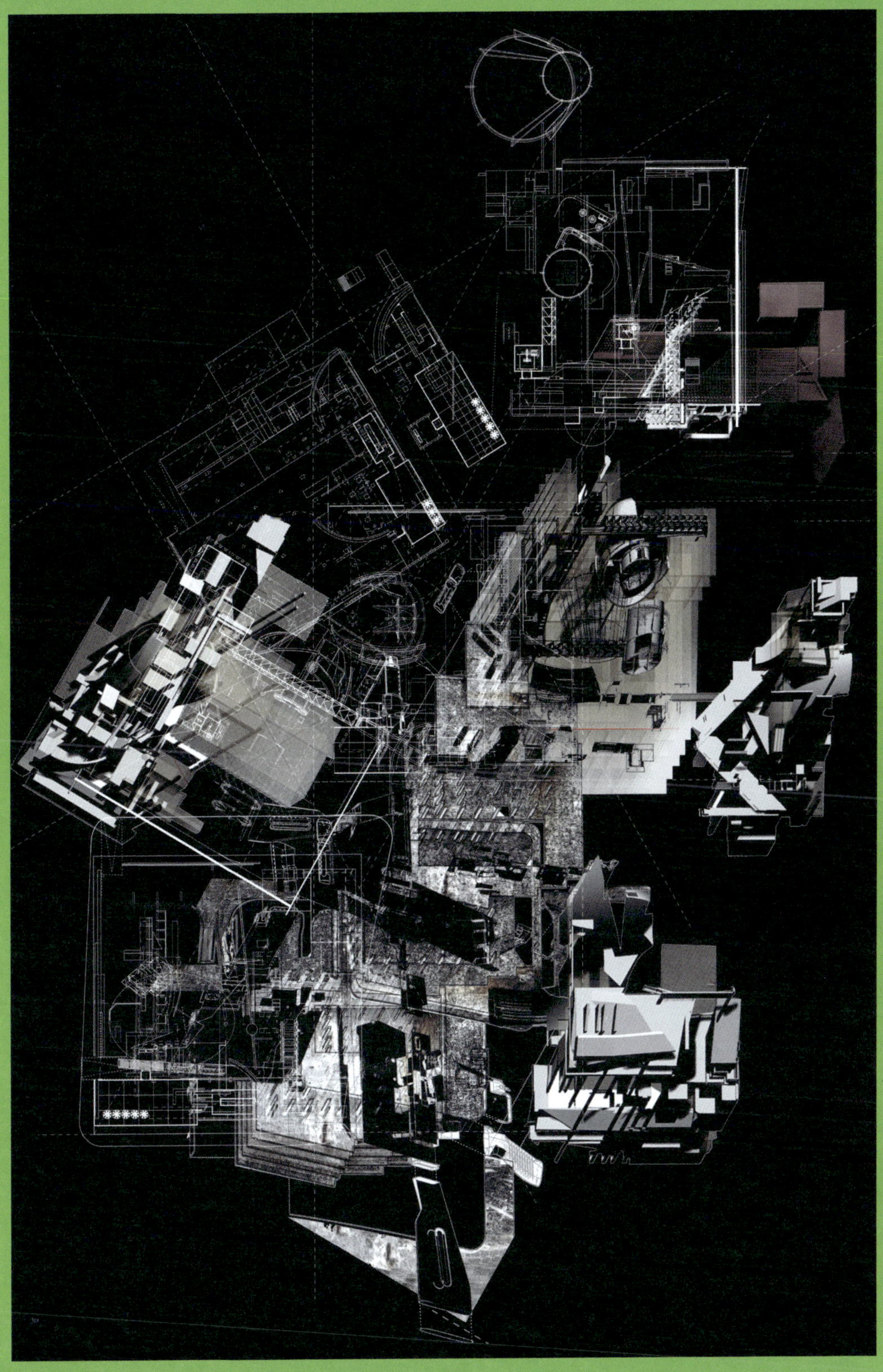



DANNY
SALAMOUN

THE NEUTRALIZING
VESSEL

In the same way that the gun mediates material and sociological intent, visual images can be decoded to mediate subjective truths and actual intent. In 2006, after a five-week war with Hezbollah, the World Press 2006 Photograph of the Year was taken by an American photojournalist in the southern suburbs of Beirut. The image captures residents returning to their neighborhoods after the bombing of infrastructure and residential suburbs. It depicts both absent and present actors in its portrayal of Beirut's conditions amidst chaos[16] by juxtaposing two seemingly opposing socio-economic divisions within the city. The visual cues facilitate comprehension, but the "real" condition is "fictionalized" by the camera and the journalist.[17]

The neighborhood, purposely targeted because of its location in a district predominantly occupied by Shia Muslims, creates a contradiction between the present camera and the absent eye. The German magazine *Der Spiegel* published an article in February 2007 falsifying the journalist's representation of the passengers in the car; they were, in fact, residents of the neighborhood and not affluent spectators.[18]

Spencer Platt, "World Press Photograph of the Year," August 15, 2006.

The photograph is an approximation of the objective world while the self-reflection of the individuals creates an alternate reality. The neutralizing vessel of the photograph is the German article's text. The text challenges the photograph's validity and becomes the objective metering of reality. Oscillating between the Western depiction and the Eastern truth, the text's structure and the image's inherent meanings create two realities at odds with one another. Over time, the camera, journalist, depicted actors, and the location of the photograph become part of the script relinquishing control to the text and the image to empower alternative ideologies.

اي قصص عم تكتب أساميـنـــا ع زمان الماضي وتمحيـنـــا
ال تتركنا أسرى امبـــــــرح الو ننطر بكرة ليليـــــــة
. جينا نحنا وغنانيـــــــــا والرقص يضوي ليالينـــــا

Oh stories writing our names to the past tense and erasing us.
Don't leave us as yesterday's captive or awaiting tomorrow.
We have come with our song and dance to light our nights.

—Julia Boutros, "Kosass" ("Stories", a popular Lebanese song), 1994.

## ABSENT OUTSIDER

Shifting demographics—resulting from the influx of Palestinian refugees—caused cultural fragmentation within Beirut, which then led to the self-assembling of militant factions. The downtown district, which became the center for urban warfare, was divided by religion along a demarcation line, with Muslims to the West and Christians to the East. Militias established checkpoints along the connecting streets to control the circulation of people. Buildings were repurposed as strategic lookouts. A pre-war sense of community once fostered by the Eastern city was violently recalibrated through weapons. As fatal ruins became the embodiment of "the other's" visual presence within the city, the streets and neighborhoods responded with reclusion and distrust. The post-war reconstruction processes of downtown Beirut further escalated this response by the local people. After the war, the desire to erase a recent and violent history manifested as a mimetic attempt by a private organization to project an image of restoration. The urgency to rebuild and reintegrate the divergent, post-war population further disconnected the people from their city. Consequently, many districts found themselves at voyeuristic odds with little to no familiarity. A society attempting to autonomously repair itself without social mediation inadvertently rebuilt itself with extreme division and inequality.

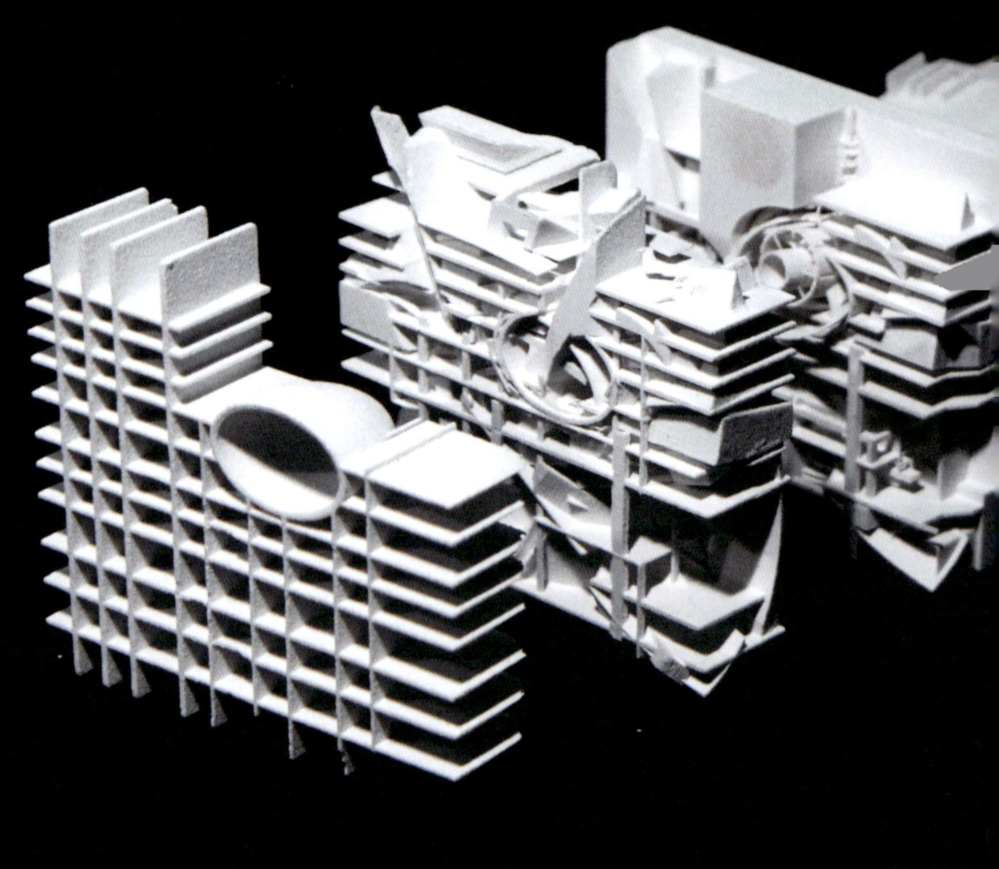

The residue of urban warfare affected the consciousness of Beirut and subsequently, the perception of its buildings and districts. The building, as an instrument of surveillance, seamlessly shifts between a symbolic agent of fear and an imaginary[19] illusion of control. Challenging the underlying laws and customs of common architecture typologies in the city allows for new scripts to emerge and incites reconfiguration. The transformation of the vernacular balcony typology captures the underlying post-war changes on an urban scale. Traditionally, the balcony extended outward beyond the apartment wall limits and receded into the residence. It connected inhabitants to their neighborhood as a communal yet individual allocation—a private display to the street. However, during the war, the balcony transformed into a violent lookout and position of vulnerability. Balconies became associated with exposure to the street and the susceptibility to attacks. This realization alludes to psychoanalyst Jacques Lacan's mirroring effect, a concept evocative of the effect children experience upon seeing themselves in a mirror for the first time.[20] Here, the subject, cognizant of their observation, loses a degree of autonomy upon realizing that he or she is a visible object.

Previous: Speculative process models of transformation from porous ruin to solid cube; This page: Collage using Alnahar Newspaper clippings and balcony postcards

Beirut's current building developments enclose most balconies with glass panels and further separate the people from the historically war-torn streets. While visual connectivity is maintained, the sociological implications of this separation extend far beyond the periphery of the horizontal surface. The neutral balcony could re-engage the people by heightening the awareness of its past and re-configuring the assembly of its parts. Forgotten stories embedded within the city and its architecture contain latent sensations and relationships to objects and texts specific to their creation. The balcony glass, once taken from the frame, can become extensive to the imagination, like the fiction of the conspiracy theory or the script surrounding a gun.

Buildings, images, guns and texts can act as instruments of fear and control in conditions of violence or conflict. Over time, their design mediates reality and fiction through the uncertainties of intent and coincidence. The city, as a testing laboratory of conflict, reinforces the opportunistic use of the instruments as an objective measure. However, as these instruments gain control over the city, they re-assemble and re-configure scripts, changing the relationship between the body and the city by propagating fear. The war ruin, as a material consequence of the instruments' control over the city, calls for the indictment of the text, object and image to demand their neutralization. To re-engage the people as social actors in the city, the neutralizing vessels can uncover disjunctions between fear and control. As the neutralized vessels relinquish control, the city becomes empowered to mediate and calibrate new meanings; people become social actors in the script because fear no longer renders a sterile fabric and control can liberate the imagination.

**1** "Architecture and the Problem of The Rhetorical Figure." *Inside Out: Selected Writings*, 1963–1988, by Peter Eisenman, Yale University Press, 2004, pp. 200–207.

**2** Gray, M. (2010) *Conspiracy theories in the Arab world*. New York: Routledge. Thomas L. Friedman (1998). From Beirut to Jerusalem.

**3** Latour, B. (2004) 'Why Has Critique Run out of Steam? From Matters of Fact to Matters of Concern', *Critical Inquiry*, vol. 30, iss. 2, pp. 225-248.

**4** Conspiracy Theory: Truth Claim or Language Game? / Bjerg, Ole; Presskorn-Thygesen, Thomas. In: *Theory, Culture & Society*, 2017.

**5** Ibid.

**6** Architecture and the Problem of The Rhetorical Figure." Eisenman, *Eisenman Inside out: Selected Writings*, pp. 200-207.

**7** The Atlas Group, (Walid Raad) 'Let's Be Honest, the Rain Helped: Excerpt from an interview with the Atlas Group' in Jalal Toufic, *Review of Photographic Memory* (Beirut Arab Image Foundation, 2004), pp. 44-45.

**8** The Game of War: Debord as Strategist by McKenzie Wark for iss. 29 *Sloth Spring*, 2008.

**9** Debord, Guy. *Comments on the Society of the Spectacle*. Verso, 1998.

**10** Kassis, Samer. *30 Ans De Vehicules Militaires Au Liban : 30 Years of Military Vehicles* in Lebanon: 1975–2005. Elite Group, 2006.

**11** Bruno Latour, *On Technical Mediation; Common Knowledge*, 1994.

**12** "Tools of Modern Terror: How the AK-47 and AR-15 Evolved Into Rifles of Choice for Mass Shootings." *NY Times* [NY] C.J. Chivers, 2016.

**13** Ibid.

**14** Bruno Latour, *On Technical Mediation*; *Common Knowledge*, 1994.

**15** Ibid.

**16** Putz, "World Press Photo Mix-Up." *Spiegel Online*, February 28, 2007.

**17** Gunthert, Andre. "Visual Journalism, or the Hidden Narration." EHESS-Ecole Des Hautes Études En Sciences Sociales, 2016.

**18** Putz, "World Press Photo Mix-Up." *Spiegel Online*, February 28, 2007.

**19** Architecture and the Problem of The Rhetorical Figure." Eisenman, *Eisenman Inside out: Selected Writings*, pp. 200-207.

**20** Ragland-Sullivan, Ellie. *Jacques Lacan and the Philosophy of Psychoanalysis*. University of Illinois Press, 1987.

# UTILITY'S EVIL TWIN: THE FUNCTION OF *VENUSTAS* AND THE FEAR OF REALITY

074

JONATHAN
OCHSHORN

PHASMOPHOBIA

## INTRODUCTION

Having taught technology classes in schools of architecture for more than thirty-five years, I'm well aware that many students worry that applying the knowledge gained from such classes could overwhelm the conceptual and abstract fantasies that are encouraged within the design studio.[1] The Roman architect, Vitruvius, would not have understood the basis for such a fear, as he considered the formal or abstract qualities of architecture (manifested in venustas) to be a complementar function of architecture, along with utilitas and firmitas. From his standpoint, there was no conflict between the expressive and utilitarian functions of architecture. So why is there one now?

The short answer is that architects, and their clients, are driven by competition to exploit the inexhaustibly mutable expressive potential of buildings. Modernist abstractions have become increasingly disengaged not just from the conventional elements of construction, e.g., columns, walls, windows, roofs, and so on, but more importantly from an appreciation of structural and control layer theories, to the extent that these building science principles may appear to threaten the hegemony of unfettered architectural expression.[2]

It is this implicit threat that drives a wedge between courses in building technology and design and affects even the production of real buildings. And whereas a design pedagogy based on such abstractions has always triggered a sense of foreboding and fear in me, I sense that the opposite is true for many of my students: for them, having internalized a design method almost completely disengaged from conventional building science principles (aka "reality," see Fig. 1), it is the discipline of structure, control layer theory, and even the rudiments of what might be called sustainable design that trigger fear, loathing, and denial.

To dig deeper into this conundrum, I propose to examine the nature of venustas, the most subjective and contentious element within Vitruvius's functional triad. Venustas will here be taken to mean not just "beauty" (or pleasure, delight, and so on) as conventionally understood, but also to include all forms of symbolic expression.

# TRIGGER WARNING

**COURSE MATERIAL CONTAINS MATHEMATICAL AND EMPIRICAL ANALYSIS OF STRUCTURAL PRINCIPLES AND, IN GENERAL, IS GROUNDED IN REALITY RATHER THAN FANTASY.**

This page, Fig. 1: The first slide in my Building Technology course; Opposite, Fig. 2: "In a stunning, though entirely symbolic, concession to economic pragmatism or, more likely, to mitigate Milstein Hall's apparent extravagance and elitist sensibility at a time when workers are being laid off and faculty salaries are frozen, Cornell has eliminated the symbolic centerpiece of Rem Koolhaas's design for its new architecture building: Ludwig Mies van der Rohe's iconic Barcelona chair has been removed from the official rendering of Milstein's glass elevator, replaced with a plain vanilla chair."[3] (By Office of Metropolitan Architecture, 2008.)

## SEMANTIC AMBIGUITY

The first thing one uncovers when examining venustas is the difficulty in pinning down its relation to functionality. This is because the word "function" is used in two ways. First, function is used to identify purely utilitarian qualities. For example, the function of a chair, in this sense, would be to provide a structurally and ergonomically adequate surface for sitting. Second, function is used in a broader sense, to include not only utilitarian aspects, but also subjective and expressive qualities. For example, the chair might also function as an article of conspicuous consumption, or as a means of aligning its owner with a particular stylistic tendency (Fig. 2).

Difficulties and confusion emerge when these two meanings of function are not made clear. For example, if "functional" architecture is defined as something, per Hermann Muthesius, without "superficial forms of decoration, a design strictly following the purpose that the work should serve,"[4] one can always argue that precisely those things excluded—decoration, ornament, or any other "superficial" elements or strategies—are also part of "the purpose that the work should serve." But this apparent paradox is just an artifact of the alternative meanings of function, nothing more.

One must be careful when arguing that the utilitarian meaning of function excludes gratuitous and symbolic elements. More precisely—since one can neither exclude "symbolism" nor, in general, prescribe what subjective responses will arise in the presence of a work of architecture—this first, utilitarian, meaning of functionality excludes only those elements considered "decorative" or gratuitous and therefore non-utilitarian.[5] Symbolic expression, on the other hand, since it is in the mind of the beholder and not in the physical material of the building,[6] will inevitably appear in the most utilitarian structures, even against the wishes (or ideologies) of its creators or critics.

A decorative element embedded in an architectural façade really is an element of the building—i.e., is actually present, can be seen, and consists of tangible material like brick or stone or paint—whereas a so-called symbolic element is little more than a theoretical sleight-of-hand in which a subjective interpretation of a building is given a tangible basis, as if it is actually present (as an "element") in the materials of the building itself. We tend to say: "This food is delicious," as if being delicious is an absolute quality of the food, rather than saying: "I find this food delicious," thereby acknowledging the subjectivity of taste.

## THE CONSTRUCTION OF MEANING

Physical or formal aspects of a building may well trigger various subjective responses in individual beholders. And just as a chef cannot create a dish that is objectively delicious, it is the beholders of architecture, rather than the building's designers, who "construct" its meaning. This does not preclude a special role for critics and connoisseurs, but, on the other hand, neither does it give their (often contradictory) opinions an objective status. And designers, working within a subculture in which particular formal strategies are recognized and valued, may well provide precisely the types of coded forms of expression that are recognized as such within those architectural subcultures. However, even in such cases, the formal codes to which they subscribe are external to the forms themselves and must be internalized by the beholder if the intended expression is to be "properly" understood. Those without knowledge of, or interest in, such codes will interpret the same forms through a different lens.

Juan Pablo Bonta provides numerous examples of just such variation in critical appraisal: "Mumford contended that Sullivan's ornament was unrelated to the forms and materials of his buildings; but Zevi, on the other hand, thought that ornament was intimately integrated into Sullivan's architectural structures."[7]

Bonta understands the materials of architectural expression as being entirely different from the physical materials with which buildings are constructed: "The materials of painting are not paints, those of music are not sounds, those of architecture are not stones, any more than the material of literature is ink. The materials of these arts are not inert matter but the creation of man, charged with the cultural heritage of a community—no more, but certainly no less than language."[8]

That symbolic expression cannot be found in the physical materials of art or architecture does not mean that such expression does not exist and has no function within artistic production. It is possible to admit some common understandings of symbolic expression within subcultures or even entire cultures, however, with the disclaimer that such subjective interpretations can be fractured, revised, or otherwise transformed by individuals or by entire groups. Tracing such movements of subjective phenomena is at best a speculative (and probably hopeless) task, given the idiosyncratic psychological content that directs any individual perception towards some subjective interpretation (Fig. 3). The Rorschach test, to cite but one example, exploits precisely this indeterminacy in attempting to draw psychological conclusions from the multiplicity of subjective interpretations that can be made from the same formal design.

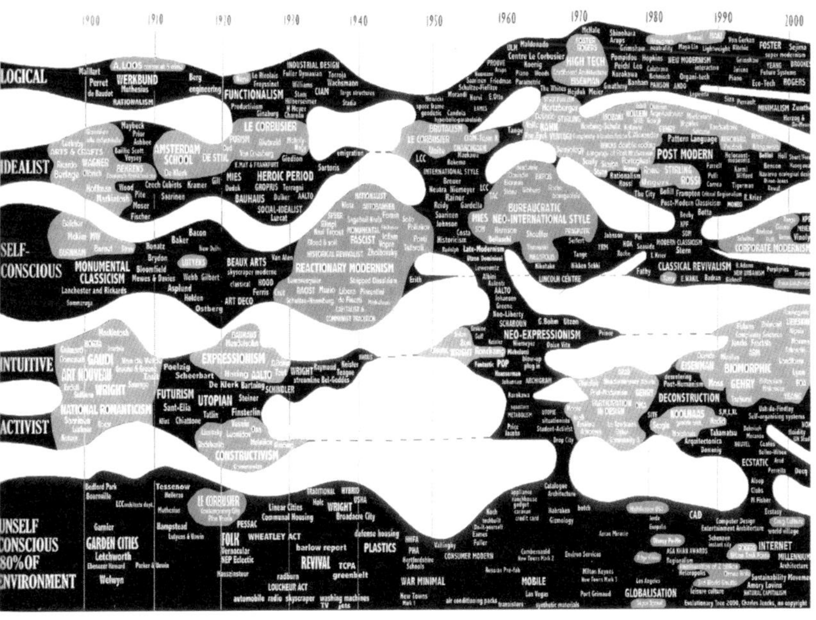


Fig.3: Tracing the movements of subjective phenomena is at best a speculative task, and probably hopeless, but Charles Jencks has certainly tried with its attractor basins. ("The Century is Over, Evolutionary Tree of Twentieth-Century Architecture." In *Architectural Review*, July 2000, p. 77.)

Art, according to E.H. Gombrich, has a social function,[9] and the idea of artistic functionality carries over to architectural expression. In fact, some architectural critics insist that being "functional" (in the sense of solving utilitarian problems) is not even architecture's primary function. Sigfried Giedion, according to Karsten Harries, "reaffirmed what he took to be the main task [i.e., the main function] facing contemporary architecture, 'the interpretation of a way of life valid for our period.'"[10]

Along these same lines, Harries proposes to extend to architecture Paul Valéry's claim that the function of poetry is "to create an artificial and ideal order of a material of vulgar origin." Harries writes that the theorists Tzonis and Lefaivre "proclaim that 'the poetic identity of a building depends not on its stability, or its function, or on the efficiency of the means of its production, but on the way in which all the above have been limited, bent, and subordinated by purely formal requirements.'"[11] In other words, according to Tzonis and Lefaivre, the function of a building (to create a "poetic identity") comes about by subordinating its utilitarian function to formal concerns.

Aside from assigning architecture the non-utilitarian function of expressing the idealized zeitgeist of the period or, perhaps, the tortured soul (poetic identity) of the individual artist, the early twentieth-century concept of "defamiliarization" is also often invoked. Here, the function of architectural expression is to "make strange" what otherwise might be taken for granted and therefore not really noticed. At the extreme, we enter into territory typically broached only by charlatans, comedians, or logicians who gleefully relate linguistic paradoxes such as that of the Cretan who claims that all Cretans are liars (and so must be telling the truth). In the realm of architecture, the analogous condition is a building with the antiheroic function of being dysfunctional. Alison and Peter Smithson, for example, proposed in 1957 that "the word 'functional' must now include so-called irrational and symbolic values."[12] This sentiment gets echoed and even amplified by some contemporary architects and engineers: Rem Koolhaas writes that the work of engineer Cecil Balmond expresses "doubt, arbitrariness, mystery and even mysticism," while Balmond's own website uses virtually the same words to describe his approach.[13]

A more conventional spin on the function of defamiliarization is attributed to Le Corbusier, who is said to have "defined architecture as having to do with a window which is either too large or too small, but never the right size. Once it was the right size it was no longer functioning."[14]

This idea of defamiliarization would have been anathema to nineteenth-century theorists like John Ruskin, or his contemporary Edward Lacy Garbett; the latter would have seen only ugliness in buildings with such "immoral" qualities: "I cannot but regard the perfection of domestic architecture as an embodied courtesy," wrote Garbett in 1850. "And will any one dare to say that this courtesy is useless?"[15] Well, yes, many architects—and not only in and after the twentieth-century—celebrated precisely this lack of courtesy, although their stance was contested. A classic confrontation over this issue occurred in the 1982 debate between Peter Eisenman and Christopher Alexander. In the following excerpt, the two architect-theorists discuss the Town Hall at Logroño designed by Rafael Moneo in 1973–1974:

> **CA:** The thing that strikes me about your friend's building—if I understood you correctly—is that somehow in some intentional way it is not harmonious. That is, Moneo intentionally wants to produce an effect of disharmony. Maybe even of incongruity.
> **PE:** That is correct.
> **CA:** I find that incomprehensible. I find it very irresponsible. I find it nutty. I feel sorry for the man. I also feel incredibly angry because he is fucking up the world... Don't you think there is enough anxiety at present? Do you really think we need to manufacture more anxiety in the form of buildings?
> **PE:**...What I'm suggesting is that if we make people so comfortable in these nice little structures of yours, that we might lull them into thinking that everything's all right, Jack, which it isn't. And so the role [function] of art or architecture might be just to remind people that everything wasn't all right.[16]

Alexander, representing the forces of politeness and comfort, asks Eisenman: "Don't you think there is enough anxiety at present? Do you really think we need to manufacture more anxiety in the form of buildings?" Eisenman's response, justifying the disorienting or upsetting qualities of some avant-garde architecture, is that people are thereby reminded "that everything wasn't all right." A similar argument is made by Herbert Marcuse, the German-American philosopher and political theorist, who writes that:

> A work of art can be called revolutionary if, by virtue of the aesthetic transformation, it represents, in the exemplary fate of individuals, the prevailing unfreedom and the rebelling forces, thus breaking through the mystified (and petrified) social reality, and opening the horizon of change (liberation)…The aesthetic transformation becomes a vehicle of recognition and indictment. But this achievement presupposes a degree of autonomy which withdraws art from the mystifying power of the given and frees it for the expression of its own truth. Inasmuch as man and nature are constituted by an unfree society, their repressed and distorted potentialities can be represented only in an estranging form.[17]

## ANAESTHETIZATION OF THE POLITICAL

But it is hardly clear that architecture has the necessary "autonomy" that Marcuse suggests it must have as a revolutionary medium. Unlike the production of literature—the art form that Marcuse is primarily interested in—the appearance of architecture (where appearance is used in the double sense of what it looks like, and its coming into existence) is contingent upon first, a patron whose interests the architecture serves, and second, the literal deployment of wealth and power in order to create (bring into existence) the physical elements of architecture. It is true that this first condition could elicit "revolutionary" form, where such formal qualities might serve the patron (client), but that alone cannot overcome the second criterion. It may well be that in literature the revolutionary thing is its printing and distribution as much as the aesthetics of the work itself. The relative ease of printing and distribution, compared to the creation of construction documents and then the actual construction of a building, is, in this respect, what separates literature from architecture.

Even if a "disturbing" work of architecture somehow comes into being, its power to "open up the horizon of change (liberation)," being based on the feelings it elicits rather than on conclusions drawn from a logical explanation, puts it immediately into competition with other emotion-based content supplied in much greater quantities by the ideologically-driven representatives and apologists of wealth and power. Neal Leach describes how Walter Benjamin, for example, "explored the problem of how fascism used aesthetics to celebrate war" and how "it could be extrapolated from Benjamin's argument that aesthetics," rather than opening up revolutionary horizons, "brings about an anaesthetization of the political…"[18]

That symbolic content can and should be expressed by a building's outward form is nevertheless taken as self-evident in much architectural theorizing. Christian Norberg-Schulz, for example, writes: "During the great epochs of the past certain forms had always been reserved for certain tasks. The classical orders were used with caution outside churches and palaces, and the dome, for instance, had a very particular function as a symbol of heaven."[19]

He goes on to argue that not only did such forms correspond to particular social functions, but that there is a psychological (emotional) basis for assigning particular forms to these functions: "The psychologist Arnheim discusses this problem [i.e., the structural similarity between content and form] in detail and maintains that we have the best reasons to assume that particular arrangements of lines and shapes correspond to particular emotional states. Or rather we should say that particular structures have certain limited possibilities for receiving contents. We do not play a Viennese waltz at a funeral."[20]

Actually, we may well play up-beat music at funerals, for example, as part of the jazz funeral tradition in New Orleans. In other words, there is no intrinsic correspondence between functional activities and the manner in which they are expressed. Some people fear tight spaces; others open spaces. How could one possibly assign some singular meaning to space given the divergent ways in which the same space is experienced? Norberg-Schulz adds that the perception requires "training and instruction…A common order is called culture. In order that culture may become common, it has to be taught and learned. It therefore depends upon common symbol-systems, or rather, it corresponds to these symbol-systems and their behavioral effects."[21] Well, of course, if one is told how to interpret a form, the connections can be memorized and regurgitated. But this is a bizarre way to understand contemporary societies, which are characterized by multiple and shifting subcultures. What, for example, would constitute the "common symbol-systems" of Peter Eisenman's House II and Archigram's Instant City (Fig. 4), both completed in 1970?

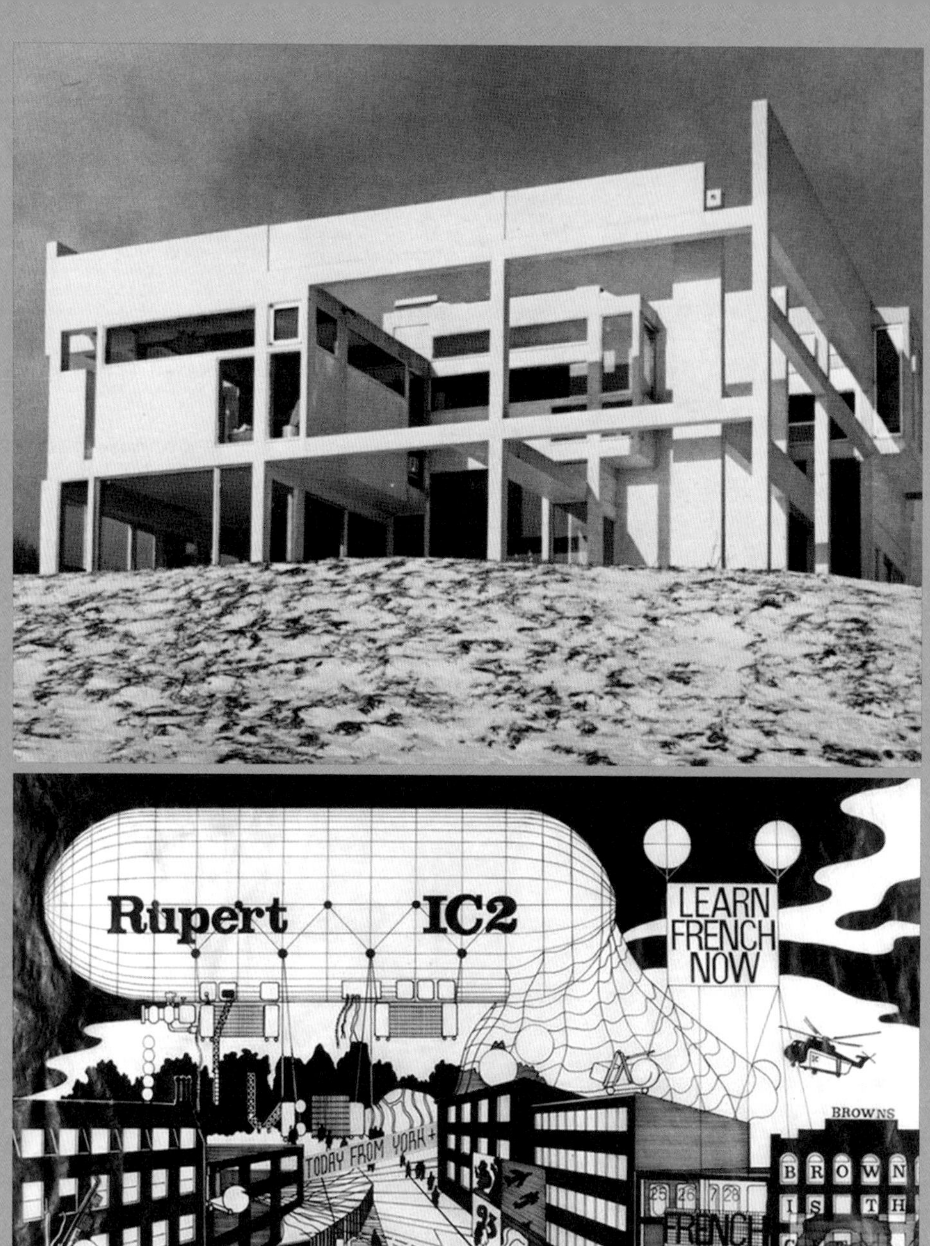


Fig. 4: Peter Eisenman's House II in Hardwick, Connecticut (top) and Peter Cook's (Archigram) "Instant City (Rupert IC 2), Airship Sequence of Effect of an English Town" (bottom), both completed in 1970, provide some evidence that no single Zeitgeist can be identified within contemporary societies.

Any answer, in my view, must distinguish between formal modes of expression ("symbol-systems"), which are evidently quite diverse, and the overarching function of such expression, which—consistent with the competition that drives the multiplicity of formal outcomes—always serves to reinforce and validate capitalist freedom and democracy.[22] In that sense, and in spite of differences in their formal attributes, the architecture of Eisenman and Archigram (and everyone else) has the same overarching cultural function. It is precisely in supporting that function that the task of reconciling the increasingly deviant manifestations of venustas with building science principles (utilitas and firmitas) grinds to a halt. Having reached this impasse, the fear of reality experienced by students of architecture—struggling to become accomplices within this insane mode of production—will not soon be assuaged.

1 The idea that architectural design might be based on "fantasy" is taken as self-evident by Colin Rowe; for example, in discussing the works and writings of Robert Venturi, he writes: "For, if it is myth—in collaboration or conflict with social and technological conditions—which is the ultimate architectural determinant, Venturi scarcely subjects this issue to examination; and, certainly, he never stipulates that the forms he admires came about through the activity of just such fantasies as he seems prone to reject." See Colin Rowe, "Robert Venturi and the Yale Mathematics Building," in *As I Was Saying: Recollection and Miscellaneous Essays: Volume Two: Cornelliana*, MIT Press (Cambridge: 1995), p. 87, first published in *Oppositions*, vol. 6, Fall 1976.

2 For a more thorough argument on questions of modernist abstraction in relation to control layer theory, see Jonathan Ochshorn, "Architecture's Dysfunctional Couple: Design and Technology at the Crossroads," *The International Journal of Design Education*, vol. 7, iss. 4, 2014.

3 Image screen-captured from Cornell's Milstein Hall web pages by the author before its removal; the caption is from the author's blog post, "Milstein Hall Loses its Barcelona Chair," Impatient Search, June 30, 2009, at http://jon.ochshorn.org/2009/06/milstein-hall-loses-its-barcelona-chair/. Denise Scott Brown has made a similar argument, but using a table rather than a chair: "…the functions of so simple and general an object as a table may be many and various, related at one end to the most prosaic of activities and at the other to the unmeasurable, symbolic and religious needs of man." See Denise Scott Brown, "The Function of a Table," in *Architectural Design 37* (1967), p. 154.

4 Muthesius is quoted in the "Function" chapter of Adrian Forty, *Words and Buildings: A Vocabulary of Architecture*, Thames and Hudson (London: 2000), p. 181.

5 Karsten Harries argues that "aesthetic components" not gratuitously added in a literal sense but still self-consciously designed—e.g., the application of the golden section to an otherwise utilitarian façade—function much like applied decoration and that such buildings therefore may be called "decorated sheds." Within my proposed framework, on the other hand, such buildings would be considered entirely utilitarian, at least to the extent that any formal manipulation or refinement was not deemed gratuitous. In making such a determination, I abstract from any "gratuitous" effort expended by the designer, and look only at the product (the building) for signs of otherwise unnecessary, or dysfunctional, elements. That such a utilitarian building may well be "appreciated" in different ways (e.g., "as a riddle with markers," or as "an ironic commentary," per Harries) is entirely consistent with my argument, and does not require that the idea of "decoration" be imposed. See Karsten Harries, *The Ethical Function of Architecture*, The MIT Press (Cambridge, MA: 1997), pp. 4-6.

6 On the importance of the beholder: "According to Riegl: 'Art is incomplete without the perceptual and emotional involvement of the viewer.' His term for this phenomenon was the 'beholder's involvement.' His successors, Ernst Kris and Ernst Gombrich, developed this idea further, settling on the term, 'the beholder's share.'" Quoted from Anne Sherwood Pundyk, "The Beholder's Share," *Artcritical*, August 22, 2017, http://www.artcritical.com/2017/08/22/anne-sherwood-pundyk-on-eric-kandel/.

7 Juan Pablo Bonta, *Architecture and its Interpretation: A Study of Expressive Systems in Architecture*, Rizzoli (New York: 1979), p. 11.

8 Bonta, ibid., p. 23.

9 Gombrich, in explaining the radical transformation within Greek art between the 6th and 4th century B.C., argues that "only a change in the whole function of art can explain such a revolution." E.H. Gombrich, Art and Illusion: A Study in the Psychology of Pictorial Representation, Princeton University Press, © 1960, third printing (Princeton, NJ: 1969), p. 127.

10 Giedion is quoted in Karsten Harries, The Ethical Function of Architecture, The MIT Press (Cambridge, MA: 1997), p. 2; the quote is from the 1967 edition of Sigfried Giedion, *Space, Time and Architecture*.

11 Karsten Harries, The Ethical Function of Architecture, op. cit., p. 24.

12 Forty, "Function", *Words and Buildings*, op. cit., p. 187.

13 The Koolhaas quote is from Deyan Sudjic, "Take a bow, Mr Balmond," *The Guardian*, 2002, accessed at http://www.theguardian.com/books/2002/oct/27/art.

14 I cannot validate this attribution with a citation to the original quote by Le Corbusier, although there are numerous secondary references, all saying essentially the same thing, and probably each assuming that their own unattributed source was accurate. This one is from Peter Eisenman, "Contrasting Concepts of Harmony in Architecture: The 1982 Debate Between Christopher Alexander and Peter Eisenman," *Katarxis No. 3*, London, September 2004, accessed May 19, 2017 at http://www.katarxis3.com/Alexander_Eisenman_Debate.html.

15 Edward Lacy Garbett, Rudimentary Treatise on the Principles of Design in Architecture as Deducible from Nature and Exemplified in the Works of the Greek and Gothic Architects (No. 18 in Weale's Rudimentary Series), John Weale (London: 1850), p. 9; quoted in Edward Robert De Zurko, *Origins of Functionalist Theory*, Columbia University Press (New York: 1957), pp. 140-141.

16 "Contrasting Concepts of Harmony in Architecture: The 1982 Debate Between Christopher Alexander and Peter Eisenman," op.cit.

17 Herbert Marcuse, *The Aesthetic Dimension: Toward a Critique of Marxist Aesthetics*, Beacon Press (Boston: 1978), p.xi and p. 9 (emphasis added).

18 Neil Leach, "Architecture or Revolution," Neil Leach, ed., *Architecture and Revolution: Contemporary perspectives on Central and Eastern Europe*, Routledge (London and New York: 1999), p. 114.

19 Christian Norberg-Schulz, *Intentions in Architecture*, The MIT Press (Cambridge, MA: 1965), p. 17.

20 Norberg-Schulz, ibid., p. 71.

21 Norberg-Schulz, ibid., pp. 72, 79.

22 "The problem is that in a world of architectural production driven by competition, any logical constraint on a designer's freedom of expression leadsthe designer—perversely but inevitably—to explore precisely those forbidden places outlawed by prevailing conventions. In defying such logic, the designer seeks to 'defamiliarize' what has become so commonplace that it is no longer capable of eliciting an aesthetic response and, therefore, serving as a useful mode of competition. This is the heroic conceit of the contemporary avant-garde: to confront danger in whichever of its manifestations appears at any given point in time." From Ochshorn, *Architecture's Dysfunctional Couple*, op. cit.

# 086

RICHARD
ROSA

PHASMOPHOBIA

**Ghost**[1]

The soul of a dead person believed to be an inhabitant of the unseen world or to appear to the living in bodily likeness[2]

Often believed to have a continued presence in some form of afterlife[3]

The spirit of a deceased person that persists in the material world (a ghost) is regarded as an unnatural or undesirable state of affairs and the idea of ghosts or revenants is associated with a reaction of fear[4]

A mere shadow or semblance; a trace[5]

Although the human soul was sometimes symbolically or literally depicted in ancient cultures as a bird or other animal, it appears to have been widely held that the soul was an exact reproduction of the body in every feature.[6]

"It was a little like that game where you have to go from sausage to Plato in five steps, by association of ideas. Let's see: sausage, pig bristle, paintbrush, Mannerism, Idea, Plato... There are always connections: you have only to want to find them."—Umberto Eco, *Foucault's Pendulum*, 2007.[7]

Rem Koolhaas—architect, historian, provocateur, and document maker—has operated at the forefront of cutting-edge disciplinary and extra-disciplinary discourse for almost four decades, in a perpetual shaping and reshaping of the contemporary debate, by positing himself firmly within the unfamiliar, the unpopular, and the unknown. His reputation as a cynical, intrepid thinker and liberated maker is galvanized by a broad spectrum of groundbreaking architectural and urbanistic design works, writings, teachings, and oratory spectacles. Ironically, his proclivity for being one step ahead of the pack is at odds with what I propose to be a deeply felt and carefully cultivated phasmophobia: a fear of the ghosts of the architectural ancestors that haunt his work and that Koolhaas fears, if not secretly desires, full acknowledgement of. From the major progenitors of twentieth-century modernism that permeate the entire oeuvre of OMA, to the peripheral figures that occupy the margins of the work, one finds that these ghosts appear sporadically to remind us of their ephemeral existence. Through readings that unpack the individual elements and devices of the projects of OMA into their distinct component sources, I will clarify the presence of both ancestral and indigenous ghosts throughout Koolhaas's body of work. With Koolhaas, an invisible presence always lingers in the background—specters haunting the work, verging on external manifestation and confrontation—threatening to reveal too much to solve the mystery of the work at hand.

## GHOST STORY ONE: PROVOCATIONS

Throughout history, architecture has maintained a dependent yet paradoxical relationship to that which preceded it. Historical precedent, while serving as the primary subject of reference, often becomes the unconscious foundation for invention and advancement in architecture; the process of transforming architectural ideas and thoughts with precise regard to cultural change and disciplinary evolution has guided the works of architects from Serlio to Stirling. Often the image of contemporary architecture masks the source material from which it was developed, either intentionally or unwittingly. This phenomenon was especially prominent in the late twentieth century when a pluralism of linguistic expression and style produced an unfamiliarity routinely mistaken for originality, often without engaging or even observing the lessons of the historical context within which it would eventually be situated. In light of the division between works of an autonomous nature and those cognizant of their relationship to an origin, this essay aims to initiate a larger study that will decipher precise relationships, and disseminate the genealogical basis of the work of Rem Koolhaas, with an emphasis on the built and unbuilt projects of the firm's first twenty-five years of production.

The central theme of this inquiry is that Koolhaas, arguably the most influential architect of our time, has crafted much of his work to produce a thinly veiled parallax view of Le Corbusier's virtuosity, and to a lesser extent that of other major figures of twentieth-century modernism. This study is focused specifically on the architectural production of buildings and projects with regard to their historical, typological, and cultural origins and references, from those deftly disguised behind a veil to those evident to all. The dense synthesis of narrative, symbolic, linguistic, and typological contents that comprise the work suggests that Koolhaas follows the Corbusian edict issued in his 1948 manifesto, *A New World of Space*: "In a complete and successful work there are hidden masses of implications, a veritable world which reveals itself to those whom it may concern, which means: to those who deserve it."[8]

Left: Charlotte Perriand, Le Corbusier, *l'Equipment Intérieur d'une Habitation*, 1929, mixed media. Right: Rem Koolhaas (OMA), *Villa Bordeaux*, Bordeaux, France, 1998.

**Annotation No.1**

In the Bordeaux House, Koolhaas references the iconic photo montage-collage constructed by Le Corbusier, Charlotte Perriand, and Pierre Jeanneret for *l'Equipment Intérieur d'une Habitation* installation for the Salon d'Automne in 1929. Here the pink-red bar floats above the field on the left side, with the glazed surface beneath the hovering mass composed of a series of variably colored

> and positioned rectangular glass panels. In both projects, the courtyard or living space is framed by an almost identical figure of blue sky that wraps the pink-red bar, extending the horizon beneath the bar, over the bar, and then back down to the courtyard or living level. It is at this connection between horizon and sky that we notice that the glazed panel system in Le Corbusier and Perriand's project becomes the two-story glass system that Koolhaas employs at Bordeaux. Finally, the lack of articulation of the ceiling or sky in the 1929 project produces the appearance of columns that are either hanging from or piercing the sky, a unique phenomenon that Koolhaas utilizes with considerable resemblance when he positions the cable for the structural counter-weight at Bordeaux.

To position within a broader disciplinary spectrum the notion of work that does not immediately sacrifice its entire range of nuance and content to the participant,[9] it is easy to understand the relationship between the major concept or image identified by the consumer and obvious to all—that which is clearly hierarchical—versus that which is hidden or symbolic, waiting to be detected at a later time or through a more sustained engagement. Some level of expertise and literacy, the ability to *read*, is required as Koolhaas operates on a multitude of literary levels, such that there is significantly more to discover after the initial encounter. What Velázquez achieves in two-dimensions in *Las Meninas* by giving us an obvious primary narrative and then contradicting this with numerous alternate but equally compelling storylines, Koolhaas achieves in three-dimensions while also satisfying the requisite utilitarian needs of architectural production.

**Left:** James Stirling, *Southgate Estate*, Runcorn New Town, Cheshire, England, 1977. Reproduced from Arnell, Peter, Ted Bickford, and Colin Rowe, *James Stirling, Buildings and Projects* (New York: Rizzoli International, 1993). **Right:** Rem Koolhaus (OMA), Villa Bordeaux, 1998. Photo by Hans Werlemann.

**Annotation No.2**

In the massing, chromatic material base, and fenestration at the Bordeaux House, Koolhaas references the bold massing of James Stirling's Southgate Estate Housing Project of 1977 in Runcorn New Town. Here Stirling develops two powerful parallel horizontal slabs that frame a horizontal sandwich of compressed space. Koolhaas constructs a similar sense of the floating bar above a base bar. But unlike Stirling, who grounds his floating mass with repetitive monolithic concrete towers, Koolhaas embraces his fascination with the modernist cantilever by erasing all visible structure in order to create the impression of an ultra-heavy monolithic red beam floating above the ground without an apparent suspension system. OMA makes direct quotations to Stirling in the shape, scale and operating mechanism for the circular windows. In both projects, the large circular openings are filled with giant windows that operate on a pivot and punctuate the otherwise monolithic suspended bars.

A deeper investigation of the work reveals an exponentially more expansive web of informants, highlighted by Koolhaas's regard for the cultural setting of each project. By unmasking the broad range of influences on the work of OMA—including technology, typology, politics, culture, and an aggressive attitude towards program—Koolhaas can be firmly positioned within the traditions of architecture, prolonging a carefully calculated lineage as opposed to the popular perception that his work is somehow ahistorical, frivolous, or driven significantly by interests in pop-culture and consumerism. The projects of Le Corbusier, Mies, Aalto, and Rietveld, among others, exist for Koolhaas as ghosts: ancestral figures whose presence in the work is palpable, but who remain elusive. By identifying the roles of both architectural history and contemporary culture in the oeuvre of OMA, it becomes possible to understand the work not only as visionary, but simultaneously as the logical and predictable product of the evolution of architecture, ultimately sharpening our ability to accurately read, decipher, and disseminate works of architecture in a way that is parallel to Koolhaas's tactics.

From left: Rem Koolhaas (OMA), *Villa Bordeaux*, Bordeaux, France, 1998.; Richard Neutra, Singleton House, Los Angeles, 1955. Photo by Julius Shulman. Reproduced from Arthur Drexler and Thomas S. Hine, *The Architecture of Richard Neutra: From International Style to California Modern* (New York: The Museum of Modern Art, 1982). Richard Neutra, *Perkins House*, Pasadena, California, 1955. Ibid.

**Annotation No.3**

In the Bordeaux House, Koolhaas makes direct references to the Case Study Houses of the mid-twentieth century, especially the structural condition of extending a beam and column beyond the line of enclosure to achieve a more theatrical, if not enigmatic, structural ensemble. The modernist ambition to develop even more seamless and dramatic effects of spatial extension are taken to a new level at Bordeaux where three visually and materially unrelated structural devices converge to discreetly suspend the weighted red block, allowing one to experience the unremitting fusion of outside and inside: in each case a black, independent trabeated device extends beyond the building to construct an exterior bay that counters the invisible glazing system, obscuring the distinction between interior space and exterior landscape.

## GHOST STORY TWO: THE HAUNTED HOUSE

In Edgar Allan Poe's *The Purloined Letter*, the antagonist sits calmly at the dining table while police examine every crevice of his home in a futile search for evidence of blackmail. Meanwhile, the thief has left, in an envelope in a letter rack and in plain sight, the instrument of his extortion. The investigators, in their zeal to find what they expect to be well-hidden, never think to look with their eyes, to look 'right in front of themselves' for the answer. The most obvious of all is often the most difficult to see.

For Koolhaas, the clear parallel is the direct quotation that is found in the deconstructed concrete and metal elements that comprise the Villa dall'Ava in the Saint Cloud district of Paris.

Here Koolhaas reconstructs with great detail the precise motif of the façades of the Villa Savoye in Poissey. The project, balanced on piloti and completed with the requisite roof garden, ceremonial ramp, and spiral stair, faces two directions. While being understood as a somewhat platonic object in the round, situated so as to command a view of the Eiffel Tower, the house exists as the physical body for Koolhaas, persistently haunted by the ghost of Savoye that, while situated more than twenty miles outside of Paris, is yet ever-present on the hill in Saint Cloud. In this regard, Rem Koolhaas is at his most audacious. He takes from Le Corbusier (among others) and gives us the most conspicous translations of Le Corbusier's own primary platonic ideas, dresses them in Prada while pulling the peasant wool easily over our eyes.

Left: Rem Koolhaas (OMA), *Villa dall'Ava*, Paris, 1991. Photo by Hisao Suzuki. Reproduced in *El Croquis* 53, pp. 160-161. Right: Le Corbusier, *Villa Savoye*, Poissey, France, 1929. Photo by Pedro Kok.

**Annotation No.4**

While the Villa dall'Ava in Paris, takes obviously and unapologetically from Le Corbusier's Villa Savoye, a closer examination of the disposition of elements and syntactical sensibilities deepens the case. A subversive effort to deform the ideal composition of the original is evident. Koolhaas, on some level a Dutch modernist, applies eccentric forces to the underlying symmetry to counter the singularity of the Swiss architect's ideal. The indoor glazing shifts to the right, one corner is grounded by the final piloti while the other corner floats freely toward the left. The existing tree serves as a cubist stand-in for the missing column, detached as a deep-space/shallow-space condition. The curvilinear garden wall at the top of Savoye—opaque and freeform—is translated into a temporary building construction fence, alluding to the orientation of Le Corbusier's wall where the purist plastic surface faces the proper front while the 'back' of the garden wall is revealed 'frontally' as we ascend the ramp, exposing its lattice structure and indicating a reorientation of primary front. Koolhaas has both stripped away the stucco covering and repositioned the curved garden fence wall from periphery to center. Further evidence of a planned deformation is presented in the façade itself where, at first glance, the horizontal wall and ribbon window appear similar. The window to surface proportion is not only different, however, Koolhaas's main façades recreate the precise proportions that Le Corbusier uses on his secondary and tertiary façades where the window marks the four-foot zone of structural setback on the façade. Here, Koolhaas registers the rotation and 90-degree reorientation of Le Corbusier's project by fusing the side onto the back-front.

This reading of the work illustrates innate and dependent connections to a vast constellation of both architecturally significant nd insignificant historical models, moments, and manifestos. Koolhaas's work can be understood—and possibly only fully understood—as a derivative collusion engaging a subset of canonical works of architecture in a way that both reinforces traditional acts of historical reference and introduces inventive and innovative tactics for their co-registration. The work is on one level entirely predictable, logical, and evident, yet at the same time it is abruptly unique, unexpected, and synthetic, producing the effect of sudden contrast coincident with overall cohesion. Ultimately, this deep reading of the work will unveil a veritable family tree of connections, references, and quotations that define an expanding network of lineages that operate as its structural and philosophical core, revealing the DNA of OMA.

Left: Rem Koolhaas (OMA), *Villa dall'Ava*, Paris, 1991. Photo by Hisao Suzuki. Reproduced in *El Croquis* 53, pp. 160-161. Right: Mies van der Rohe, *Berlin Building Exposition*, Berlin, 1931. Reproduced from Barry Bergdoll and Terence Riley, *Mies in Berlin* (New York: Museum of Modern Art, 2001).

**Annotation No.5**

In the Villa dall'Ava, Koolhaas remakes the domestic model constructed by Mies van der Rohe for the Berlin Building Exhibition of 1931. Here the glazing, metal frame, proportions, and position of the glass box derive from lessons offered by the Mies prototype. The asymmetrical cantilever reveals a ceiling pushing in two directions, with Koolhaas taking greater liberties with the extreme structural ambitions. The central column in Koolhaas's glass chamber is positioned as a thinner version of the radius container of the bathroom in Mies's demonstration. The floor pattern of broken naturalistic stone that extends Mies's interior space to the private garden beyond is made rhetorical by Koolhaas, who constructs a faux paved surface under his cantilever. He then transposes Mies's pattern to the vertical surfaces of the front of the house. These acts of dismembering and recombining elements of canonical modern models speak to a reverence for the lessons offered by modernism, with a liberated spirit of expression, language, space-making, and programmatic activity, positioning Koolhaas comfortably between the historical and the present, relying on both to construct new responses to contemporary contexts.

Koolhaas—who has always operated with a Madonna-esque knack for being *ahead of the curve*, as a trend-setter and a force that directs us to the next thing before it is a thing—could have had his star cast in a different cosmological light were his eager disciples to have the OMA curtain pulled back to reveal the true mechanical-historical workings of the Koolhaasian empire. The cultural icon who invested in and celebrated new conflations of program, and who introduced us to and celebrated congestion, shopping, lagos, junkspace, elevators, bigness, elements, preservation, and recently the countryside, might appeal to a different constituency were his indebtedness to, or obsession with, the canonical figures of high modernism to be revealed as the requisite framework for his platform of vision and invention. Similarly, the comprehension of his promotion of a version of globalism might be altered were his deeply rhetorical acts of vernacular, iconographic, and cultural contextualism to be illuminated.

To be clear, the critique here is not of Koolhaas in any way, but of the limitations of a populist audience, rabid to consume a set of political aspirations that are rapidly shifting and buzzword-driven. Koolhaas, I argue, understands and has consciously crafted his position as the next worthy addition in the linage of the Dutch Masters from Rembrandt to Mondrian to van Doesburg and so on. At the same time, he has constructed a parallel set of narratives—a body and a soul—a collection of works that at once satisfy the mainstream culture of consumption just enough to appeal to and appease the mass's desire for a neatly packaged reductive caricature. As a second ghost-like project, it embeds multiple ambitions, bodies of knowledge, references, and revelations within its construction. The latter project is what defines the work of Koolhaas as operating on a level inaccessible to many, alternately internal to and external to the discipline. These works do not presuppose that architecture is an elitist or esoteric enterprise, but rather a work of art, one that exists as a multi-layered proposition as opposed to a one-liner, and one that operates in a multitude of capacities and levels of decipherability. These range from the idea that there are fundamental consumable ideas evident and available to all, and that there are texts and subtexts, layers, stories, and references, combinations and contradictions that exist within a work that are available for anyone interested in and able to identify, extract, and engage the content. Viktor Shklovsky's premise is not lost on Koolhaas: "The purpose of art…is to lead us to a knowledge of a thing through the organ of sight instead of recognition. By 'enstranging' objects and complicating form, the device of art makes perception long and 'laborious.' The perceptual process in art has a purpose all its own and ought to be extended to the fullest. *Art is a means of experiencing the process of creativity. The artifact itself is quite unimportant.*"[10]

**Left:** Rem Koolhaas (OMA), *Casa da Musica*, Porto, Portugal, 2000. Photo by Eugenio Aglietti. **Right:** Marcel Breuer, *Begrisch Hall*, Bronx, New York, 1961. Photo by Jason Woods.

**Annotation No.6**

In the Casa da Musica, Koolhaas lifts the modernist theater awkwardly from its delicate perch to construct an otherworldly contextual figure in Porto that finds its origin in Marcel Breuer's Begrisch Hall at Bronx Community College (1956-61). Where the Breuer building finds its literal expressive external form in the geometric shape of the internal programmatic activity of lecture halls and theaters, Koolhaas constructs the 'image' of the apparent theater, reflecting the expected sectional form, raked seating, and wedge shaped container of Breuer. However, in the Porto project, the exterior form has absolutely nothing to do with the actual spatial form of the concert hall inside. Koolhaas constructs an internal oxymoron by employing the three-dimensional theater form motif, signifying function and iconography, when in reality the music hall is modeled after the ideal form for a symphony hall, an elongated shoebox. Begrisch Hall, a paradigm for the modernist ambition to clearly express and represent function in the form of the building is countered by the postmodernist sensibilities of the Casa da Musica where the relationship between internal figural voids and the external image-based packaging is negotiated by a generous and malleable mass of poche.

## GHOST STORY THREE: THE CONSTRUCTION OF THE BODY + SOUL

Koolhaas' interest in historical sources that predate twentieth-century modernism is often manifest in the form of references to cultural, vernacular, political, and iconographic traditions endemic to the *genius loci* of the project's context. Koolhaas promotes rhetorical political and cultural commentary, both positive and negative, through content that is difficult to detect, embedded within carefully crafted three-dimensional collages presented as program-driven logics: red herring from the beginning. To arrive at the core of the matter requires rigorous analytical reading and dissection of the typological genesis and absorbed deformations of the works in question. By looking at Koolhaas through a series of carefully defined and revealing analytical filters one can address and begin to repair the deepening schism between late-twentieth, early twenty-first-century architecture and the past.

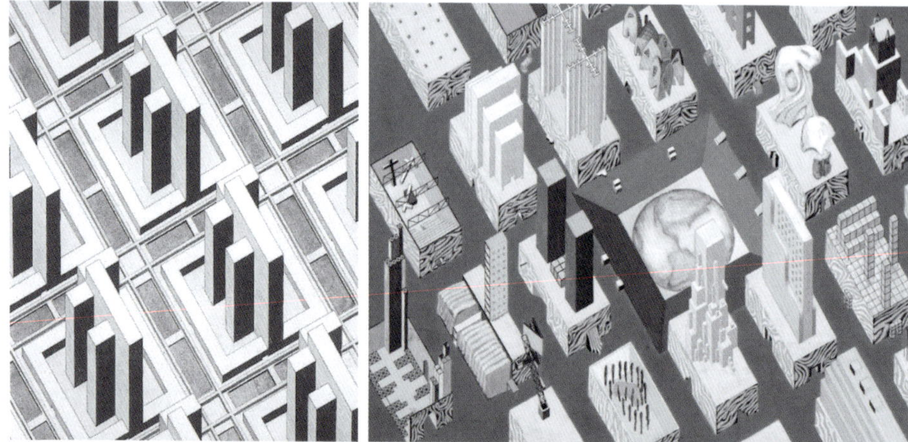

From top left: Cornelis Van Eesteren, *Optimal Relationship Between Skyscrapers and Traffic*, 1926. Reproduced in *ReD Magazine*, iss. 2 (1929), p. 227.; Rem Koolhaas, *City of the Captive Globe*, 1972. Reproduced by Rem Koolhaas and Zoe Zenghelis, *Delirious New York* (England: Oxford University Press, 1978).; Raymond Hood, *Daily News Building*, New York, 1930. Reproduced from the website *A View on Cities*.

**Annotation No.7**

In the *City for a Captive Globe*, Koolhaas makes direct references to two independent, unrelated sources: his interests in the works of the Amsterdam urban planner Cornelis van Eesteren and American architect Raymond Hood, van Eesteren for his model of formal urban structure and Hood for his symbolic and tactical importation of iconographic content as spectacle. The 1972 polemical study of the contrasting duality of New York's unrelentingly uniform grid and the unrestricted freedom of function and expression utilizes Cornelius van Eesteren's proposal for the optimal relationship between skyscrapers and traffic. This relationship is the formal and structural substrate for a project that employs the suspended and captive globe borrowed from Raymond Hood's Daily News Building Lobby in Manhattan—the iconic symbol of New York as the world. Van Eesteren provides Koolhaas and then-partner, Elia Zenghelis, with the utilitarian ideal, complete in its form, syntax, proportion, and overall geometric strategy, for organizing the relationship between mass, space, light, and infrastructure that provides the perfect foil for the delirium of a Manhattan that can at once represent the globe and hold it captive.

The projects, buildings, and ideas of Rem Koolhaas are characterized by a paradoxical line of contradiction—presenting thesis then counter-thesis with seamless ease—a lesson materialized and mastered by Le Corbusier in work that could be at once Pompeian, industrial, utilitarian, sculptural, cinematographic, and ritualistically primal. A filmmaker before he studied architecture, it is with a film editor's sensibility that Koolhaas employs methods of cross-cut, splice, montage, dissolve, and the counter-shot with great agility, from constructing architectural scenes that directly quote their references to embedding phantom content invisible to all but the most discerning of readers. The act of constructing present but elusive content represents the most temporally engaging of all his combinative operations. The work, overtly cloaked in literal quotations, mimicry, and borrowed fragments, countered by hidden symbolic content, becomes a game of references and sub-texts, cues and clues about precedent, cultural context, political content, and ultimately, the construction of meaning within otherwise functionalist propositions.

It is Rem Koolhaas—and for the purposes of this study I take the position that it is precisely Koolhaas and not the fluid confluence of persona that is OMA—that holds central responsibility for the dense and cryptic associations that underlie the oeuvre of OMA. While it is popular to claim that Koolhaas has limited control or specific input on the projects from typological variance to architectural detail, and that it is the endless collection of talented employees, associates, and disciples that he has amassed and surrounded himself with since the 1970s who are responsible for the invention and vision, I contend that it is singularly Rem Koolhaas who is responsible for the deeply rhetorical and substantively layered work that has been evident since his *Berlin Wall—Voluntary Prisoners* diploma project at the Architectural Association. Koolhaas's demonstrated flirtations with the major figures of high modernism is evidenced in his more blatant homages to Le Corbusier and Mies van der Rohe—and as Randy Shear states, "Architecture has always been a game of looking forward and looking backward,"[11] and Koolhaas plays this game with Corbusian vitality, fearless of friction, kitsch, or bad taste, aggressively embracing the widest peripheral view of targets and sources. It is the ability to embed within a work of obvious primary origin an unrelated collection of references while deftly smoothing the relationship into one singularly clear and symphonic construct that distinguishes the work of OMA from that of other firms, and firmly places it in the pantheon of great works of rhetorical depth and achievement in architecture. Typically the combination of unrelated content is understood against the background of a unified construction, the primary tactic being the relentless reliance on the overbearingly clear and dominant formal diagram, often in the form of a perimeter limit.

Le Corbusier reconceptualized an aspect of architectural theory by synthesizing the lessons of that which came before with the particulars of a fluid contemporary condition. One might say the same of Koolhaas. Where Le Corbusier exploited early twentieth-century technological advancements in the evolution of concrete and steel, Koolhaas today works with structural glass and transparent concrete, reimagining the performative and perceptual terms of the cantilever and the capacity of a structural system for gravitational hijinks. Koolhaas has turned the living unit into a distinct mechanistic enterprise in Bordeaux, a dismembered Villa dall'Ava in Saint Cloud, and a tension of sheared slabs in the Dutch House. Le Corbusier was responsible for creating a unique and demonstrable historically-inclined modernism in architecture, one where his historical references and idealized sources were identified and celebrated, their transformation put on display in compliance with the doctrines of modernism. Koolhaas operates with slightly less openness when it comes to revealing the origins and depth of content from which he borrows and sometimes steals. Only the tip of the iceberg is revealed here.

Left: Mies van der Rohe, *National Gallery*, Berlin, 1955. Right: Rem Koolhaas (OMA), *Kunsthal*, Rotterdam, 1989. Photo by Richard Rosa.

**Annotation No.8**

Here we compare Koolhaas's Kunsthal in Rotterdam with Mies's National Gallery in Berlin: the paradigmatic model of modern museum as origin; a simulacra of museums; Mies as manifesto. In these two low-rise, square, steel boxes the debt owed by the Dutch assemblage of rhetorical contradictions to the Berlin original is palpable. Koolhaas glazes his roadside showroom with a mullion system, cantilevered portico, glazing format and reconstituted ground plane largely in line with the lessons delivered by the National Gallery. The literal quotation of the black steel beam punctuated by regulated vertical braces that caps both projects is similar enough to instigate a fiction about the Kunsthal being constructed from surplus steel from the Mies masterpiece.

Unlike the deeply nationalistic and typologically motivated work of Giuseppe Terragni in 1930s Italy, a body of work at once emancipated by the lightless, language, and tectonic opportunities afforded him via the Gruppo Sette and simultaneously and permanently both enshrined and encumbered by the weight of the Italian architectural historical reverence that few architects of the peninsula had escaped. Unlike the new spatial language of Mies in Germany with his direct Wrightian and Dutch sources, Le Corbusier demonstrated a greater sense of fluidity, flexibility, and combinative agility in his invention and especially in the transformational tricks he played while rethinking and revising typological, compositional, and organizational schema across the globe. Did Le Corbusier make Swiss, Parisian, modern-industrial, or 'Indian' buildings in Chandigarh and Ahmedabad? Yes, all of the above, and all fused together into composite constructions. While Zaha Hadid brings her brand to your home town, Frank Gehry delivers his wreckage of metal to the highest bidder, and Herzog & de Meuron detail with irony combined with the attentiveness one might expect of the Swiss, Koolhaas, aware of the limitless potentials of embracing the global game, has exploited the notion of the architect as globetrotting magician, able to produce culturally appropriate buildings anywhere, anytime, while simultaneously redefining the aesthetics of cool and the image of tomorrow through his icy smooth, shockingly unpredictable provocations.

From the beginning of his formal architectural education, Rem Koolhaas's work has operated as part political manifesto, part extension of high modernism, part redefinition of the terms of contemporary architecture, and surprisingly, part nostalgic catalogue of a collection of seemingly disparate histories of architecture–histories that provide the continuum of soul for Koolhaas's otherwise enigmatic and fractured body of work.

## GHOST STORY FOUR: AN INCONCLUSIVE CONCLUSION

In an age of apparent innovation, one that has reexamined and redirected the discipline in areas of technology, fabrication, ecology, representation, and functionality, while introducing ideas about new origins—and Koolhaas has influenced, if not defined the leading discourse in some of these areas with major contributions including *Delirious New York, Junkspace, Harvard Project on the City*, and the 2014 Venice Architectural Biennale *Fundamentals*—he has simultaneously constructed a lesser-celebrated and largely undetected shadow career of works based on a densely layered integration of multiple, unrelated historical models. In this capacity, the work situates OMA's obsessive commitment to the contemporary urban and associated cultural condition within a framework of an archeology of typological ghosts, distinct from an architecture discarded by most critics as less relevant in addressing the questions facing architecture in the third millennium.

**Annotation No.9**

The Kunsthal in Rotterdam, provides a different light and insight into the Koolhaasian sensibility about context. Here he displays the tactics for making a building that advances and mutates a lineage of earlier typological

Top: Rem Koolhaas (OMA), *Kunsthal*, Rotterdam, 1989. Photos by Richard Rosa. Bottom left: Port of Rotterdam, 1962.; Bottom right: *De Hef Railway Bridge*, Rotterdam, 1939. Photo by Menno Janssen.

KUNSTH

> experiments in Dutch functionalism and the making of cultural artifacts, but that also serves as an intervention into and born of a specific place. Here the qualities endemic to Rotterdam's image and industrial sensibility manifest as architectonic elements embedded within the project and serve as the impetus and source for linguistic, material, and symbolic representation of the project's context. Rotterdam, the largest container shipping port in Europe, is identified by the industrial character of the functional constructs that populate the harbor. Koolhaas produces a museum, one without a collection that is then perpetually involved in the act of shipping and receiving, that is a reflection if not extension of the industrially scaled and naked steel equipment that give the city its most identifiable features.

The thesis presented here operates on the assumption that Koolhaas has surreptitiously examined in great detail the entirety of Le Corbusier's oeuvre with a particular interest in the less celebrated works published by Le Corbusier in his *Oeuvre complète*. Regarding Koolhaas's investment in the domestic, institutional, and urban scaled projects and competition entries of the last four decades, there is ample evidence of Koolhaas scouring the B-sides in search of unfulfilled potential, unused diagrams, unrealized dreams, and the barely visible masterworks in the margins. It is in this context that Koolhaas may be at his most ingenious.

It is his ability to recognize the quantity and quality of unfinished business that was left behind by Le Corbusier, and then to be able to extract from the literal pages of his legacy—a legacy in front of our eyes, hidden in plain sight, a well-preserved gold mine of architectural thought—and to then unapologetically translate the range of organizational schema into the most radical, most modern, most visionary and layered architectures of his time. So supremely seductive are these frigid constructs that they are blindly consumed by the most fashion conscious of architecture audiences, while at the same time able to intellectually engage the most discerning of historically minded and scholarly literate skeptics. That Koolhaas is able to do both simultaneously, without claiming to do either, is evidence of his absolute control of the production of his work, and the cunning construction of his own self-image: a case of the careful manipulation of the mind's-eye of the public's imagination.

Left: James Stirling, *Nuestaatsgalerie*, Stuttgart, Germany, 1982. Photo by Steve Silverman. Right: Rem Koolhaas (OMA), *Kunsthal*, Rotterdam, 1989. Photo by Richard Rosa.

## Annotation No.10

Koolhaas's Kunsthal in Rotterdam, a museum project centered on an outdoor public passageway that connects two distinct sections of the city, borrows the urban and ultimately political concept from James Stirling's Neue Staatsgalerie in Stuttgart. To focus here on a signifying accent feature, both projects contrast the beige stone boxes with a pop-postmodernist expressionism in the form of matching brightly colored hollow steel railings that punctuate marble clad museums—buildings that have significantly more in common than this essay has the opportunity to elaborate on.

1 Editor's Note: This essay is an excerpt from the first chapter of a significantly more comprehensive book, *The DNA of OMA*, to be released in 2020.

2 Merriam-Webster Dictionary, online edition, © 2019 Miriam-Webster, Incorporated.

3 en.wikipedia.org re; Ghost, Fear of Ghosts.

4 Ibid.

5 Dictionary.com re; Ghost.

6 Oxford English Dictionary, online edition, © 2019 Oxford University Press.

7 Eco, *Foucault's Pendulum*, Harcourt Books, 2007, p. 217.

8 Le Corbusier, *New World of Space* (New York: Reynal & Hitchcock, 1948), p. 8. In 1996 In Charlottesville VA the quote, excluding the final phrase, was shared with me by my colleague, Jeffrey Hildner. Seven years later, he shared with me the final seven words, "which means: to those who deserve it."

9 One might make the comparison to the academic disciplines of comparative literature or film studies.

10 Viktor Shklovsky, "Art as Device," *Theory of Prose*, trans. Benjamin Sher (Normal, IL, Dalkey Archive Press, 1990), p. 6.

11 Internet Reference, posted December 18, 2019, https://www.facebook.com/shear1.

# between reality & represent

Tension

its

tion

108

RUBÉN
ALCOLEA

# SCIOPHOBIA

There is a willow grows aslant a brook,
That shows his hoar leaves in the glassy stream;
There with fantastic garlands did she come
Of crow-flowers, nettles, daisies, and long purples
That liberal shepherds give a grosser name,
But our cold maids do dead men's fingers call them:
There, on the pendent boughs her coronet weeds
Clambering to hang, an envious sliver broke;
When down her weedy trophies and herself
Fell in the weeping brook. Her clothes spread wide;
And, mermaid-like, awhile they bore her up:
Which time she chanted snatches of old tunes;
As one incapable of her own distress,
Or like a creature native and indued
Unto that element: but long it could not be
Till that her garments, heavy with their drink,
Pull'd the poor wretch from her melodious lay
To muddy death.

—Queen Gertrude, *Hamlet*, Act IV, Scene VII.

# THE THRESHOLD OF FLOATING

Captured in this beautiful fragment, the death of Ophelia is contextualized within an intimate garden overtaken by cold, broken imagery. John Everett Millais' *Ophelia* (1852) captures this tragedy by shifting the viewer's perspective from the stage to the eyes of Queen Gertrude. Ophelia has fallen into the river from a tree while gathering flowers and singing, unaware of the danger as her clothes growing "heavy with their drink, / Pull'd the poor wretch from her melodious lay" down "to muddy death." John Guille Millais, the son of the painter, described the incident during the production of the painting, which could have resulted in the death of the model:

> Miss Siddal had a trying experience whilst acting as a model for Ophelia. In order that the artist might get the proper set of the garments in water and the right atmosphere and aqueous effects, she had to lie in a large bath filled with water, which was kept at an even temperature by lamps placed beneath. One day, just as the picture was nearly finished, the lamps went out unnoticed by the artist, who was so intensely absorbed in his work that he thought of nothing else, and the poor lady was kept floating in the cold water till she was quite benumbed.[1]

The idea of having Miss Siddal benumbed, or deprived of complete physical or emotional feeling by being suspended in chilly water, establishes a direct connection between the model and the young Ophelia in an unintentional, but acute way. It bestows an intensity latent in previous sketches. Millais' *Ophelia* is, in fact, one of the most suggestive portraits of the tragic Shakespeare's character, although the art critics of its time judged the work as "completely inaccurate… There is no pathos, no melancholy, no brightening up, no last lucid interval. If she dies swan-like with a song, there is no sound of melody, no poetry in this strain."[2] It is precisely this absence of pathos, or her emotionless and obliviousness to her doom, that permits Millais' *Ophelia* to transcend other portraits of the drowned lady-in-waiting. It protects the beauty of youth and pure love by embalming it; her garments encapsulate the body within the natural stream of water. As planned in preliminary drafts, the corpse floats facing up with rigid, open arms and a clear expression of dismay. Indeed, the poor Ophelia shown in Millais' painting does lay, although perhaps not as melodiously as Shakespeare imagined.

**Previous:** Sir John Everett Millais (1829-1896), *Study for the head of Elizabeth Siddal for 'Ophelia,'* 1852.; Sir John Everett Millais, *Ophelia*, 1887. Tate Images. **From top:** Simeon Solomon (1840-1905), *Ophelia*, 1851-2. From the collection of © Tullie House Museum, Carlisle.; Theodor von der Beek, *Ophelia*, 1901.; Paul Delaroche, *La Jeune Martyre/Ophelia*, 1855. Paris, The Louvre.

The Pre-Raphaelites, a secret society of young artists founded in 1848, popularised the character of Ophelia throughout London as her cold portrayal gained prominence. This practice extended beyond painting into the work of early photographers like Julia Margaret Cameron.[3] Other famous representations of Ophelia include Simeon Solomon's medieval *Ophelia* (1887), Theodor von der Beek's crying, floating *Ophelia* in 1901, or more recently Paul Delaroche's *Young Martyr* (1955) where the juvenile lady floats with her hands bound together.[4] The Pre-Raphaelites depict the young lady as static while floating on her back, reinforcing the impossibility of the body to embrace the aquatic medium. The human figure is protected by white fabric garments, avoiding as much contact as possible with the liquid of her death. Eugène Delacroix's romantic vision in *Death of Ophelia* (1853), quite contemporary with Millais', followed the lithographies developed by the French artist over the course of that decade. In this rendition, the young lady, afraid of slipping into the water, is depicted in a strange, half-fallen stance while gripping a tree branch. We now imagine Ophelia rhythmically swinging within the pool, nearly dancing, with both her hair and garments welcoming water while gently pulling this non-rigid and still warm body down the stream.

Left: Eugène Delacroix, *Death of Ophelia*, 1843, New York, The Metropolitan Museum of Art. Right: Eugène Delacroix, *Death of Ophelia*, 1853, Paris, The Louvre.

What makes Millais' work so compelling is not just the presence of water or Ophelia's lifeless flotation, but the poignant illustration of an intimate and common fear. *Aquaphobia*, the irrational, persistent anxiety felt towards water or other liquid states is one of the most common phobias, as we consider it our non-natural environment. Around 45 percent of American adults are frightened of deep water in pools, and 65 percent are distressed by deep open water.[5] Various reasons trigger the instinctive fear of water, but the most important one remains the fear of drowning.[6] This feeling is caused by tension experienced when the swimmer moves their head out of the water to inhale, something not just restricted to beginners.[7] Aquaphobia produces anxiety even after recognizing an ocean, river, lake, or bathtub poses no imminent threat. Nevertheless, science has demonstrated that fear in general—aquaphobia in particular—may be controlled and treated through certain activities and anticipation, with the potential to transform the fear into pleasure.[8] As generally happens, the deviation of the phobia into its opposite goes far beyond the romanticized philia. The term *aquaphilia* typically refers to the love of practicing water activities, although also commonly used as a fetish term, a kind of sexual paraphilia, which involves images of people swimming or posing underwater, as well as practicing sexual activity in or under water.[9] Fear and love of water do not come as an abstraction, as both involve the body and its interaction with the liquid state. To that extent, it is the specific condition of the body floating in water which then becomes something stronger than an obsession. Perhaps it is precisely that border, the fine line where water merges with air, where the transition from life to death seems to be easier.

One of the first literary suicides that many students experience comes from *The Awakening* by Kate Chopin, originally published in 1899. Edna Pontellier's suicide is eerie as she walks into and drowns in the Gulf of Mexico:

> The water of the Gulf stretched out before her, gleaming with the million lights of the sun. The voice of the sea is seductive, never ceasing, whispering, clamoring, murmuring, inviting the soul to wander in abysses of solitude. All along the white beach, up and down, there was no living thing in sight. A bird with a broken wing was beating the air above, reeling, fluttering, circling disabled down, down to the water.[10]

Kate Chopin's sublime description of Edna's final moment conveys a reality of relief, juxtaposed with the psychological suffering of being a mother, wife, and lover. The rhythmic prose depicts not only the act of death as an act of freedom, but describes the swinging movement of the ocean surface, once a joyful playground, now a dramatic crime scene.

**Top:** Toni Frissell, *A woman floats in Weeki Wachee Springs*, Florida, 1947. **Bottom:** Edmund Teske, *Mineral Baths*, 1967, photo, 7.625" × 9.825". Los Angeles, The J. Paul Getty Museum.

The presence of water has undergone its own transformation throughout history, whether through engagement with a subject or by means of abstraction. The work of both Toni Frissell[11] and Edmund Teske[12] demonstrate photographic explorations of underwater bodies during the mid-century. Here, not only is the body bordering on playful, it highlights the symbiotic relationship allowing these images to evolve from intriguing visual compositions to something more emotive—and cinema does not fall far behind. One of the earliest experiments in immersive representations of water is Thomas Edison's two minute short film, *Panorama of Gorge Railway*.[13] Edison attached a camera to the front of a moving train, close to the edge of a river, and ascended the grade at high speed. The motion of the train opposed to the water creates an astonishing sensation. Impeded by the rocky path and interrupted in its course, spray and foam soar through the air. This short movie made an impression upon the audience as it shocked the viewers, produced anxiety and, in some cases, a genuine fear of drowning in front of the screen.[14]

The cinematic experience introduced and practiced sensorial communication to a curious audience. Described as an unforgettable experience resulting from watching a film or movie, the expression encompasses a richer meaning than either "cinematic" or "experience" do individually.[15] The authentic cinematic experience allows the viewer to enjoy not only perceptive, surface-level stimulation, but breaches further to the uncontrollable, subconscious nature. As a result, it produces something closer to the supernatural than physical reality.

As cinema matured in the 1920s, the avant-garde incorporated the word "cinematic" into their own vocabulary when referring to experimental films. Dadaists and surrealists explored the fresh opportunities of the "moving image"; László Moholy-Nagy referred to cinema as the natural evolution of photography and the only possible way of perceiving and expressing the complexities of the modern world.[16] Photography and film were no longer considered mere tools as a real and profound admiration spread among modernists. Moholy-Nagy stated that "the magic possibility of framing a certain space and time is what brought me to photography."[17] Moholy's admiration transformed into nearly a religious devotion, pointing to the cinematic media as something sacred that "emanated from an inner vision."[18] He illustrates early experiments as a personal journey: "When the light-prop was set in motion for the first time in 1930,

I felt like the 'sorcerer's apprentice.' The mobile was so startling in its coordinated motions and space articulations of light and shadow sequences that I almost believed in magic."[19] Artists have since pushed the boundaries of modern story-telling through the narrative of film to access deep, obscure feelings.[20]

Thriller and horror films soon took advantage of primitive cut-and-paste techniques when manipulating frames to execute the first terror-inducing cinematic tricks. One of the oldest movies, *Arrival of a Train* by the Lumière Brothers in 1895, is a fifty-second silent film showing the entry of a train to the French town of La Ciotat. Although not a horror movie by contemporary cinematic standards, the single, unedited shot induced panic as the audience witnessed a life-size train about to barrel out of the screen. Just a year later in 1896, French illusionist Georges Méliès produced what was considered the first true horror film. *Le Manoir du Diable*, or *The Haunted Castle*, was the first in a series of short movies in which Méliès explored the potential of film to scare the audience and create an imaginary world behind the screen. His film *Faust aux enfers*, or *The Damnation of Faust*, produced in 1903, is based on the classic Faust legend, but Méliès pays less attention to the story itself and instead, focuses on the special effects representing hell. The presence of waterfalls throughout the journey allow demons and monsters to float back and forth between liquid curtains before the protagonists reach the final stage of hell itself.[21]

While film as a medium challenges the creative expression of water, the motif of floating bodies becomes prevalent in both popular and cult cinema. While filming his movie *Frenzy* (1972), Alfred Hitchcock photographed himself floating down the River Thames for the movie's trailer, though actually using a mannequin of vague resemblance to the director. Hitchcock himself says: "I dare say you are wondering why I am floating around London's river like this. I am in the famous Thames River, investigating a murder. Rivers can be very sinister places, and in my new film *Frenzy*, this river you may say is the scene of a very horrible murder."[22] Contrary to his skyward gaze and hands crossed over his chest, Brenda is found floating facedown in a limp cruciform. The director avoids the possibility of making the viewer believe that his body was acting unconsciously. Entirely clothed, he floats like a log, shielded from the water. His fake death alludes to Millais and Solomon's paintings where the limits of the body are preserved, yet the actress performed her death explicitly by exposing every inch of her body to the deadly liquid.

Top: "Floating Brenda." Film still from Alfred Hitchcock, dir., *Frenzy*, 1972, London, England. Universal Pictures. Bottom: "Alfred Hitchcock floating in the River Thames for the the trailer of the movie Frenzy." Ibid.

Both classic and contemporary film take great measures to explore each iteration of the body in relation to water. Its presence, whether flowing in a stream or stagnant inside an enclosed room, is a recurring leitmotif in Andrei Tarkovsky's movies. In *Stalker* (1979), Aleksandr Kajdanovsky (the stalker), lies down in a stream and engages in a personal connection with the sinister soul of the Room while whispering and reflecting on the meaning of life. The Room, a place where "everybody gets what they need," is described as "the threshold" at the end of an introspective journey where "your innermost wishes will be made real."[23] The stalker and his friends gradually transform into water themselves, as sweat and tears cover their bodies and connect them to the spirit of the unknown. Their phobia transforms into love via an intense desire to find the ultimate meaning of their existence, even if requiring their own passing.

The duality between phobia and philia of the liquid medium becomes present in more recent movies, such as *A Cure for Wellness*, directed by Gore Verbinski in 2016. It depicts a contemporary use of the term aquaphilia, referring to the medical condition recognized by Central European physicians

From top: "A visitor lying inside the sand and water room." Film still from Andrei Tarkovsky, dir., *Stalker*, 1979, Russia. Mosfilm.; "The Stalker's hand." Ibid.; "Floating." Film still from Gore Verbinski, dir., *A Cure for Wellness*, 2016, Germany, Luxembourg, United States. 20th Century Fox.; "Floating." Ibid.

in the nineteenth century. Joy through immersive engagement with water characterizes this condition whether for recreational or therapeutic uses. Aside from the plot, this psychological horror film combines the beauty of its visually compelling shots with a literally saturated environment. Water is everywhere, whether liquid or fog, and complements the perception of the interior spaces as the plot evolves. Water not only transforms the way the senses perceive the different rooms, but is simultaneously the disturbance and the cure as the original fear gradually transitions to an irrational philia. Not only do human bodies float or sink deep into pools, but they also float and dance through dense foggy atmosphere, like a psychological journey that brings both actors and viewers to the threshold of life and death, or love and hate.

It is through examining these cinematic explorations that we can better understand the repulsive but also intriguing feeling towards unconscious bodies in water. Cinema offers the chance to gradually alter the body's positioning and reaction to water, exposing simultaneously the philia and phobia by provoking our senses into an immersive experience. In a way, this was ultimately how Gertrude was describing Ophelia's death.

1 Cfr. Millais, John Guille, *The Life and Letters of Sir John Everett Millais*, President of the Royal Academy (New York: Frederick A. Stokes Company, 1899).

2 Altick, Richard D., *Paintings from Books: Art and Literature in Britain,* 1760–1900 (Columbus: Ohio State University Press, 1985), p. 301.

3 The photographer Julia Margaret Cameron made several photographic studies on Ophelia, described in: *Rhodes, Kimberly, Ophelia and Victorian Visual Culture: Representing Body Politics in the Nineteenth Century* (Aldershot, England: Ashgate, 2008), chap. 4.

4 Gustave Klimt painting *Ria Munk on her Deathbed* (1912) usually is interpreted as a variation on Millais's *Ophelia*. In this occasion, Klimt shows the beauty of the young woman without visible traces of death.

5 According to data in 2009: Popke, Michael, "Back to swim school" in *Athletic Business*, 2009, pp. 52-61.

6 Bakar, Rofiza, Bakar, Jazredal, "Aquaphobia: Causes, Symptoms and Ways of Overcoming it for Future Well-Being," in *International Academic Research Journal of Social Science*, 2017, vol. 3, iss. 1, pp. 82-88.

7 Ibid.

8 LeDoux, Joseph E., "Coming to terms with fear", in *PNAS Proceedings of the National Academy of Sciences of the USA*, February 25, 2014, vol. 11, iss. 8, pp. 2871-2878.

9 Ramsland, Katherine M., McGrain, Patrick Norman, *Inside the Minds of Sexual Predators* (ABC-CLIO, Praeger, 2009), pp. 61–62.

10 Chopin, Kate, *The Awakening* (New York: Bantam Classic, 1981).

11 Antoniette Frissell Bacon (1907–1988) was an American photographer well known for her fashion, WWII and portrait photography. Cfr. Stafford, Sidney, *Toni Frissell: Photographs 1933–1967* (New York : Doubleday in association with the Library of Congress, 1994).

12 Edmund Rudolph Teske (1911–1996) was an American photographer with a prolific output of experimental photography. Cfr. Teske, Edmund, *Images from Within* (Carmel: Friends of Photography, 1980). Cox, Julian, *Spirit into Matter: The Photographs of Edmund Teske* (Los Angeles: J. Paul Getty Museum, 2004).

13 Thomas A. Edison, Inc, and Paper Print Collection, *Panorama of Gorge Railway* (United States: Edison Manufacturing Co, 1900). Video. *https://www.loc.gov/item/00694268/. 2 min.*

14 Edison was particularly interested in attaching cameras to the front of moving vehicles, and he did it in cars, trains, streetcars, and even subways. Cfr. Bruno, Giuliana, *Atlas of Emotion: Journeys in Art, Architecture and Film* (New York: Verso, 2002), p. 20.

15 The term 'cinematic' gets its definition as "of, relating to, suggestive of, or suitable for motion pictures or the filming of motion pictures." The word 'experience' has a more complex meaning, including "a practice derived from direct observation of on participation in events or in a particular activity," as well as "something encountered, undergone, or lived through." Definitions extracted from Merriam-Webster dictionary.

16 Moholy-Nagy, László, *Malerei, Fotografie, Film*, (Munich: Albert Langen, 1925). Published in English in Moholy-Nagy, László, *Painting, Photography, Film*, (Cambridge: MIT Press, 1969).

17 "This process of recording elements of three dimensions in the flow of time, and fixing them in a two-dimensional image, creates a new context for the elements of the photograph, and now they are detached from their original surroundings. They are involved in a close world in which they only relate to each other: all the rest of 'reality' has vanished." Moholy-Nagy, László in *Creative Camera*, (November 1976), p. 367.

18 Moholy-Nagy, László, *Vision in Motion* (Chicago: P. Theobald, 1947), p. 142.

19 Moholy-Nagy, László, "Abstract of an Artist," quoted in Kaplan, Louis, *László Moholy-Nagy: Biographical Writings*, (Durham: Duke University Press, 1995), p. 158-159.

20 Cutting, James E., "Narrative Theory and the Dynamics of Popular Movies." in *Psychonomic Bulletin & Review*, 2016, vol. 23, iss. 6, pp. 1713-1743.

21 Cfr. Frazer, John, *Artificially Arranged Scenes: The Films of Georges Méliès*, (Boston: G.K. Hall & Co., 1979); Rosen, Miriam, "Méliès, Georges," in Wakeman, John, *World Film Directors: Volume I, 1890–1945*, (New York: The H.W. Wilson Company, 1987), pp. 747–765.

22 Transcript of Alfred Hitchcock's presentation trailer for his film *Frenzy*, 1972.

23 *Stalker*, directed by Andrej Tarkovsky. USSR: Mosfilm, 1979. DVD.

122

# ELIE BOUTROS

# SCIOPHOBIA

B.Arch Thesis
Advisors: Aleksandr Mergold
& Sasa Zivkovic

Through studies of the existing Burj el Murr tower in Beirut, this thesis seeks to challenge the hoarding of memorials and the objectification and fetishization of destruction and war ruins as physical artifacts. The thesis investigates an alternative way of reinventing deteriorating structures in post-war Beirut through an analytical process of a participatory, delayed, selective, self-contained top-down demolition, which would allow the city to reclaim the post-traumatic coping phase of “remembrance and mourning” that was taken away by Beirut’s violent, “forward-looking” reconstruction strategy. Rather than a merely physical artifact, Burj el Murr becomes a set of relationships, urban dynamics, and readings to be used to generate an emerging architecture stemming from the complexities left on site, bringing the tower’s embodied richness into the everyday.

## THE MOURNING AFTER: ON EXHAUSTING RUINS

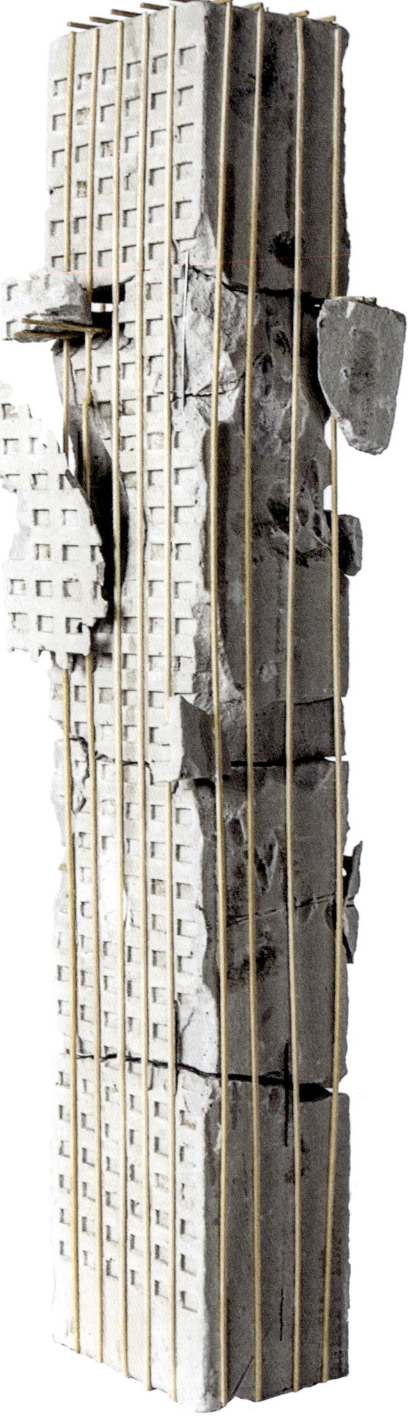

This page: Exploration of deterioration and preservation armature (Elie Boutros, 2018.); Opposite: Trace and impact studies

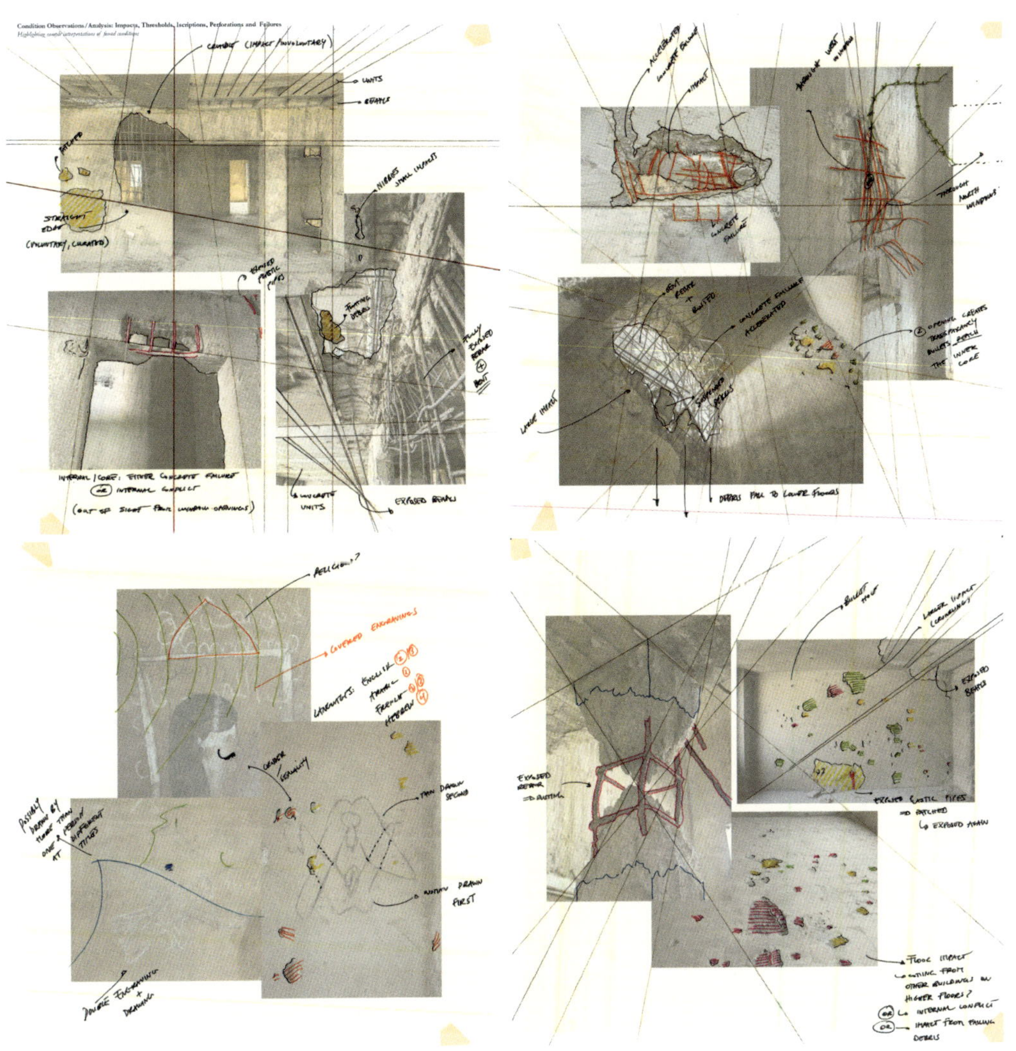
Condition Observations / Analysis: Impacts, Thresholds, Iscriptions, Perforations and Failures
EXPOSED REBAR
DEBRIS FALL TO LOWER FLOORS
LARGE IMPACT
RELIGIOUS?
COVERED ENGRAVINGS
LANGUAGES: ENGLISH, ARABIC, FRENCH, HEBREW
DOUBLE ENGRAVING + DRAWING
BULLET HOLE
FLOOR IMPACT

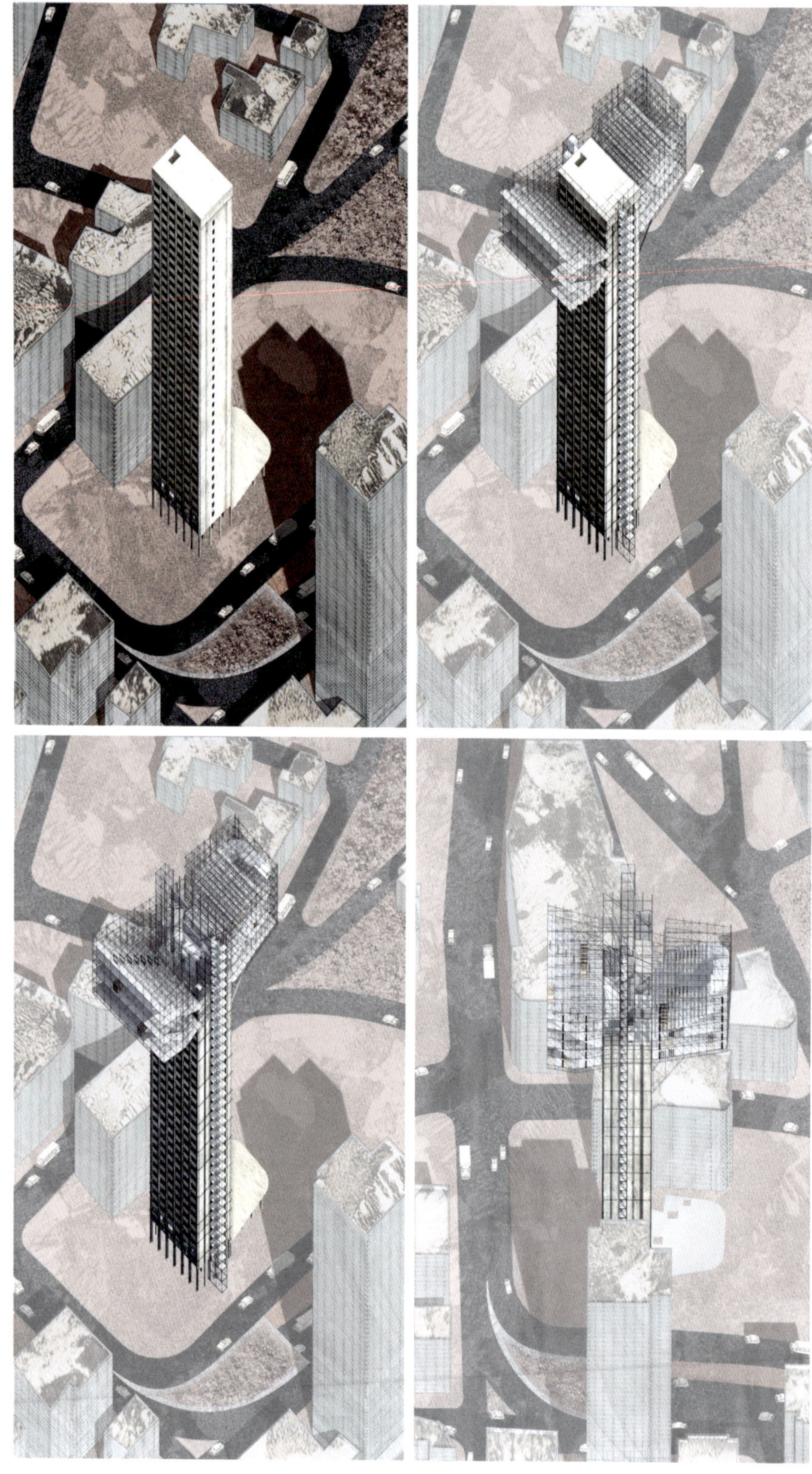

This page: Stills from demolition animation. Opposite: Network of structures involved in the war of the hotels

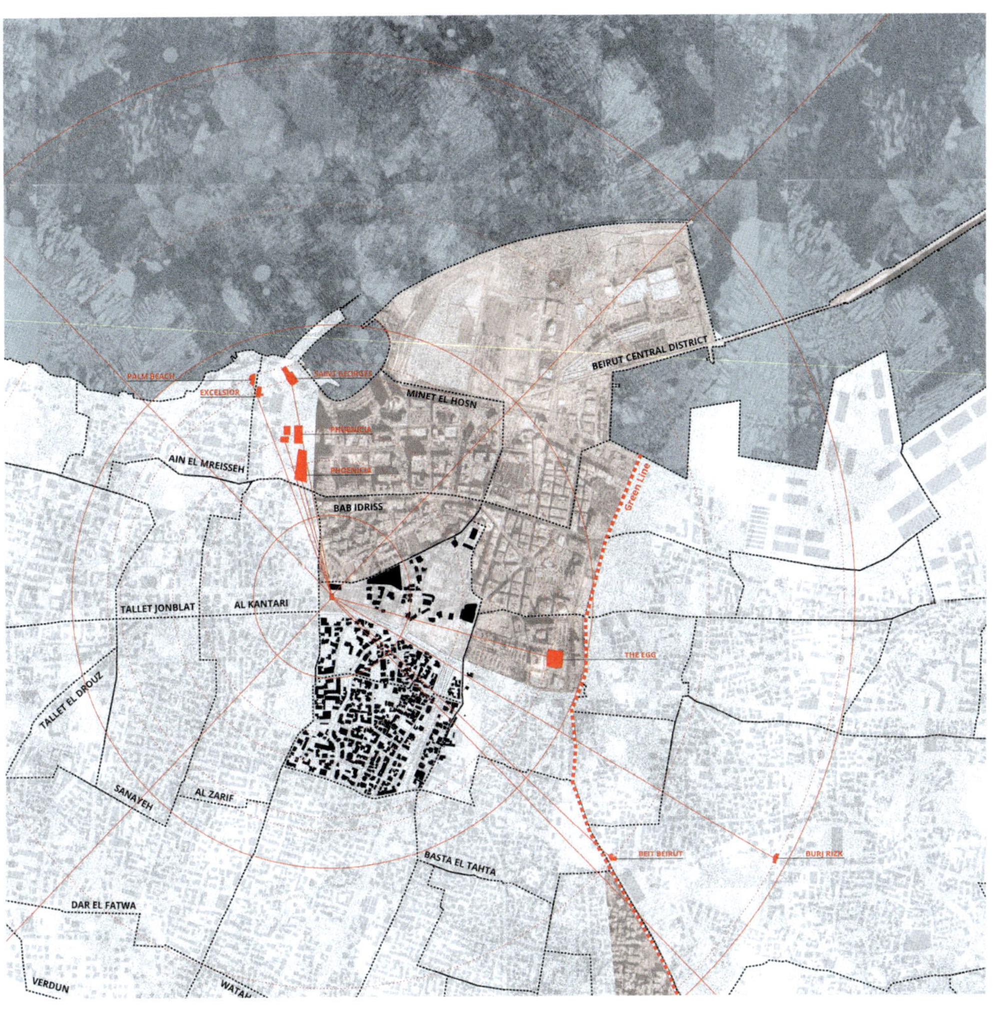
PALM BEACH
EXCELSIOR
SAINT GEORGES
PHOENICIA
PHOENICIA
AIN EL MREISSEH
BAB IDRISS
MINET EL HOSN
BEIRUT CENTRAL DISTRICT
Green Line
TALLET JONBLAT
AL KANTARI
THE EGG
TALLET EL DROUZ
SANAYEH
AL ZARIF
BASTA EL TAHTA
BEIT BEIRUT
BURJ RIZK
DAR EL FATWA
VERDUN

Citizens operate in limbo between a ***fear*** of recent history, and a ***fear*** of remembering it. The building itself sits frozen as a reminder of the failure of the older generation, and the impotence of the younger generation, twenty-eight years later. It is as potent as it is powerless in the amalgam of buildings with similar fates scattered around Beirut. As architects, we love to ponder the strength of such looming structures and their important role in collective memory. However, paired with the ignorant and misinformed youth, the disillusioned elderly and the misguided developer the building stands defeated. As architects, we ***fear*** erasing history, rewriting it and altering it. Do we reconstruct? Should we mimic the past or set the stage for the future? We ***fear*** misreadings and misinterpretations. We dabble with the ***fear*** of intervening in such complex conditions. That ***fear*** is often suppressed, but is also often quite justified. When faced with a rich and complex set of elements, we are quick to deploy all our best tools, some having been "successfully" put to the test in similar past projects—a dangerous simplification we are so often guilty of. We build, fabricate, add and recreate. We make. We ***fear*** leaving any trace that is not curated, calculated, and completely rational. We ***fear*** losing control, we ***fear*** failing our cultures and fellow citizens by destroying our heritage, and we ***fear*** meddling with the isolated, frozen idea of what our identity ought to be. We rely on safe methods, we museumify, we renovate at the mercy of aesthetic trends, and we relinquish any sort of responsibility for contributing to transformations to our cultures and the evolution of our identities. We ***fear*** public intervention; we ***fear*** giving the public more power over such potent architectural artifacts. We ***fear*** the public's lack of training and practice; we ***fear*** the public's ignorance. Seeing how subjective and indoctrinating an architectural education can be, we also ***fear*** other architects. We ***fear*** digressions and non-linear progressions. We ***fear*** defamiliarization, and we have no faith in process and the natural state of affairs. We ***fear*** the lack of closure, but we love open-endedness when looking to evade responsibility. We ***fear*** loss of ownership and shared credit. Our sense of self is merely a set of ideas and concepts. However, we ***fear*** exactitude, and the accountability that comes with it. We ***fear*** slowness but thrive in it. We are impatient; our clients are impatient. We ***fear*** misguided development yet thrive through it. We cannot bite the hand that feeds us, but we can contaminate the soil where it gathers its food. We ***fear*** impotence yet criticize those who try. For architecture is an ongoing infinite experiment through which we constantly challenge the past, and every ***failure*** is but a step forward. Some of us ***fear*** God, some of us think we are one.

This page: Ascending site and context documentation; Opposite: Collage timeline made with mold of cast models; Next spread: Stills from demolition animation

LIBANAISE
الشام

WARISARA SUDSWONG

# SCIOPHOBIA

M. Arch. Thesis
Advisors: Mark Morris & Andrea Simitch

# ALIEN INTERFACES: EXPLORING A WORLD BEYOND REALITY

Can there be life on other planets? Is there anyone else out there?

Humans have always stared into the night sky and wondered what could exist beyond Earth's atmosphere. Despite having explored more of space than our ancestors, our modern understanding of paradoxically infinite and ever-expanding space gives rise to existential fear. To consider the rest of the universe empty is to indulge in a fear that we are masters of an impossibly large territory, that human consciousness and subjectivity is the only source of meaning there can ever be. It is a fundamentally self-centered and earth-centered fear.

Alternatively, one may consider that there are enough galaxies and enough carbon to produce nearly-infinite possibilities, meaning there is a near-definite possibility that other life forms exist. There is another fear embedded in this version of the universe: the familiar fear of the foreign unknown. If there are possibly other forms of consciousness, and other perspectives, then one must generate new ways of understanding, documenting, and depicting not only other life forms, but ourselves as well. Thus, this is a generative fear, an imaginative, conspiratorial, and visionary fear.

One such visionary was Carl Sagan, an astronomer and interlocutor of scientific principles for the public. Sagan believed that if extraterrestrials exist, then we could allay their potential fear of humans by sending a welcoming communication from our species to theirs. His *Golden Record* project recorded everything that Sagan imagined could convey our consciousness to a foreign entity. Scientific hieroglyphics, illustrations of human bodies in welcoming positions, visual art, music, and sounds from Earth were all sent into space on the Voyager spacecraft.

Embodied in the project of the *Golden Record* is the idea that traces of human existence can be recorded as we experience them, and presented to another planet's life form. Sagan's hope was that an alien entity may understand and value our existence when presented with the products, traces, and performances of our societies.

"Alien Interfaces" inverts the premise of the *Golden Record*, imagining instead what extraterrestrial beings would observe on a visit to Earth. In other words, how might an alien perceive the traces of our existence in our own homes? As Earth's first interlocutors, the visitors find Carl Sagan in his private study, his interior universe, and attempt to understand our whole world through his. In this way, his study is proposed as the primary mediator between this world and the other worlds.

The project aims to construct the world of Carl Sagan and his obsessions with the extra-terrestrial through a series of drawings depicting his study.

It aims to develop a working methodology for seeing and drawing through the eyes of extraterrestrial beings. These drawings attempt to capture the fantastical character of Sagan's study of the universe, and enable viewers to envision his world. There, Saturn's rings become a cast-iron balcony on which the inhabitants of the planet take air in the evening, or the skylight acts as a portal between Sagan's world and the worlds of the "other." The drawings include everything from Sagan's mundane objects of everyday use to the cosmos. By pursuing each element of the drawing to its extremity, one can begin to disclose its nature.

As Walter Benjamin once said, "The interior is not only the universe but also the etui of the private person. To live means to leave traces."[1] In the drawings, traces of objects that are imprinted in both the visible and invisible worlds, are meticulously documented. The occupant—their life force, their emitted brain waves—also leaves their impression on the room. These traces unravel a story through the use of layering, juxtaposition, and superimposition. Alien x-ray vision, hyper-vision, hyper-color, tone and shading, multiple realms of dimensional projections, and magnification of time and space are explored as methods that may suggest an alternate reality.

1 Benjamin, Walter. "Paris: Capital of the Nineteenth Century." *Perspecta*, vol. 12 (1969), pp. 165-72.

p. 135: The drawing suggests a fracture in time where planes becomes repetitive and active as the lines begin to superimpose with slight misalignments to create a new visual depth. (Warisara Sudswong, *Bookshelf Rift #4*, 2017.) This page: *In Landscape #8*, the drawing introduces a perspective-warping landscape, which means the various "wave" forms become fields that stretch onto the landscape. The slight folding and undulation suggests an infinite expanse as the landscape wraps and warps along the vanishing points along the Earth's curving surface.

**This page:** *View through a Portal* depicts a (possible) alien's view through the skylight portal into Sagan's study. This spatial and dynamic drawing begins to highlight Sagan's obsession with his bookshelf—a space where he no longer sees the walls of his house but instead sees the touchstones within his study. Here the walls become translucent as the landscape warps, distorts, and bleeds. **Next spread:** These drawings allow the viewers to understand Sagan's world through various lenses, whether it's the aliens looking into Sagan's world or Sagan's view of his study through the eyes of the alien. (**Left:** *Composite #12.*; **Right:** *Key Drawing #3.*)

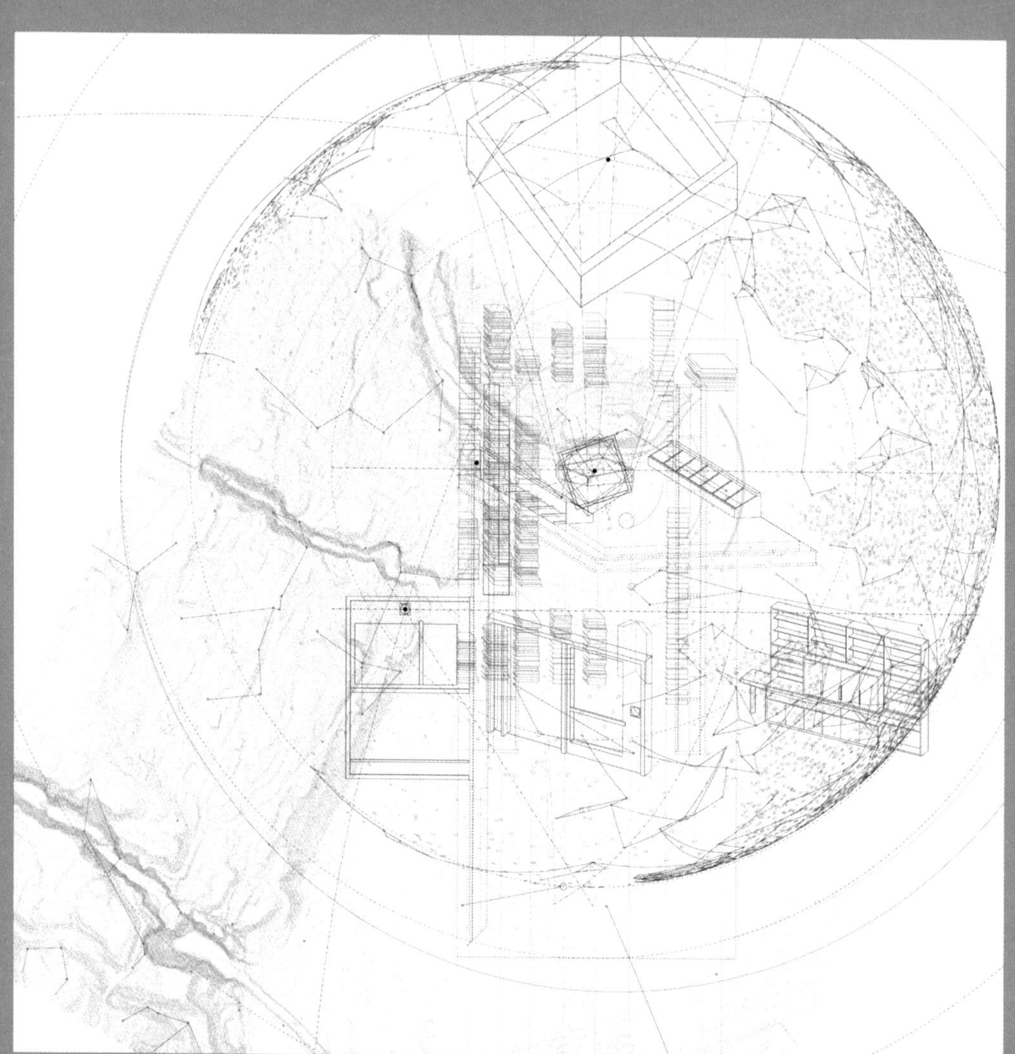

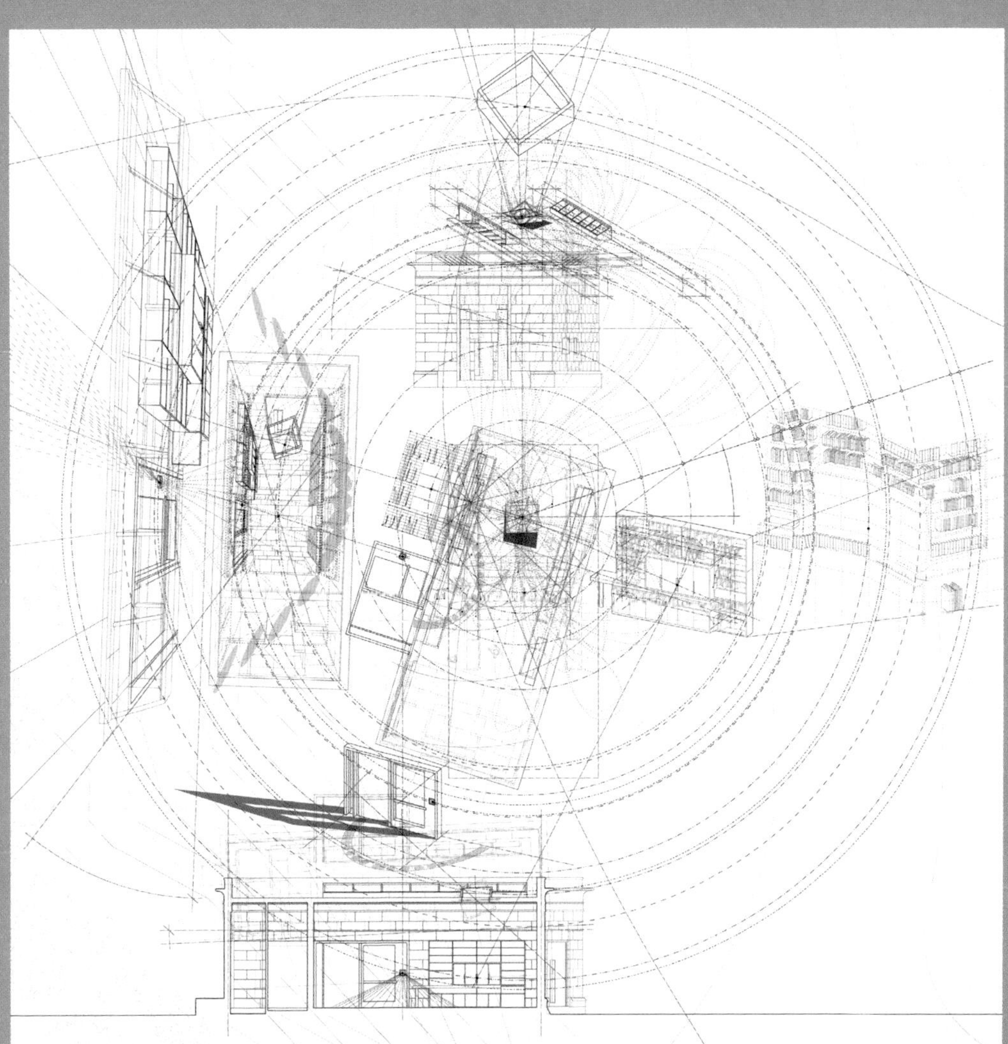

*Space of Encounter* is a new proposal where Sagan and the aliens can simultaneously experience a shared connection where one world slips into another. Through the superimposition between our world and their's, elements such as Sagan's door begins to slowly collapse into a single line and then tranforms into the alien's world upon a single horizontal plane.

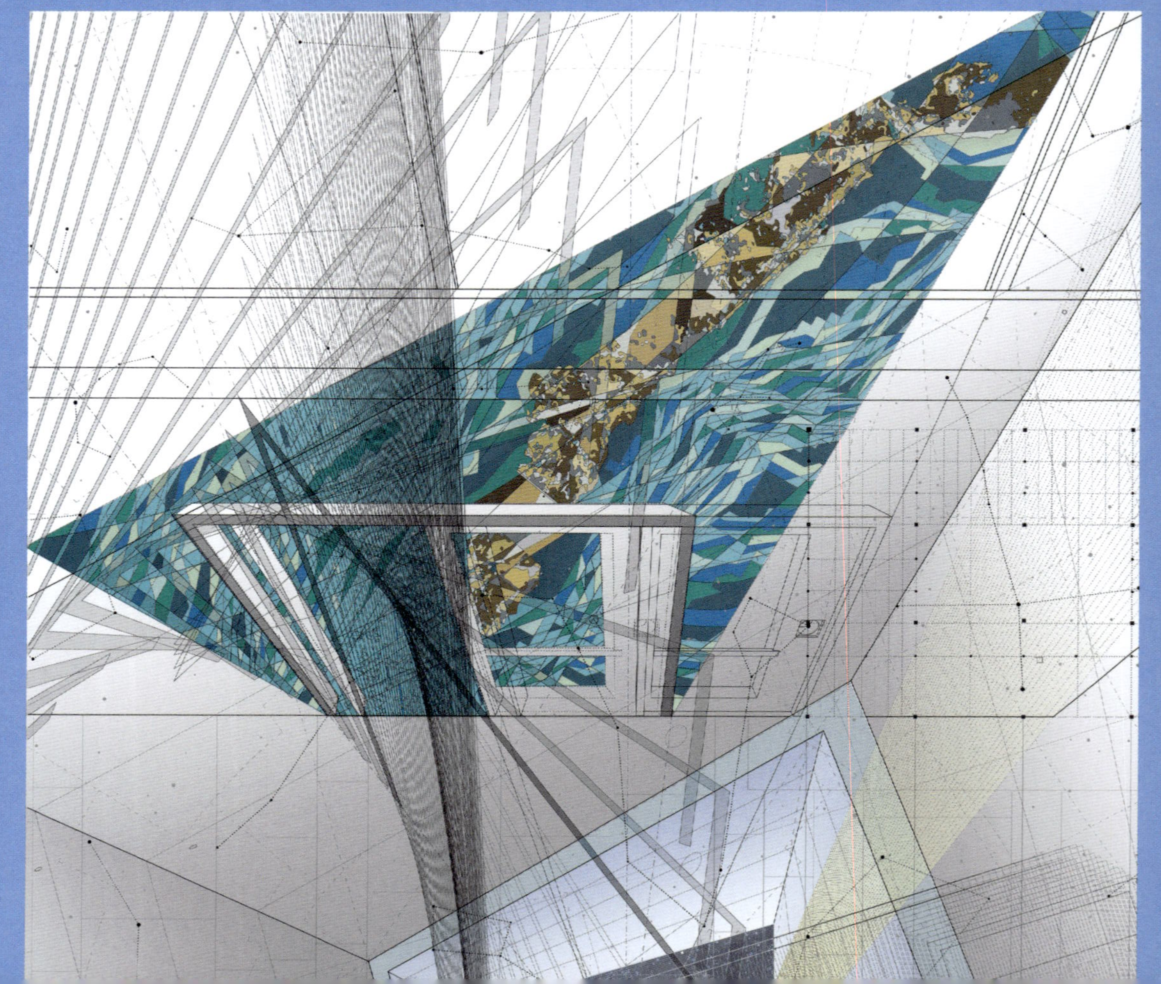

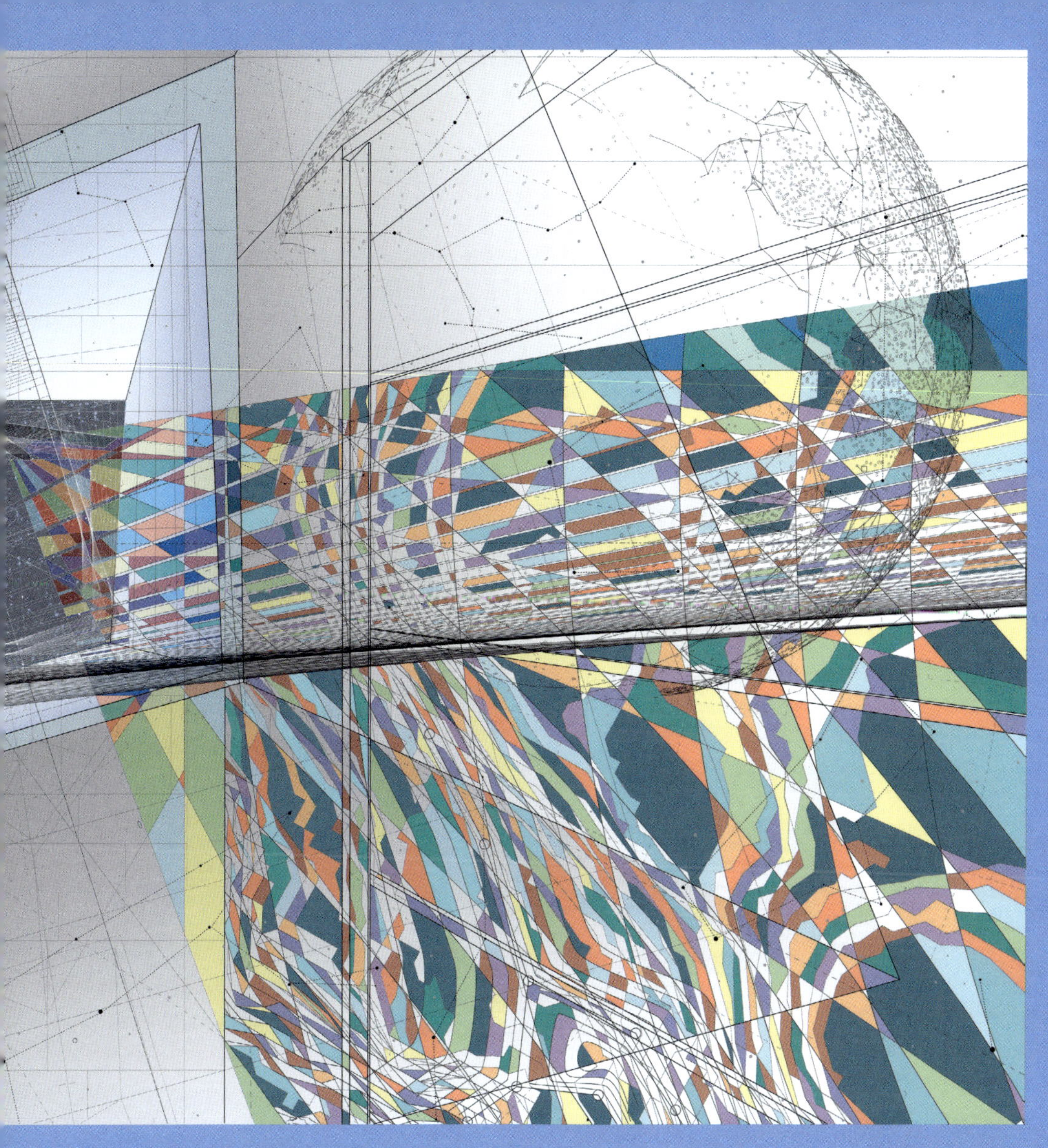

146

# MICHAEL YOUNG

# SCIOPHOBIA

> Photography did not become an art because it employed a device opposing the imprint of bodies to their copy. It became one by exploiting a double poetics of the image, by making its images, simultaneously or separately, two things: the legible testimony of a history…and pure blocs of visibility, impervious to any narrativization, any intersection of meaning. This double poetics of the image as cipher of a history written in visible forms and as obtuse reality, impeding meaning and history, was not invented by the device of the camera obscura. It was born before it, when novel writing redistributed the relations between the visible and the sayable.
>
> —Jacques Rancière, "The Future of the Image," 2002.[1]

# FEAR OF THE MEDIATED IMAGE

Architecture has a troubled relationship with images. As an embodied physical experience, an architectural environment is always more than its mere visual appearance. These qualities, beyond the optical, include affective haptic and aural sensations, dynamic shifts of attention, and the contingencies of context in all of its manifestations, from the material to the social to the conceptual. To reduce this dense block of experience to an image loses much of the richness of reality. But, if we consider this issue more broadly, all mediations miss some aspect of the real. We could even say that one of the conditions of what we term reality is that it always has qualities that withdraw, eluding sensation and cognition.

The problematic relation between the image and the real becomes substantially more pressing considering that architects do not make buildings, they make representations. These representations, these images, establish a base for a significant amount of architectural discourse. It thus not only becomes crucial to articulate which modes of mediation will best aid an architect in an accurate forecast of future projections, but also equally important to dig deeper into the roles that representations play in the construction of discourse. As the discipline of architecture developed, a curious divide occurred in the classification of representations. Images that abstract aspects from reality are given a place of privilege, while images that "look like" reality are devalued. In fact, many architects will use the word "image" only for the second species, reserving the word "drawing" for the first. Part of this judgment relates to a deeply ingrained distrust of visual similitude in picturing practices, but another aspect is determined by how architecture uses representation as a basis for an ethics of labor and the delineation of disciplinary knowledge. This second aspect was initiated by the control of construction through measurable drawings, but also speaks to the discursive history that linked architecture to the humanities through geometry and rationality as the basis of aesthetic judgment.

If we directly evaluate our digital image culture and its ceaseless flow through internet dissemination, it becomes ever more difficult to divide the production of architectural representation into two clear-cut species. The images formerly known as drawings are behaving socially more and more like the images formerly known as photographs. And if we peer just a bit deeper, we find that the mediations we construct as architects

Previous: Thomas Ruff, *jpeg ib01*, 2006, chromogenic print with Diasec, 68.5" × 127.6".

through digital software are much closer to the world of images than they are to the world of drawing. It is becoming apparent that the genres architecture has used to value certain representations over others will no longer be sufficient for our current situation. In order to have some modicum of hope for architectural discourse within this image deluge, it may be necessary to question several of our disciplinary assumptions regarding the fear of the image. Specifically, we may need to look a little closer at photography's relation to veracity, at digital versus mechanical reproduction, and at the ties between aesthetics and politics when considering images.[2]

The veracity of the photographic image to what it represents is not a simple equation. I will propose that there are two general tensions that need to be untangled: one is epistemological, the other aesthetic. The first concerns the photographic image as a sign of the real. A common belief is that traditional mechanical or chemical photography faithfully represents occurrences in the world. This is often explained through the double sign system of the photograph as both icon and index.[3] As icons, photographs look like the things they represent, producing similitude with many qualities of our unmediated vision. As an index, light passes through a lens, focuses on an emulsified strip of film, chemically reacts to the intensity of the stimulus, and is recorded as a physical trace. This process occurs without the so-called intervention of the human hand, and the photograph develops an unadulterated copy of real phenomena in the world. This dual nature of icon and index has been discussed at length throughout the history of photography. It is an epistemological question regarding knowledge through systems of signification.[4] This double bind is found in dismissals of photography as true art (Baudelaire).[5] But, it is also present in arguments for how photography *is* an art different from other picturing practices (Krauss).[6] It is there in the establishment of mechanical objectivity in nineteenth-century science (Daston, Galison).[7] It underlies our belief in reportage through the documentation of past events (Barthes).[8] The double signification of icon and index typically align, but there are moments—common enough that we have all experienced them—where they diverge. These are photographs where the image indexes phenomena that do not align with our assumptions of visual resemblance. This split is primarily explained in two manners. In the sciences, these images reveal truths that the senses failed to predict; in the arts, they are intriguing phenomena for aesthetic contemplation. Both explanations for the contradiction between iconic resemblance and indexical record are curious. If it is true that we trust a photograph because of its double signification in representing the world, then why is it that when the iconic and indexical referents diverge, we explain the discrepancy as either a deeper scientific truth or as an art object? Why do the misalignments become more interesting, more valuable, more real? It would appear that the glitch between these two sign systems cannot easily be explained away as an anomaly, and we should be encouraged to question the stability of photography as a true representation of reality.

Secondly, there is an aesthetic tension. David Campany writing on the photographs of Jeff Wall provides a description of this condition.

> A photograph is apprehended as a tableau if it is given to be seen, by whatevermeans, as an internally organised image that compels on the basis of that organisation. It may be documentary in origin or highly staged, but what is important is that the mode of attention and aesthetic judgment solicited by the tableau is itself a way of 'artificing' it....Of course, this premise existed before photography in painting, but when it appears in photography it produces a tension between the picture's status as record or evidence, which locates it in the past, and its pictorial organisation, which conjures an imaginary, contemplative dimension.[9]

This aesthetic tension challenges assumptions of the epistemological tension, for in order to experience a photograph as an art object there must be an intervention, an "artificing." This intervention goes directly against the veracity of an un-tampered documentary index. Manipulations can occur before the photograph is taken, or afterwards, through what is now commonly known as post-processing. They can occur intentionally through the desires of an artist, but they can also be produced accidentally as a quality of a specific affect caught in the image. It could be argued that all photographs experienced as art engage this conflict as a tension between fact and fiction, between reality and its representation. Photos as art disturb the relations between an object and its qualities; they initiate doubt then deeper contemplation regarding the content of what is displayed. These are the aesthetic questions of realism. They do not originate in photography and are not medium specific. As Jacques Rancière argues, the aesthetics of realism began in nineteenth-century painting (e.g. Gustave Courbet) and literature (e.g. Émile Zola, Gustave Flaubert). These aesthetic experiments flattened the hierarchy of traditional genres, introduced high levels of specific episodic detail, appropriated aspects from the everyday, and deployed abstraction of matter and technique as an estrangement of the real.

The relationship between ethics, epistemology, and aesthetics is a complex one, and we will obviously not be able to track its philosophical history in the space of this essay. The entanglement extends back to the formation of Western philosophy where Plato feared the forsaking of moral essence through the seduction of the senses, in other words ethics compromised by aesthetics.[10] It is important to note that conflations between ethics, epistemology, and aesthetics often underlie arguments regarding the uses and abuses of the image. Most often these arguments are critical, claiming that aesthetics masks what is true regarding a situation. *Images conceal knowledge*. Furthermore, this belief often gains an additional valence. *Images conceal knowledge for nefarious intentions*. This statement implies that images are not just problematic, but unethical because they disturb access to truth. The ethical process following from this would be to analyze, critique, and dismantle images in order to raise awareness and reveal underlying motivations, that is, using ethics and epistemology as foundations to critique aesthetics. The problem with this is that the three distinct modes of engagement become ranked, with aesthetics always as a subservient and secondary concern.

Within architecture, fear of the mediated image is as old as the modern establishment of the discipline, initiated with Leon Battista Alberti's advisement against perspective for architects. The perspective image produces "deceptive appearances," while the orthographic drawing is true on account of its fidelity to "certain calculated standards."[11] Despite this advice, architects have used rendered perspectival images throughout the last five centuries to both construct disciplinary arguments and engage extra-disciplinary audiences. Examples can be found in Peruzzi, Piranesi, Boullée, Soane (Gandy), Schinkel, Wagner, Wright, and Le Corbusier. The École des

Beaux-Arts had a thoroughly developed pedagogy around rendering through the tripartite techniques of *entourage*, *poché*, and *mosaïque*, applicable to both orthographic and perspective images. A shift in attitude is noticeable after the democratization of photography in the early part of the twentieth century. The drawing merged with photographic images for both public presentation and utopian critical discourse. Through an engagement with photography, rendering became more realistic in some instances and more abstract in others, such as using photos as fragments in collage. Architectural discourse would largely focus on the second path of collage, leaving the more traditional naturalistic visual image in the wasteland of professional marketing. This divide only accelerated with the advent of digital imaging.

On first glance, the digital image would seem to be a complete rupture between iconicity and the indexical, as visual qualities are rendered illuminations of information signals. John May elucidates in his article "Everything is Already an Image" that digital images are in no way photographs. Instead he likens them to photon detection.

> Unlike photographs in which scenic light is made visible during chemical exposure, all imaging today is a process of detecting energy emitted by an environment and chopping it into discrete, measurable electrical charges called signals, which are stored, calculated, managed, and manipulated through various statistical methods. Images are thus the outputs of energetic processes defined by *signalization*, and these signals, in their accumulation, are what we mean when we say the word *data*.[12]

May is observant and precise regarding the differences between chemical and digital image making. Coded signals do not look like a visual image. A digital camera detects energy, stores this data through computation, and then at another location, at another time, through another machine, translates these signals as an array of illuminated pixels. This process of digital photon detection is obviously different than the chemical trace of light on film, and it brings with it different techniques, interfaces, and methods for the construction and manipulation of images. But, given our concerns in this essay about the relations between images and truth, how different is this really regarding the relationship between image and reality? There is a common belief that digital images are more easily manipulated in the production of deception, more difficult to decipher as artificial. I will suggest that the collusion between the two registers of icon and index in traditional chemical photography was an epistemological error. There was never a natural connection between the two. Both chemical and digital images are indexical, and both can be used to create fictions and truths regarding the iconic resemblance to things in the world. A chemical image is created through material processes of energetic translation, but its value as an iconic resemblance remains outside of these techniques. A digital image is created through technical processes of energetic translation, and its value as an iconic resemblance remains outside of these techniques as well. There is an ingrained bias for the material as natural and the technical as cultural, tainting assumptions regarding the veracity of digital images, but this bias ignores the fact that digital processes are also always material processes and naively assumes that there is no technology in a chemical emulsion. Discrete imaging is much older than the computer. Images can be considered marks in matrices (painting) as opposed to lines on grounds (drawing).[13] All technologies of reproduction work through some discrete transfer involving a resolution of the mark that can be located, verified, and copied. W.J.T. Mitchell reminds us that, "Digitization of the image is a consistent technical feature from mosaic tile to the mezzotint to the Ben-Day dots of newspaper photographs."[14] Regardless of the informational capture, storage, and computational processes, as soon as the data is displayed for human perception we are in the realm of images, which opens aesthetic concerns.

To manifest the data of digital images as "photo-real rendering" is an aesthetic choice. A digital image is a collage of discrete independent pixels. The same data can be assembled and reassembled in multiple manners. The images of Philipp Schaerer activate tensions between the aesthetics of photography and the discrete resolution of independent pixels. His images are not photographs, they are montages. The difference from many traditional collages is that Schaerer removes the seams and ruptures from the visual surface and pushes the artifice into the reality the image presents, triggering a conceptual doubt

regarding veracity. This uncanny feeling is a result of the tensions between reality and its representation—an aesthetics of realism.

Photography automatically brings with it issues of reproduction fundamental to its ontology. A photographic image can be reproduced as a potentially infinite number of identical copies. These reproductions can be inserted into any form of publication, printed and distributed as books, portfolios, journals, newspapers, or pamphlets. Walter Benjamin famously described the result of these reproductions as a "loss of aura," for now the artwork was divorced from its context in time, place, materiality, and reception. The qualities of the unique singular original are lost under the spread of mechanical reproduction.[15] "The Work of Art in the Age of Mechanical Reproduction" contains many of the seeds that would become media studies in the twentieth century, eventually leading to postmodern theories of societal immersion in the simulations of spectacle. Furthermore, Benjamin's argument has been an important foundation for theorists attempting to understand the transformations of digital reproduction. The most common view is that digital images spread via the internet are a massive increase in reproduction, thus an even more intense loss of aura, an even deeper immersion in simulation, and even more distant from the original reality.

But what if this transference of Benjamin's argument from mechanical to digital reproduction is too quick? Yes, images on the internet spread rapidly and in a manner that can seem so out of control that we give them the biological metaphor of going "viral." But Benjamin's mechanical reproduction argument is based on the idea of a single original and an infinite amount of identical copies. What makes the original special, is its uniqueness in time, material, and place—three aspects which architecture prides itself on. But let's consider for a moment what is literally being reproduced in a digital image. When an image file is copied, it is data that is being reproduced, a discrete set of numeric signals compressed into a format that machines can translate into visible images. The data can be copied infinitely, but these coded signals are not the visual image itself. Every digital image will appear visually different based on the machine translating it. Any display device—a phone, a tablet, a monitor, a projector—will scale the image differently, have different resolutions, different color settings, and furthermore, each software platform will interpret the coded information differently, altering the image's

Philipp Schaerer, *Bildbauten No 2*, 2007.

appearance. The data is closer to the abstraction of a written score in music or dance. As Boris Groys suggests, the visual image of a digital file is a performance, sometimes even a one-off occurrence.[16] This makes each opening of a digital image something singular, something that in Benjamin's language would have its own unique "aura." Only now, it is fruitless to consider any of these unique occurrences an original.[17] Instead of originals without auras, we have auras without originals. This furthermore suggests that the consumer takes on aspects of the producer of an image. What matters is less the original image as a single material artifact than how it is manifested, manipulated, and released into the wilderness of the internet, knowing full well that it will come back transformed after passing through the hard drives of unknown places. This change in dissemination and manipulation is a profound difference between mechanical and digital reproduction.

Mechanically reproduced images were circulated through a limited number of portals. These were regulated, curated, verified, and legitimized by the institutions that produced and published them. It is important to consider that one of the roles these institutions played was to manipulate (distort) images to serve their desires, regulating aesthetics through disciplinary knowledge. Within architecture, these images were crafted by professors wishing to instruct, architects trying to promote, and critics establishing an argument. The aesthetics of reproduction have political implications in terms of the communities they generate, described as the "distribution of the sensible" by Jacques Rancière.[18] The journals that began to appear in the early part of the twentieth century embraced mechanical reproduction and created a discursive space radically different from the portfolios of the academies that preceded them.[19] Consider the redistribution that took place between a portfolio such as Letarouilly's *Edifices de Rome Moderne* (1840-1855) and a journal like *L'Esprit Nouveau* (1920-25) edited by Le Corbusier and Amédée Ozenfant. The aesthetics of the portfolio instilled a close reading based on an epistemological construct of disciplinary knowledge through formal analysis. A student was disciplined through drawing overlaid layers, studying the underlying geometry, proportions, and ornament. The aesthetics of *L'Esprit Nouveau* used images in blunt juxtaposition. These were images of architecture, but also images of machines, airplanes, factories, fashion designs, household objects, etc., all combined with text and the experiments of modern graphic design.[20] The journal was a very different discursive space for architectural thought. It constructed a new constituency for architecture in relation to modern culture, one that was politically and socially less regulated by the academic and professional institutions of the nineteenth century.

The internet is our contemporary platform for the dissemination of architectural imagery. The discipline of architecture needs to consider how this alters image consumption and the production of discourse. The spread of images through websites, blogs, image boards, and social media are regulated along completely different terms than mechanically reproduced books and journals. These are no longer controlled by a single institution. Rather, it is often an algorithm that selects what appears on millions of devices. Furthermore, there are frequently no human eyes witnessing or evaluating the reproduction of these images. For instance, a Google image search tests an array of data signals, stored as an image file, looking for similarities of adjacent pixel patterns to determine resemblance.[21] This is a very different iconology.

The reproduction and distribution of images on the internet often requires a compression of image resolution. For Hito Steyerl, these low-resolution images are called "poor images."[22] This is deliberately provocative, with a relevant aspect for our current discussion. She argues that the low-resolution JPEG and AVI files are the raw material of our internet-image culture. Typical image consumption online is not of the high print resolution of art photography, but the misnamed, compressed, clipped, pixelated assemblages that appear on our screens. These are the images that we view and manipulate. These establish the reality of image distribution, consumption, trade, monetization, and influence.

> The poor image is no longer about the real thing the originary original. Instead, it is about its own real conditions of existence: about swarm circulation, digital dispersion, fractured and flexible temporalities. It is about defiance and appropriation just as it is about conformism and exploitation. In short: it is about reality.[23]

All images are captured at a resolution. The images we term "high" are those that eclipse the specific scalar perceptions of our eyeballs. In traditional photography, this is the grain of the image;

in digital images, this is DPI (Dots Per Inch). There is an assumption that the high-res is more real, more similar to the appearance of reality, while the low-res is a bad copy that misses the richness of real experience. High-res is a misnomer though. All images are at a lower resolution than the reality they represent, regardless of the technology of mediation. To push the issue even further, our unmediated vision is also at a lower resolution than the real object. There are always qualities we cannot perceive, aspects that are withdrawn from the senses. The threshold that we use to qualify images is an aesthetic decision. Above a threshold, the image looks like unmediated vision (icon), below the threshold, the grain or pixel is visually present (index).

Ruy/Klein. *Apophenia: The Form of Los Angeles in the Style of the Himalayas as Seen by a Convolutional Neural Network*, 2017.

Since digital devices all work in a fragmented and discrete manner, the exposure of the chunk, the unit, or the pixel appears to be true to the medium, in that it reveals its abstract artifice. There are several contemporary arguments that suggest that lowering the resolution of an image will open a better understanding, and in accordance, produce a more critically engaged aesthetic.[24] This critical revelation will allow an escape from the false simulations of smooth high-res image seduction and all of its ethical quagmire. There is an aspect of this argument that ties into traditional architectural drawings where abstraction provided the distancing mechanism believed necessary for criticality. This argument also seeks to epistemologically ground the digital image as a specific medium. A digital image automatically brings up issues of resolution, but this does not mean that this is what determines its "medium specificity" in terms that align with the arguments of Clement Greenberg.[25] The contemporary image world is an assemblage of multiple resolutions, and its medium is one of constant exchange and manipulation throughout a multitude of devices, software, algorithms, producers and consumers. Take for example the JPEG image from Thomas Ruff that opens this essay. This is an image of an iceberg that was found on the internet and appropriated by Ruff. It was then blown up to the scale typically associated with painting, at roughly four by three feet. This transforms the low resolution of the image into large visible squares. But look closer: within each of these divisions there are other squares, other resolutions, and at the lowest level, we have the mark that eludes our vision—the pixel of the print resolution itself. Ruff has not given a simple exposé of the digital nature of contemporary images, he has built worlds within worlds of resolutions as abstract color field studies, and simultaneously, it is still an image of an iceberg. Another example of the multi-resolution image is provided by Ruy/Klein's project *Apophenia*. In this series of images, two satellite photos are combined using a convolutional neural network. In this process the pixel information of two images are analyzed to filter features. The algorithm "learns" these features through thousands of passes through the data of the image signals. This allows the images to be collaged along a fine grain of resolution—a sequencing that could only be processed through the digitally discrete. The resultant image fuses the organization of one image with the features of another. The observer sees two images simultaneously, but not as layered, woven, or visibly fragmented. The image appears as a "real," single satellite photo, yet it evokes a reality other than the one we assume to exist.

Does one find truth in the similitude of an image to the way the world appears to vision? Or, is it more true to expose the technology and the abstractions that a medium is composed of? As noted before, realism is not medium specific. It is the production of a tension between reality and its representation. This can include techniques of producing doubt through the grain of a medium, but just as often, this tension is produced as a friction between mediums—photography in tension with painting (Wall), painting in tension with photography (Gerhard Richter), photo-collage in tension with digital rendering (Schaerer), and satellite data in tension with satellite photography (Ruy/Klein). Furthermore, images do not cross into our attention as singular objects. They are received as sets, as searches of associations, even if the associations subscribe to a logic outside of human control, motivation, or comprehension. A better description of digital images may be as quasi-objects that manifest, circulate, and redistribute visual information. Resolution is tied to how images travel, to the context they are received in, to the audiences they build, to the portals that disseminate them, and to the aesthetic engagement they intensify. Internet-image cultures build collectivities around these redistributions—the political opens from the aesthetic. Architecture could find possibilities for speculation on alternate plausible realities by appropriating these contexts to actively disturb them. To estrange this background, to challenge it to be other, opens a space for the development of an architectural discourse that no longer fears the image, but respects the anxiety of operating in a mediated reality.

> But if images start pouring across screens and invading subject and object matter, the major and quite overlooked consequence is that reality now widely consists of images; or rather of things, constellations, and processes formerly evident as images. This means one cannot understand reality without understanding cinema, photography, 3D modeling, animation, or other forms of moving or still image. The world is imbued with the shrapnel of former images, as well as images edited, photoshopped, cobbled together from spam

and scrap. Reality itself is post-produced and scripted, affect rendered as after-effect. Far from being opposites across an unbridgeable chasm, image and world are in many cases just versions of each other. They are not equivalents however, but deficient, excessive, and uneven in relation to each other. And the gap between them gives way to speculation and intense anxiety.[26]

**1** Jacques Rancière, "The Future of the Image", (2002) from *The Future of the Image* (London: Verso, 2007), pp. 11-12.

**2** Ibid.

**3** W.J.T. Mitchell, "Realism and the Digital Image", from *Image Science* (Chicago: University Chicago Press, 2015), p. 49.

**4** Charles Sanders Pierce, "Logic as Semiotic: The Theory of Signs" from *Philosophical Writings of Peirce* ed. Justus Buchler (New York: Dover Publications, 1955), p. 102.

**5** Charles Baudelaire, "The Salon of 1859" from *Strangeness and Beauty* ed. Eric Warner & Graham Hough (Cambridge: Cambridge University Press, 1983).

**6** Rosalind Krauss, "Notes on the Index: Part 2" from *The Originality of the Avant-Garde and Other Modernist Myths*, (Cambridge: MIT Press, 1986).

**7** Lorrine Daston & Peter Galison, *Objectivity* (New York: Zone Books, 2007).

**8** Roland Barthes, *Camera Lucida* (New York: Hill & Wang, 1981) .

**9** David Campany, Jeff Wall *Picture for Women*, (London: Afterall Books, 2011), p. 39.

**10** Plato, *The Republic*, translation 1955 Sir Desmond Lee (London: Penguin Publishing, 1955), pp. 429-431.

**11** Leon Battista Alberti, *On the Art of Building in Ten Books* (Cambridge: MIT Press, 1988) .

**12** John May, "Everything is Already an Image", from *LOG 40* (New York: Anyone Corporation, 2017), p. 12 .

**13** Walter Benjamin, "The Work of Art in the Age of Mechanical Reproduction" from *Illuminations* (New York: Schocken Books, 1968), pp. 220-221.

**14** Boris Groys, *In the Flow* (New York: Verso, 2016), pp. 142–145.

**15** Ibid.

**16** Jacques Rancière, *The Politics of Aesthetics* (London: Continuum, 2004).

**17** Huyngman Pai, *The Portfolio and the Diagram* (Cambridge: MIT Press, 2002).

**18** Beatriz, Colomina, *Privacy and Publicity* (Cambridge: MIT Press, 1994), pp. 118, 128.

**19** Lowe, David G. (2004). "Distinctive Image Features from Scale-Invariant Keypoints" from *International Journal of Computer Vision*, vol. 60, iss. 2, pp. 91-110.

**20** Hito Steyerl, "In Defense of the Poor Image" from *The Wretched of the Screen* (Berlin: Steinberg Press, 2012).

**21** Hito Steyerl, "In Defense of the Poor Image" from *The Wretched of the Screen* (Berlin: Steinberg Press, 2012), p. 44.

**22** Clement Greenberg, "Modernist Painting" from *The Collected Essays and Criticism Vol. 4* ed. John O'Brian (Chicago: University of Chicago Press, 1993).

**23** Hito Steyerl, "Is the Internet Dead" from *Duty Free Art* (London: Verso, 2017), p. 148.

**24** These are varied in their objectives and should not be lumped together, but I have in mind here, Michael Meredith's exhibition at the Princeton School of Architecture, *44 Low-Res Houses*, Mario Carpo's *The Second Digital Turn*, and the voxel based designs of M.Casey Rhem and Gilles Retsin.

**25** Clement Greenberg, "Modernist Painting" from *The Collected Essays and Criticism Vol. 4* ed. John O'Brian (Chicago: University of Chicago Press, 1993).

**26** Hito Steyerl, "Is the Internet Dead" from *Duty Free Art* (London: Verso, 2017), p. 148.

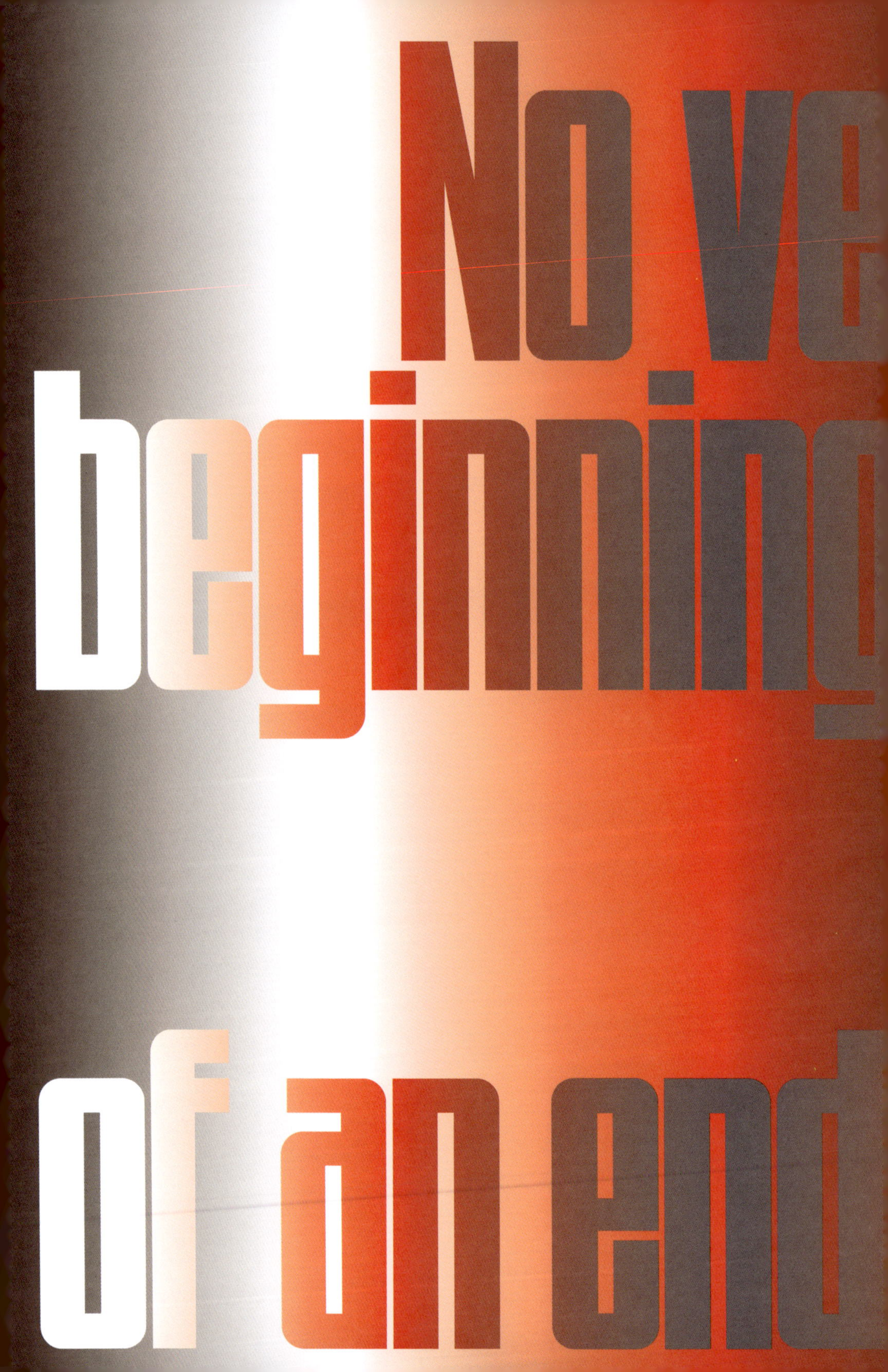
No ve
beginning
of an end

# stige of a no prospect

IGNACIO
GALÁN

# MNEMOPHOBIA

# DISLOCATING NATIONALISM: SPATIAL GENEALOGIES OF PRESENT FEARS, NEW YORK ITALIANS CA. 1900

165

## I.

In an interview with British tabloid *The Sun* published July 13th, 2018, right after a trip to Brussels for a NATO summit, the United States president Donald Trump lamented the transformation of Europe he perceived in his visit. In a series of statements, he sought to instigate fear for the dissolution of the continent's alleged identity: "I think you are losing your culture. Look around."[1] The new image of the continent was threatening, in his mind, the possibility of providing a recognizable representation of what he understood to be European culture. The trigger for this loss was, to Trump, clear: "Allowing the immigration to take place in Europe is a shame. [...] I think it changed the fabric of Europe and, unless you act very quickly, it's never going to be what it was and I don't mean that in a positive way."[2]

His arguments characteristically located European identity, as he has repeatedly done for America, in an indeterminate past confined within its territories.

Trump's rhetoric has been grounded, since his earlier campaign rallies, in the dissemination of fear. While migration has consistently been used to this purpose, he paradoxically highlighted, in these statements, his own migrant background, even if just to evidence his connection to Europe: "Don't forget, essentially I'm a product of the European Union, between Scotland and Germany."[3] Trump's mother, Mary Anne MacLeod, was originally from Scotland while his father, Fred Trump, a native of New York City, had a German father. Friedrich Trump arrived to New York in 1885—a time when the United States of America was an increasingly welcoming destination for his compatriots, after decades of anti-German nativism among other forms of exclusionary politics.

## II.

Italy is one of the places where such fear has resulted in a more visible political response, contemporaneous to these statements. The country's politics have been personified in the figure of Matteo Salvini, Minister of the Interior of the coalition government between the populist Movimento Cinque Stelle and the Lega. Salvini has been responsible for the transformation of the former Lega Nord, a regionalist party advocating for more independence for the northern regions in Italy, into a nationalist party (dropping the "Nord" from its name), with a program

Previous: Jacob A. Riis, *Italian flat in South Fifth Avenue*, 1887. Museum of the City of New York.

paradigmatically encapsulated by the electoral slogan "Italians First"—echoing Trump's own "America First." It is not the abstract notion of Italy, but its more concrete inhabitants, Italians, that are considered in need of protection and privilege. This is particularly interesting when, right after the Italian unification (completed in 1871), the young country was considered to lack a characteristic population. Given the internal diversity of the regions encompassed within the newly formed national territories, Massimo d'Azeglio (a central figure in the process of national unification) allegedly claimed: "We have created Italy, now we have to create the Italians."[4] The Italian nation remained an exercise of representation or, in the conceptualization proposed by Emilio Gentile, "an empty simulacrum."[5]

The recently drawn boundaries of the country were probed at that time not only by the internal diversity of its population, but also by its diaspora. This outward migration resulted in more than thirteen million people leaving the country throughout the period of national formation broadly known as Risorgimento (following from the unification to the rise of fascism in 1922)—outnumbering any other population outflow in modern history.[6] It was precisely New York, Trump's own place of birth, that became the destination of great numbers of these migrants, to the point of becoming the fourth largest Italian city in the first decades of the twentieth century, after only Rome, Milan, and Naples.[7] Migrants contributed to cement Italy in a decisive way throughout those decades. The remittances that they sent to the homeland contributed to the national economy to a degree that cannot be disregarded, and might have been instrumental to the country's progress.[8] However, beyond this material contribution, theorists including Edward Said have argued that nationalism flourishes in response to uprootedness,[9] and the role that this unprecedented diaspora might have played in the consolidation of an "imaginary community" for Italians would need to be further explored.[10]

## III.

Despite their material contribution to Italy's economy, Italian migrants residing in New York were considered by some to be "not Italians, because they have never been Italians." That is how Giuseppe Prezzolini, manager of the Casa Italiana (the house of Italian culture in the city) put it at the end of this period of national consolidation in 1931: "Here they have taken on certain American habits, but at base they have remained southern peasants without a culture, without learning, without a language, people for whom the moment of 'italianità' has never arrived. They leave Italy before being Italians. They have settled here but have never become real Americans."[11]

Following Étienne Balibar, "the exercise of citizenship appears inseparable from belonging to a nation, whether through inheritance or naturalization (by descent or by 'choice'),"[12] but none of these seem to apply to Italians here. Regardless of the legal definition of citizenship for this migrant people—either through *jus soli* (associated with their place of birth) or *jus sanguinis* (inherited from their parents)—it is the possibility to "'produce' noncitizens" based on cultural differences (following Balibar) that is made evident here.[13] Prezzolini's allusion to "the moment of 'italianità'" renders contingent the process of citizenship manufacturing (in d'Azeglio's quest), beyond the association of citizenship and nation-state that many theorists have discussed.[14]

The social and cultural project at play in Prezzolini's arguments regarding citizenship was, in fact, pervasive throughout the Risorgimento, and depended on the differences between Northern Italy and Southern Italy, where most migrants in New York originated from. This project considered the Northern bourgeoisie to be the model inhabitants for the nation. This preference given to Northern Italians characterized a process that might be regarded as internal colonization, as the founder of Italy's communist party and political theorist Antonio Gramsci put it.[15] This process was based on a lack of recognition of Northern and Southern Italians rooted in cultural and racial stereotypes—in ways that mirror contemporary exclusionary politics and their racist base. An envoy of Cavour (a key political figure in the country's unification) manifested this disconnection prior to the completion of the project: "What barbarism! Some Italy! This is Africa: the Bedouin are the flower of civilized virtues compared to these peasants."[16] It is significant that the lack of identification by certain populations with the nation was bi-directional. Only 2 percent of Italians voted in the plebiscite that led to the creation of the State.[17] If not identified with their own nation and not recognized by their own compatriots, Southern Italians were also not particularly welcomed in the United States. They were thought to be less prepared than other European migrants and were subject to the same racial stereotypes that excluded them from Italy. They were darker skinned than Europeans stood in the imaginaries of Americans, and consequently remained "doubly alien"—set apart from the Northern Italians as the model for Italy both locally and abroad.[18]

## IV.

Despite the pursuit for unity, the internal heterogeneity of the Italian state was furthered throughout the Risorgimento due to the consolidating transnational circulatory operations linking Italy with territories beyond its borders. These operations came as a result not only of migration, but also of expanding trade, displacements relating to colonialism, and developing media. Fascism resulted, at the end of this period, from a will to internally homogenize the country and simultaneously counter the aforementioned processes, with the will of producing a "new total word—view or nomos," identifiable with the nation.[19] Still, by 1935, the chronicle provided by writer Carlo Levi reported how the everyday life of the southern households in the Italian countryside was not only connected with the images described by family members battling in Abyssinia, but was also "entirely American in regard to mechanical equipment as well as weights and measures." From Rome, he said, "came nothing [...] but the tax collector and speeches over the radio."[20] Written just four years apart, Prezzolini and Levi's words account for the complex territory in which Italian nationalism aimed to ground its project. Against the essentialist ideology underlying Salvini's claim to protect the Italian people's identity and rights, one could dislocate the fears of nationalist rhetoric by connecting the history of nation building in Italy with the contemporaneous reality of diasporic migration.

## V.

The quest of this migrant population for a space of belonging abroad, and the complex identity negotiations at stake within that pursuit, are critically embodied in the housing debates in New York at the turn of the century—the time witnessing the largest flow of Italian migration. Documentary photographer, social reformer, and housing activist Jacob A. Riis was a prominent voice in those debates, and was particularly attentive to the way they framed the life of Italians in the city. A migrant himself, born in Demark in 1849, Riis was particularly relevant at the time for casting light on the housing conditions of what he called "the other half." This process of "casting light" might be considered literally, since his work was significantly aided by the innovative use of flash photography and was importantly disseminated through "magic lantern" lectures.[21] His account situated housing concerns in relation to the distribution of migrant communities in the city—linking the history of housing in New York and the search for a space of belonging abroad. In fact, Riis's famous evaluation of the city's tenements in *How the Other Half Lives* (1890), was significantly organized with chapters dedicated to the communities of different backgrounds settling in the city. Thus it not only attended to the more general technical housing problems, but also considered how housing was occupied by diverse populations.[22]

His attentive analysis linked the flows of migrations with urban distribution logics, and social articulations both internal to, and between each community: "As emigration from east to west follows the latitude, so does the foreign influx in New York distribute itself along certain well-defined lines that waver and break only under the stronger pressure of a more gregarious race or the encroachments of inexorable business. A feeling of dependence upon mutual effort, natural to strangers in a strange land, unacquainted with its language and customs, sufficiently accounts for this."[23]

His text described a landscape of interlocking bands of populations of different origins defining the city: "A map of the city, colored to designate nationalities, would show more stripes than on the skin of a zebra, and more colors than any rainbow."[24]

However, he was quick to acknowledge that these distributions were not naturally shaped, as the definition of the different "rainbow" bands depended on diverse factors. Landlords, for example, had the capacity to intervene in the drawing of the city. "The color line must be drawn through the tenements to give the picture its proper shading. The landlord does the drawing, does it with an absence of pretence, a frankness of despotism, that is nothing if not brutal."[25]

## VI.

Riis often fell into generalizations of these different populations, dwelling on stereotypes associated with their different origins and ethnicities. That applied to the Italians as well: "Here [the Italian] promptly reproduces conditions of destitution and disorder which, set in the frame-work of Mediterranean exuberance, are the delight of the artist, but in a matter of-fact American community become its danger and reproach. The reproduction is made easier in New York because he finds the material ready to hand in the worst of the slum tenements."[26]

Riis regarded the tenements as the natural environment for the reproduction of these attitudes deemed to be both typical and dangerous. In fact, his work chronicled the genealogy of the tenements not only as a spatio-technical reality resulting from the densification of the Manhattan grid, but in relation to a series of social patterns and collective forms of occupation characteristic of the migrating populations establishing within them: "There had been tenant-houses before, but they were not built for the purpose [of collective living]. Nothing would probably have shocked their original owners more than the idea of their harboring a promiscuous crowd."[27]

Despite repeatedly establishing in his writing a deterministic relation between the architecture of the tenements and the conditions of life that they harbored, he was careful to note the role that landlords and speculation played in exacerbating those conditions: "[A] sanitary inquiry brought to light the fact that more than one-half of the tenements with two-thirds of their population were held by owners who made the keeping of them a business, generally a speculation."[28]

Riis specifically wrote about the Italians as tenants, and as victims of those abusive behaviors. Regarded as "a tenant who 'makes less trouble'" in comparison to those originally from Ireland and Germany, Riis recorded the Italian tenant's submission "to robbery at the hands of the rent-collector without murmur."[29] Though Riis tended towards generalization, one might consider that the Italians' disempowered position and virtual lack of citizenship (following Prezzolini) might be related to this attitude. Italian immigrants were barred from imagining themselves as full citizens of either Italy or the United States.

## VII.

In connecting architectural and social patterns, Riis was not only concerned with the resolution of technical problems in the tenements. He was also guided by a pursuit for the normalization of the populations that lived within them, particularly the family

Jacob A. Riis, *Lodgers in a crowded Bayard Street tenement—"Five cents a spot."*, 1889. Museum of the City of New York.

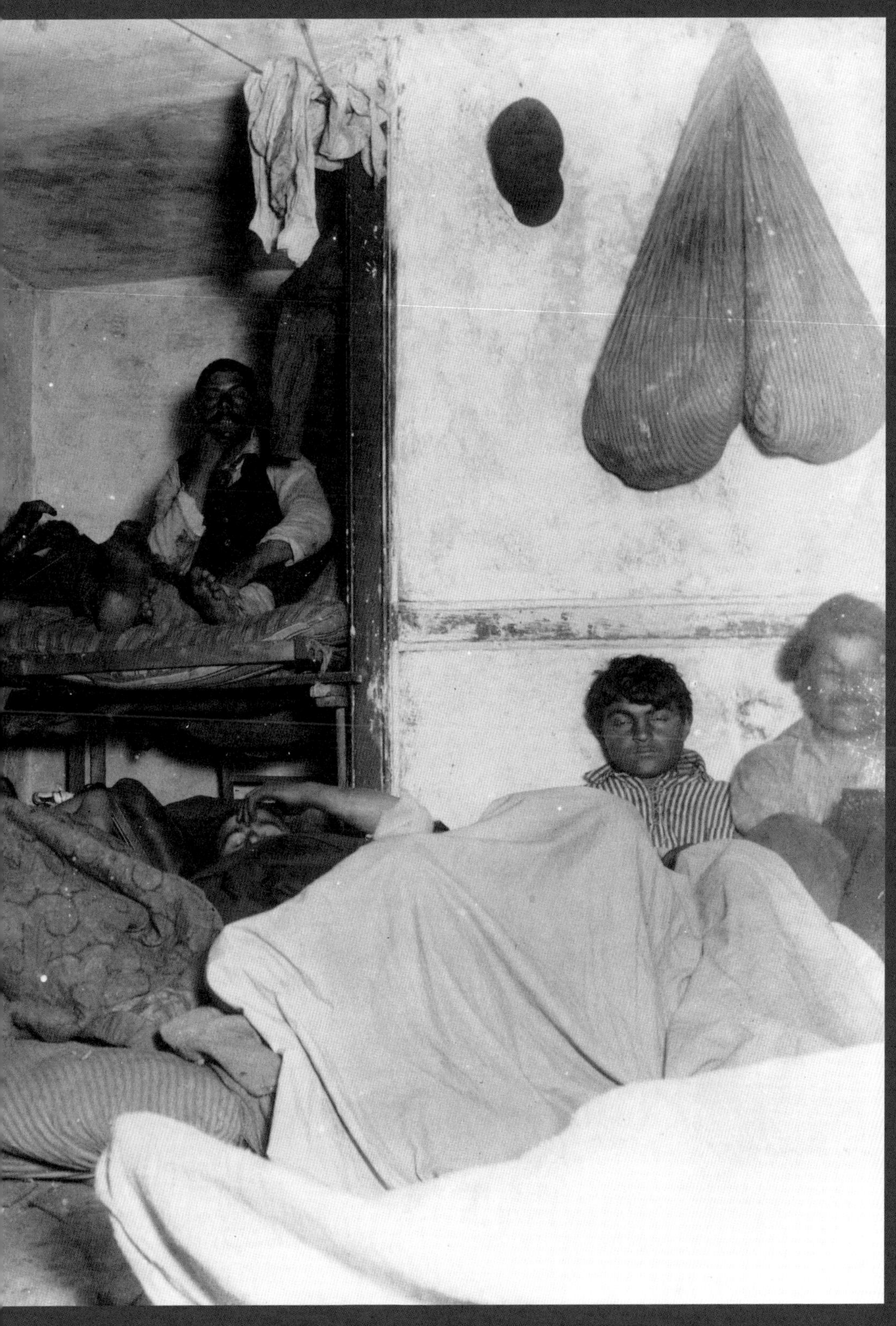

as a naturalized form of belonging guaranteed by the home. In fact, in the introduction of his book, Riis quoted the Secretary of the Prison Association of New York, linking social maladies and deprived architectural conditions with the dissolution of the family: "By far the largest part—eighty per cent, at least—of crimes against property and against the person are perpetrated by individuals who have lost connection with home life, or never had any, or whose homes had ceased to be sufficiently separate, decent, and desirable to afford what are regarded as ordinary wholesome influences of home and family."[30] Appropriating this argument, Riis emphasized the delimitation of familial boundaries at the core of his project. He particularly applied this framework to his observations about Italians, noting elsewhere how Sicilians, for example, gather two and sometimes three families in each apartment,[31] in what the census called at the time "partner households."[32]

While the Italians' occupation of the tenements might be analyzed as a response to their mistreatment by landlords, when one considers their virtual lack of citizenship, it could also be seen as an impulse to form alternative networks of support and spaces of belonging. These networks need to be evaluated beyond the limitations of the nuclear family privileged by social reformers such as Riis.[33] Donna Gabaccia's groundbreaking research has already considered the "partner households" in the tenements and what she calls "malleable households" (resulting from the temporary incorporation of boarders), not only as a response to the economic need to split rents, but as the articulation of alternative social networks.[34] The evolution of the tenement's typology might have favored some of those social formations because increasing density and new policies required the introduction of small courtyards in the sides of each building. Some rooms might have opened directly to the corridor and consequently facilitated those processes of social malleability, allowing for families sharing an apartment to continue to live independently.[35] Regarding the further consolidation of familial and social networks, Gabaccia records, "closer relations to the *parenti* [relatives] and, to a lesser extent to the *paesani* [members of the same village] would be further reinforced by urban life in the United States."[36] Furthermore, she polemically poses that "*la famiglia*—the immigrant network of close and extended kin living in several neighboring households—[...] appears to have emerged during migration to and life in a new urban environment," locating the origin for this characteristic association with Italians, in New York, rather than in their home country.[37] While it would be difficult to draw a deterministic link between this social formation and the architectures of the tenements, her arguments unravel the multiple genealogies that need to be accounted for in the understanding of what many times is regarded as a natural space of belonging for the Italian population.

## VIII.

Simultaneously, Italians looked beyond these networks of kin and village, to include people from other Italian regions as well. Architectures of belonging articulated the life of Italians in New York beyond the tenements, through performances that, following Riis, were often mediated by religion: "To the Italian who came over the sea, the saint remains the rallying-point in his civic and domestic life to the end of his days."[38]

Religious performances described the city in ways that provided more detail for the urban distributions that Riis had previously drawn. Writing for *The Century* in 1899, for example, he reported on the internal diversity of Italians in the city, with sections within Little Italy establishing spatial and geographic correspondences with different Italian regions, as they were rendered visible through their patron Saints:

> As St. Roch rules Mulberry street, so Thompson street is preempted by St. Anthony of Padua; but over there there are no back-yard celebrations—at least, I never heard of any. The reason is found in the latitude, not of Thompson Street, but of Padua. [...] In the whole schoolful of these children whom I questioned one day, I found only seven who knew 'Santa Lucia,' and they would not sing it. Any little Neapolitan or Calabrian would have sung it as naturally and as joyously as the robin warbles its love-song in the twilights of spring.[39]

While religious performances were many times consolidated around regional demarcations (and around different dialects spoken in each of those regions), other times they challenged those divisions and shaped larger social articulations. In emphasizing the importance of the Saints to the Italian communities, Riis

Jacob A. Riis, *Celebrating the feast of St. Rocco in Bandit's Roost, Mulberry Bend—May 23, 1895.* Museum of the City of New York.

chronicled that someone told Theodore Roosevelt (then president of the New York police board) "He [the saint] is just-a lik'-a your St. Patrick here."[40] Particularly important was the Lady of Mount Carmel, based in the Little Italy of East Harlem, which defied the atomization of the Italian population along different regions: "Not only from New York and Brooklyn, but from the far towns of New Jersey and the railroad camps of Connecticut, come hosts to kneel at her shrine."[41]

In fact, these performances increasingly went form reinforcing regional clusters and their associated indentities, to building an Italian—national—one.[42] The relevance of this social association of national reach could be regarded not only for the diasporic community of Italians in New York, but also in Italy, considering the massive return of migrants after the 1929 crash. However, beyond these effects, understanding the nation (just as the family) as a framework resulting from shifting performances rather than as a stable unit, remains fundamental to the goal of destabilizing naturalized identities.[43]

## IX.

The understanding of the transformation of both the family and the nation in relation to the occupations of architecture and to urban performances in New York, adds to the contorted genealogies of both of those frameworks of belonging as they have been naturalized to justify diverse politics of exclusion. The relation between family and nation has also been instrumental in cementing the exclusionary goals of different political paradigms: The nuclear family, for example, was appropriated by Italian fascism[44] and, more recently, the family has been theorized as a substitute for welfare support within neo-liberal regimes.[45] The case explored in this article draws different boundaries for the family and the nation—in the form of the *famiglia* and the diasporic community—and casts their relation as fundamental to the forms of support countering the virtual lack of rights, supposedly granted by the nation, for these displaced and unrecognized Italians.

Most importantly, the complex genealogies of both the *famiglia* and the nation reaching to New York come to complicate the assumptions of contemporary nationalist rhetoric, by understanding the way in which they might have been shaped beyond Italian national boundaries. Contemporary exclusionary nativism will have difficulty finding any safe ground within these genealogies. Accounting for the entanglements of architecture and urbanism within the histories of migration and nationalism, is essential to dismantling the forceful—if hollow—fears that are being spread in our time.

1 "The Sun exclusive interview with President Trump," *The Sun* (July 13, 2018), https://www.thesun.co.uk/news/6766531/trump-may-brexit-us-deal-off/.

2 Ibid.

3 Ibid.

4 For the attribution of this sentence see Carlo Fomenti, "Siamo una nazione, ma chi ha fatto l'Italia?" *Corriere della Sera* (July 17, 1993), p. 23.

5 Emilio Gentile, *Né stato né nazione. Italani senza meta* (Bari and Rome: Lateza, 2001), p. 97. According to Stephanie Malia Hom, "The Risorgimento made its form, but the contents of the Italian state remain unsettled and indeterminate." See Stephanie Maila Hom, *The beautiful Country. Tourism and the impossible state of destination Italy* (Toronto: University of Toronto Press), p. 9.

6 See Mark Choate, *Emigrant Nation. The Making of Italy Abroad* (Cambridge, MA: Harvard University Press, 2008), p. 1. See also the earlier studies of Robert F. Forrester, *The Italian Emigration of our Times* (Cambridge, MA: Harvard University Press, 1919) and the publications of the journal *Altreitalie* since 1989. See also *Ercole Sori, L'emigrazione italiana dall'Unità alla seconda guerra mondiale* (Bologna: Il Mulino 1979); and Gianfausto Rossoli and Francesco Baletta ed., *Un secolo di emigrazione italiana 1876–1976* (Rome: Centro Studi Emigrazione, 1978).

7 See *Modern Italy. Images and History of National Identity*, vol. 1, p. 317. Nine million people crossed the Atlantic between 1900 and 1914.

8 Ibid., p. 319.

9 See Edward Said, "Reflections on exile," [1984] in *Reflections on Exile and Other Essays* (Cambridge, Mass.: Harvard University Press, 2000). Mark Choate has also argued, for the Italian case, that rather than challenging the process of national unification, the outward flows of Italians played a key role in the consolidation of the Italian nation. See Choate, *Emigrant Nation*, pp. 145-148.

10 Benedict Anderson has described the nation as an "imaginary community" in Benedict Anderson, *Imagined communities. Reflections on the Origin and Spread of Nationalism* (New York and London: Verso, 2006), [1983].

11 Giuseppe Prezzolini [1931], cited in *R.J.B. Bosworth, Italy and the Wider World* (New York; London: Routledge, 1995), p. 137.

12 Étienne Balibar, "Propositions on citizenship," *Ethics* vol. 98, no. 4 (July, 1988), p. 726.

13 Balibar, *Citizenship* (Malden, MA: Polity Press, 2015), 76: "*[...] it is always citizens*, 'knowing' and 'imagining' themselves as such, *who exclude from citizenship and who, thus, 'produce' non-citizens in such a way as to make it possible for them to represent their own citizenship to themselves as a 'common' belonging.*"

14 See, among others, Hanna Arendt, "We Refugees," *Menorah Journal*, no. 1 (1943), pp. 69-77 and Giorgio Agamben, "Biopolitics and the Rights of Man," in *Homo Sacer: Sovereign Power and Bare Life* (Stanford, Ca: Stanford University Press, 1998), pp. 126-35. Esra Akcan has recently discussed the implications of these arguments to the politics of housing in Berlin in Akcan, *Open Architecture. Migration, Citizenship, and the Urban Renewal of Berlin-Kreuzberg by IBA-1984/87* (Basel: Birkhauser, 2018), pp. 32-33.

15 Antonio Gramsci, "Some aspects of the Southern question," [1926] in *The Gramsci Reader. Selected Writings (1916–1935)* (New York: The New York University Press, 2000), pp. 171-185.

16 John Dickie, "Stereotypes of the Italian South, 1860–1900," in Robert Lumley and Jonathan Morris, eds. *The New History of the Italian South: The Mezzogiorno Revisited* (Exeter: University of Exeter Press, 1997), p. 122.

17 See Donna R. Gabaccia, *Italy's Many Diasporas* (Seattle: University of Washington Press, 2000), p. 36. It is important to note that many Italians were denied voting rights at the time. As Gabbacia discusses, "[a]fter 1881, about 6 percent of Italian citizens, including a very few ordinary workers, could vote; few of the other 94 percent felt much loyalty to a nation of Italians."

18 Joseph Cosco, *Imagining Italians. The Clash of Romance and Race in American Perceptions, 1880–1910* (Albany, State of New York Press, 2003), p. 8. See also John Higham, *Strangers in the Land: Patterns of American Nativism, 1860–1925* (New York: Atheneum, 1970), p. 66.; Alan M. Kraut, *The Huddled Masses: The Immigrant in American Society, 1880–1921* (Arlington Heights: Harlan Davidson Inc., 1982), pp. 19-21.; John Dickie, "Imagined Italies,"in David Forgacs and Robert Lumley, eds., *Italian Cultural Studies: An Introduction* (New York: Oxford Univeristy Press, 1996), pp. 28-29.

19 See Roger Griffin, "Modernity, modernism, and fascism. A 'mazeway resynthesis,'" *Modernism/modernity*, vol. 15, no. 1 (January 2008), p. 18.

20 Carlo Levi, *Christ stopped at Eboli* (New York: Straus and Company, 1947), pp. 131-132.

21 See Bonnie Yochelson, *Rediscovering Jacob Riis: Exposure Journalism and Photography in Turn-of-the-Century New York* (New York: New Press, 2007).

22 Jacob A. Riis, *How the Other Half Lives. Studies among the tenements of New York* (New York: Charles Scribner's Sons, 1890).

23 Ibid., p. 24.

24 Ibid., p. 25.

25 Ibid., p. 148.

26 Ibid., p. 48.

27 Ibid., p. 7. Also, p. 17: "To-day what is a tenement? The law defines it as a house 'occupied by three or more families, living independently and doing their cooking on the premises; or by more than two families on a floor, so living and cooking and having a common right in the halls, stairways, yards, etc.'"

28 Ibid., p. 4. His arguments continued: "The complaint was universal among the tenants that they were entirely uncared for."

29 Ibid., p. 48.

30 Ibid., p. 2 (italics in the original).

31 Jacob A. Riis, *Ten Years' War: An Account of the Battle with the Slum in New York* (Boston: Mifflin and Company, 1900), p. 53.

32 See Ibid., p. 75. It is difficult to determine with precision the average occupation for these apartments, since both the tenements' sizes and their inhabitants diverged greatly. Riis provides some extreme examples, mentioning reports accounting for "one room 12' × 12' with five families living in it, comprising twenty persons of both sexes and all ages with only two beds (...)." Riis, *How the Other Half Lives*, p. 11.

33 The nuclear family is conventionally defined by a couple and their dependent children. Extended understandings of the family are conventionally understood to include other relatives beyond this nucleus.

34 See Ibid., p. xvi.

35 See Lillian W. Betts, "The Italian in New York," *University Settlement Studies*, no.1 (1906), p. 98 cited in *Gabaccia, From Sicily to Elizabeth Street*, p. 75.

36 See Gabaccia, *From Sicily to Elizabeth Street. Housing and Social Change Among Italian Immigrants* (Albany: State University of New York Press, 1984), p. 68.

37 Ibid., pp. xv-xvi. See also ibid., p. 115.

38 Jacob A. Riis, "Feast-Days in Little Italy," *The Century Magazine* (August 1899), p. 494. He continued: "To the homesick peasant who hangs about the Mott street café for hours, hungrily devouring with his eyes the candy counterfeit of Mount Vesuvius in the window, with lurid lava-streams descending and saffron smoke ascending, predicting untold stomach-quakes in the block, the saint means home and kindred, neighborly friendships in a strange land, and the old communal ties, which if anything, are tightened by distance and homesickness."

39 Ibid., p. 495.

40 Ibid., p. 493.

41 Ibid., p. 496. On the Lady of Mount Carmel see Robert Anthony Orsi, *The Madonna of 115th Street. Faith and Community in Italian Harlem, 1880–1950* (New Haven and London: Yale University Press, 1985).

42 See Denise Mangieri DiCarlo, "The Role of the Italian Festa in the United States," in Harral E. Landry, ed., *To See the Past More Clearly: The Enrichment of the Italian Heritage, 1890–1990* (Staten Island, NY: The American Italian Historical Association, 1994), pp. 198, 204. Cited in Cosco, *Imagining Italians*, p. 47. These religious performances might need to be considered among other ways of consolidating networks including businesses, societies, and others. See Harry M. Shulman, *Slums of New York* (New York: Albert and Charles Boni, 1938), p. 105.

43 It would be possible to relate this de-naturalizing impetus to the way in which feminist and queer theorists including Judith Butler originally discussed gender not to be inherent to bodies, but as adopted through a series of performances deemed characteristic of femininity or masculinity. See Judith Butler, *Bodies that Matter: On the Discursive Limits of "Sex"* (1993).

44 Vitoria De Grazia has argued how "the family was regarded as the most distant outpost of government power. Accordingly, no conflict should exist between family obligations and patriotic duty." However, families were also a "private haven" that the fascist government understood it should let without interference as a way of letting them develop its mandate to perpetuate the raze. See Vitoria De Grazia, *How Fascism Ruled Women: Italy, 1922–1945* (Berkeley: University of California Press, 1993), p. 79.

45 See Melinda Cooper, *Family Values: Between Neoliberalism and the New Social Conservatism* (Cambridge, MA: MIT Press, 2017).

MARRIKKA
TROTTER

# MNEMOPHOBIA

# DEAD LIFE: ROBERT ADAM AND THE GEOLOGICAL ANXIETY

181

During the last decades of his life, Scottish architect Robert Adam (1728–1792) embarked on the production of a thousand landscape watercolors, of which roughly four hundred finished compositions and sketches in his hand are known to survive today.[1] Adam was an enthusiastic topographical artist, often finding time in his busy professional life to take sketching tours across Scotland and parts of England with his close friend and brother-in-law, John Clerk of Eldin. As a friend and pupil of Giovanni Battista Piranesi—the great architect-antiquarian of eighteenth-century Rome—and a designer whose own eclectic brand of neoclassicism relied on the imaginative recombination of historical motifs from across architectural history, Adam was also naturally attentive to the castles, keeps, and brochs that populate the territory he sketched. However, the watercolors he produced in what was to be one of the last great creative outbursts of his life do not depict any known scenes, nor do the castles included in nearly every composition reflect any actual fortification. Rather, the scenes are composites: fictional views that often include real topographical features and nod toward historical structures and types without faithfully recreating any place in particular (Fig. 1).

In Adam's obituary, *The Gentleman's Magazine* singled out these paintings for their "luxuriance of composition" and "effect of light and shadow"[2] and indeed the highly designed arrangements of individual elements—many of which are vaguely recognizable to eyes familiar with British landscapes—continue to vie for attention with the dramatic effects (including long white shafts of sunlight, deep purple shadows, and tumultuous atmospheric conditions) used to bring these elements together. With their striking combinations of mountains, rivers, bridges, and fortresses, these paintings affiliate with the Romantic landscape fantasies just coming into vogue in Britain: they follow the prescriptions of William Gilpin and echo the fictional compositions of another of Adam's friends and sketching partners, the topographical artist Paul Sandby.[3]

Yet on closer inspection, unique traits appear. Fortresses and landforms confront each other or cooperate as if equal entities. In some cases, rocky outcrops and castles possess the same apparent heft; in others, somber ridgelines follow the outline of the architectural compositions they overshadow. In one painting, a rock seems to march toward a hilltop castle like an attacking army. There is, moreover, a laminated quality to many of these works, as though the planes of various two-dimensional tableaux have been stacked together like so many layers of stage scenery. This is a deliberate

Previous, Fig. 1: A rocky outcrop seems to lay siege to an equivalently sized fortress. (Robert Adam, *Landscape with a Castle, Lake and Farm Animals*, about 1780. D 454: National Galleries of Scotland. David Laing Bequest to the Royal Scottish Academy transferred 1910.) This page, Fig. 2: This preparatory watercolor composition (top) is more unified than the finalized iteration; foreground, middle ground, and background seamlessly blend into one another. (Robert Adam, *Mountain with castle on a rocky promontory in loch*, 1781. London, Sir John Soane's Museum.) Fig. 3: In the final version of the sketch he had made the year before (bottom), Adam cropped the foliage to leave a clear highlighted gap between the rocky outcrop framing the view at right and the trees immediately beyond. The hill with a second castle on it in the distance on the left side of the composition is similarly held apart from the landscape beyond with a thin pale highlight. (Robert Adam, *Drawing of Picturesque Scenery*, 1782. Scotland, Blair Adam Muniments.)

effect, rather than a lack of ability, as can be seen by comparing a surviving rough sketch from the Sir John Soane's Museum in London (Fig. 2) with the extensive collection that remains at Blair Adam's family home in Scotland (Fig. 3). The draft is much more seamless than the final iteration, in which a thin white border has been inserted between the layers of foreground, middleground, and background, as if to highlight the piece's combinatorial nature. In fact, in several of the more highly finished compositions, various perspectival vantages seem to be combined, producing the vertiginous sensation that the landscape before which the viewer is placed is capable of flying apart at any moment.[4]

Such anomalous characteristics suggest that these paintings might be more productively considered in the context of Adam's architectural output than landscape art proper. For example, the kind of visual fracture that appears in Adam's landscape compositions is also used in his architectural vedute to signal that some foreign element has been allowed to invade the composition (Fig. 4). For example, Adam placed a Piranesian depiction of the Pyramid of Cestius into one of his own Rome-inspired scenes with a slightly different vanishing point, allowing a piece of his mentor's world to exist within his own composition under the banner of its separate representational logic. The intentional nature of this maneuver is emphasized by leaving the construction lines for the larger two-point perspective visible.[5]

Fig. 4: Like many of Adam's landscapes, this composition appears to combine multiple perspectival vantages into one scene. (Robert Adam, *Romantic Landscape with Castle*. London, Sir John Soane's Museum.)

Analogues for this open display of heterogeneity can also be found in Adam's approach to his architectural commissions. An early example of Adam's technique is the anteroom he designed for Syon House in 1761, just five years after he returned from his Grand Tour. As Doreen Yarwood has summarized, the composition contains column shafts supposedly dredged from the Tiber River—allegedly real, ancient elements of classical antiquity—that Adam embellished with ionic capitals, an entablature modeled on that of the Greek Erecthion, and necking decoration inspired by those of Roman baths. The coffered ceiling follows William Kent's design for Houghton Hall, and the gilded trophy panels are based on an engraving of the trophy of Octavianus Augustus by Piranesi.[6]

It is likely that Piranesi himself encouraged the younger architect in this approach; the Italian treated history as a jumble of fragments available for endless combination and recombination in his own archeological fantasies. In Adam's case, the simultaneous treatment of disconnected architectural events went further than diverse assemblages of ornament. His Roman anteroom at Syon House, with its riot of color, pattern, and detail, is spatially and sequentially adjacent to his severely Grecian, black-and-white design for that house's Great Hall, and both exist within a crenellated, preexisting Elizabethan box that bears no relation to the interiors within.

If Adam's uniquely combinatorial technique connects his landscape paintings to his larger architectural oeuvre, the question that still remains is why he felt compelled to transfer his design approach to the landscape in the first place. While his practice with his two younger brothers certainly suffered after the financial implosion of their Adelphi speculative development in London, and there was less money for large-scale work in England after the American colonies rebelled, the period that witnessed the bulk of his painting production also corresponded to a renaissance in his architectural practice, as he began picking up a number of public and private commissions in his native Scotland.[7] Many of these projects were also designed as aggregates of discrete elements sourced from a broad range of architectural history, but the material these late Scottish works engaged with were largely drawn from a different, more bellicose catalogue than the neoclassical motifs that informed Adam's earlier works. Roman fort elements were collaged together with French bartizans and machicolations, pre-Caledonian brochs from Scotland, and British medieval keeps.[8] The architectural language of attack and defense, threat and resistance, permeated Adam's "Castle Style," as this period became known, at precisely the same time that Adam began populating imagined landscapes with similar structures. It is as if Adam aimed to explore architectural defense in its full potential, unconstrained by the limits of commissioned projects (Fig. 5).

It is important to note that the turn from the eighteenth to the nineteenth century witnessed a major upheaval in the way the landscape was understood. Discoveries across the earth sciences contributed to a new and deeply challenging picture of the earth as an entity with a history of its own—one that dwarfed both human history and that of all life. The Scotland of Robert Adam's day was particularly involved in this intellectual revolution. At the scale of daily experience, the burgeoning Industrial Revolution brought with it a persistent chronological regulation of quotidian existence, termed "clock time" by E. P. Thompson.[9] At the scale of national consciousness, the framework of history began to be assembled. Figures like Adam's friend David Hume claimed that this was "the historical age and this is the historical nation" as he wrote his magisterial History of England (1754–61).[10] At the same time, Britain's great era of mineral exploitation had commenced, particularly in Scotland. Locating, extracting, and transporting coal, lead, and iron-ore exposed an uncanny netherworld beneath familiar agricultural surfaces. As more mines were opened, caves were explored and quarries were established, the more the newly synchronized tick-tock of daily existence and the freshly systematized historical past dwindled beside the gulf of time exposed by mattocks and mapped by commerce.

This new and threatening temporal scale comes into sharp relief in the geological theory of James Hutton. A prominent member of the Scottish Enlightenment, Hutton was an agricultural theorist and deistic philosopher who viewed the planet as a productive base for human life. In his schema, the earth was locked in an immense cycle of erosion and lithification, where old land decayed at the same rate as new land formed under the sea. There was no such thing as primary rock, existing since an originary event; there were simply different densities of soil. The earth's contemporary

configuration was an amalgamation of the recycled detritus of an endless succession of former worlds, and ceding its own material, granule by granule, to a world yet to come.[11]

Hutton famously concluded the published version of his ideas, *Theory of the Earth; or an Investigation of the Laws observable in the Composition, Dissolution, and Restoration of Land upon the Globe* (1788), with the unsettling remark: "We find no vestige of a beginning, no prospect of an end."[12] As Stephen Jay Gould has observed, this view of geological time is radically ahistorical. Time passes, but the record of its passing is being continually effaced; and while evidence of great duration can be identified, it cannot be interpreted as part of a directional progression.[13] In Hutton's work, the narrative arc that had been so central to the Western view of the world since the rise of Christianity, was lost, and with it, any assumption of an intuitive human affinity with the landscapes that ultimately supported life.[14] Time and matter looped in upon themselves. What had happened before was happening again, very slowly, and would happen once more in a future too remote to imagine.

The incommensurability Hutton's theory proposed between lived experience and the vast and indifferent rhythms of the planet exemplifies the Enlightenment's contradictory attitude toward the earth. In his study of the impact of geology on British poetry, Noah Heringman puts the situation succinctly: on the one hand, the Industrial Revolution was based on an instrumental view of the mineral landscape as a static reserve of economic resources. On the other, its meticulous investigation of this reserve revealed abundant evidence of large-scale activity and change, forcing Romantic culture to confront the earth "in its otherness; its non-human aspect."[15] For example, Hutton attributed fundamentally life-like qualities of motion, circulation, and self-repair to inorganic matter. In his *Theory of the Earth*, he insisted that the world is not simply a machine but also an "organized body" with a "reproductive operation, by which a ruined constitution may again be repaired, and duration of stability thus procured."[16] The transfer of organic rhythms to a mineral kingdom so old that it might well have existed forever imbued this previously inert substrate with eerie agency.

John Playfair, Hutton's biographer, recounted the experience of comprehending Hutton's interpretation of the rock formation at Siccar Point, Berwickshire, in 1788:

Fig. 5: Although rendered with the same techniques as Adam's watercolors, this is an unbuilt "Castle Style" design commission. Adam's monumental design for additions to Barnbougle Castle surrounded the original tower house with a book-matched Roman scrim that emphasized the stark symmetry of the ancient keep. (Robert Adam, *A Fortified Castle or Palace, Surrounded by a High Wall, Corner Towers and a Central Gateway (Barnbougle Castle)*. D 467: National Galleries of Scotland. David Laing Bequest to the Royal Scottish Academy transferred 1910.)

We felt ourselves necessarily carried back to the time when the schistus on which we stood was as yet at the bottom of the sea, and when the sandstone before us was only beginning to be deposited, in the shape of sand or mud, from the waters of a superincumbent ocean. An epocha still more remote presented itself, when even the most ancient of these rocks, instead of standing upright in vertical beds, lay in horizontal planes at the bottom of the sea, and was not yet disturbed by that immeasurable force which has burst asunder the solid pavement of the globe. Revolutions still more remote appeared in the distance of this extraordinary perspective. The mind seemed to grow giddy by looking so far into the abyss of time.[17]

Playfair's dramatic depiction represents one end of a sophisticated gradation of sensual responses that had been devised over the last half of the eighteenth century: if the landscape is beautiful when cultivated for pleasure, and picturesque when worked for profit, then when it reveals what Hutton called "the exquisite mechanism and active powers of things," it is sublime.[18]

Playfair's account of Siccar Point followed a particularly Scottish notion of this effect. Although geological features had been included in the repertoire of sublime objects since this aesthetic category had been formulated. (Longinus, the ancient Roman author whose treatise formed the basis for eighteenth-century theories, included the volcano of Mount Etna in his catalogue.[19]) Scottish philosophers placed a unique emphasis on temporality. In his *Treatise on Human Nature* (1738), Hume asked, "Why a very great distance encreases our esteem and admiration for an object: Why such a distance in time encreases it more than that in space: And a distance in past time more than that in future."[20] He concluded that, while the imagination perceived space as a smooth continuum, time was envisioned as a "broken up jumble." The greater difficulty in imagining a remote past than a remote place thus produced a more complete sense of disorientation, followed in turn by the attainment of "a more vigorous and sublime disposition."[21] Yet there is also the sublime menace of time itself, couched as a ruinous counterforce that erases not just mankind's physical productions, but also mankind's mental constructs. The Scottish associationist philosopher Lord Kames, a contemporary of both Hume and Hutton, and also an influential friend and correspondent of Robert Adam's, speculated that the most basic reduction of a sublime encounter could be produced by "a huge mass of rubbish, the ruins perhaps of some extensive building, or a large heap of stones, such as are collected together for keeping in memory a battle or other remarkable event."[22] This ambiguous index of opposite processes is sublime because it reveals the indifference and unmeaning of Hutton's "medium of things." The past reaches up to touch the present in muteness. Ruins perpetually enact forgetfulness; cairns forecast failures of memory to come. The stones will outlive their arrangements, will again become part of the larger effacing upheaval of the earth, and will go down to darkness and dust, as they have come from these only temporarily, reluctantly, into the landscapes of the living.

These new concepts placed particular pressure on architecture's relationship to the landscape. The historian John Dalrymple, an associate of Hume, Hutton, and Kames, and also a friend and patron to Adam, wrote in an influential 1774 treatise on landscape:

> The chief natural defect of a highland situation is that, being generally ill-inhabited, it has too much the appearance of dead life: that appearance, added to the vastness of the objects, creates a kind of despair in the mind, which considers itself as nothing amidst that stupendous and solitary scene it beholds.[23]

Coupled with Hutton's extension of an eerily biological "reproductive operation" to the entire surface of the globe, this sense of "dead life" becomes part of a deeper eighteenth-century intuition of a negative force, hostile to life itself. For Dalrymple, the ever-present threat of the barren Scottish landscape required extensive defensive bulwarks. His solution was architectural. As he put it, "though the little finishings of art on the face of the ground would in such a situation be lost, yet the great efforts of art would please, because that very art is a sign of cultivation." The "great efforts" he specifically had in mind were castles:

> The slenderness of an Ionic or Corinthian pillar, placed at the side of a vast mountain, would create a ridiculous comparison; and therefore in a highland situation, the principle house should be in the form of a castle. The elegance and fineness of execution belonging to the Grecian architecture, would here be totally misplaced. If in that castle, added to the greatness and solid

> appearance of the main building, there should shoot up in the middle a Gothic tower, pierced and of hardy execution, a sentiment similar to the sentiment of terror, added to that of grandeur, would still more correspond to the natural genius of the place.[24]

In this, Dalrymple echoed a roughly contemporaneous remark by Lord Kames that a Gothic ruin "exhibits the triumph of time over strength; a melancholy, but not unpleasant thought: a Grecian ruin suggests rather the triumph of barbarity over taste; a gloomy and discouraging thought."[25] But embedded within Dalrymple's preference for hardiness over slenderness was a sense that architecture possessed a sublimity of its own, one capable of rising up against the inorganic hostility of an ancient and vitalized landscape. This illuminates one of the underlying attractions of the sublime in the context of the enlightened estrangement between culture and the natural world. From Longinus to Burke, the sublime had permitted a sense of parity, however fraught, between the works of man and the works of nature. Doomed as such efforts were ultimately acknowledged to be, there was yet something in the artifice of human achievements, architecture in particular, that could resist the overpowering force and temporality of nature, even as it gave way before it.

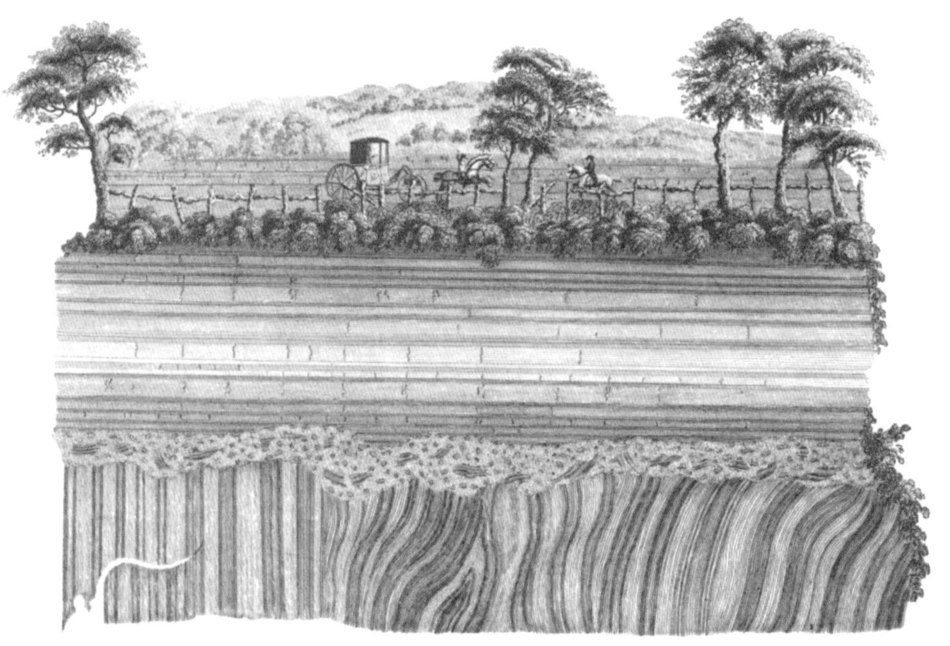

Opposite, Fig. 6: In this early geological drawing, the quick surface pace of human life, represented by the moving carriage and the horse and rider, is contrasted with the immensity of time it must have taken for horizontal layers of sediment to accumulate, harden, buckle, upend into their current vertical positions, and be covered again in turn by new horizontal strata. (John Clerk of Eldin, *Sketch of the Unconformity at Jedburgh, Borders, Scotland*, 1787. Midlothian, Scotland, Clerk of Penicuik Muniments.) This page from top, Fig. 7: In Adam's version of this composition (left), the landscape seems more changeable and active than the Italianate castle. (Robert Adam, *Castle on rocks above lake with figure and cart in foreground*. Scotland, Blair Adam Muniments.) Fig. 8: Clerk of Eldin's version of Adam's composition (right) puts the inhuman landform and the human fortress in direct confrontation, as if to signal the overpowering scale of geological time and processes. In contrast to Adam's Italianate fortress, Clerk of Eldin's castle is a more Scottish type. (John Clerk of Eldin, *Castle in a Landscape after R. Adam*. National Galleries of Scotland.)

Like Hutton's cyclical mechanism, which assembled new mineral formations from old ruins, Adam's collage-like approach crafted entirely unique spaces and views from the existing repertoire of architectural elements and images. Their similarity of approach is not purely coincidental. Hutton and Adam were closely associated via Clerk of Eldin, a polymath who produced the illustrations for Hutton's *Theory of the Earth* and was so involved in that project's conceptualization that Playfair felt it was impossible to tell where the work of one man stopped and the other began.[26] It is in light of the intellectual connections of Clerk of Eldin, Hutton, Hume, Kames, and Dalrymple (a network of luminaries not uncommon during the Scottish Enlightenment) that Adam's late landscape watercolors must ultimately be understood.

**From top, Fig. 9:** The waterfall shown here is a vertically exaggerated view of Cora Linn, one of the Falls of Clyde in South Lanarkshire, Scotland. (Robert Adam, *Fortress above a Waterfall*, 1782.) **Fig. 10:** The mountains in the background of this composition are recognizable as the "Three Sisters" of Glencoe, Scotland. (Robert Adam, *River Landscape with a Castle, Lake and Sailing Boat*. D 444: National Galleries of Scotland. David Laing Bequest to the Royal Scottish Academy transferred 1910.) **Fig. 11:** Here the fictional form of the castle in Fig. 10 is recycled, while the mountains in the background echo but exaggerate Glencoe's Three Sisters in the above composition. (Robert Adam, *Mountain landscape with two castles and smaller towers beside a loch*. Scotland, Blair Adam Muniments.) **Next page: Fig. 12:** Here the fictional form of the castle in Fig. 2 is recycled, while the mountainous forms in the background echo but exaggerate the "Three Sisters" in Adam's other composition. (Robert Adam, *Mountain landscape with two castles and smaller towers beside a loch*. Scotland, Blair Adam Muniments.)

A pair of paintings by Adam and Clerk of Eldin presents a striking inversion: in Adam's watercolor (Fig. 7), a mountainous mass, blurred as if in motion, surges by an inert fortress on an equivalently scaled hill. Clerk of Eldin's take on his friend's composition (Fig. 8), *after R. Adam*, takes this scenario to a new extreme, repositioning the castle in front of a rushing landform that rears back as if to engulf the fortress. Taken together with Clerk of Eldin's position as the likely conduit of Hutton's theories and the amount of time these men spent in each other's company during Adam's Castle Style period, this startling composition raises the possibility that Clerk of Eldin was a more catalytic figure in Adam's creative life than previously credited.[27]

As mentioned, Adam had a tendency to include real Scottish landforms in his fictional compositions. A looming ridgeline that overshadows a fortress, mimicking its contours, is a view of the Grampian Mountains near Cluny Castle (Fig. 9). The waterfall that drops away from an Italianate tower is recognizable as Cora Lin, a famous feature of the River Clyde (Fig. 10). The "Three Sisters" peaks of Glencoe appear in several paintings (Fig. 11), and the distinctive cone of Ben Lomond dominates the middle distance of a scene with a ruined tower (Fig. 12). Fictional elements are also reused: castles from one landscape will appear in another, or invented landforms will be recycled. Treated as a series, the paintings give the impression of a typology that includes both real and projected objects, as well as built and natural forms. The net result of such maneuvers is to signal that Adam was treating the landscape as source material for his designs. Even mountains were as available for imaginative recombination as the cornices and capitals he sampled at Syon House. Moreover, in so blatantly articulating the artificial manner of their composition, these sublime scenes invite the power of reason to eclipse the dazzled gaze.

In the Scottish Enlightenment, one of the final props supporting an anthropocentric view of the world slipped—the latest in a series of recognitions that included the discovery of infinity and the Copernican establishment of a heliocentric planetary system. What was at stake was no less than humanity's right to regard itself as the end to which all nature was the means. In this light, while Adam's landscape paintings seem to register an awareness of the earth's inhuman dimension, they fundamentally propose nothing more than a way to operate in spite of its overtaking flood.

Adam's archaeology was always one of fragments rescued willy-nilly from the annihilating crush of time. His embrace of the past as a hodgepodge accepted that any meaning gained would always be a contemporary artifact predicated on present tastes. Architecture is a humanistic endeavor. Adam met the Scottish Enlightenment's new and frightening understanding of the earth by extending his disciplinary logic to the landscape.

1 Robert Adam's brother-in-law and close friend, John Clerk of Eldin, refers to this project as a "thousand landskips" in his unfinished "Notes for a Life of Robert Adam," Clerk of Penicuik Muniments, NAS, GD18/4981. It is unclear how many Adam actually completed in addition to the ones that have survived today. Adam viewed these landscape works as offering some financial security for his family, and during one particularly bad bout of illness in 1786 gave them to his three sisters in London in case of his death. Margaret H. B. Sanderson, *Robert Adam and Scotland: Portrait of an Architect* (Edinburgh: HMSO, 1992), p. 103.

2 "Obituary: Robert Adam," in *The Gentleman's Magazine*, vol. 62, iss. 1 (March 1792), pp. 282-283.

3 Adam and Clerk of Eldin were familiar with Gilpin's work and even went so far as to copy his compositions. See, for example, BA151 and BA110 from the Blair Adam Muniments. Both men were also influenced in their art by the work of Paul Sandy, who became a friend of the Adam family through his role as a draughtsman to the Board of Ordnance at Fort George, near Inverness, in the early 1750s, when Robert and James Adam were engaged on construction work there for the family practice. See Fleming, pp. 84-86, 100-101, 259-260; and Tait, *Robert Adam: Drawings and Imagination*, pp. 13-15. The Adam–Clerk–Sandby circle is also discussed in A. A. Tait, "Robert Adam and John Clerk of Eldin," *Master Drawings*, vol. 16, iss. 1 (1978), pp. 53-77, 109-111.

4 I am grateful to Stephen Astley for first pointing out these perspectival anomalies to me. In addition to Fig. 4, *Romantic Landscape with Castle*, 1782, other particularly striking examples include 68.1.7 in Sir John Soane's Museum, and D462, D463, D465, and D466 in the National Gallery of Scotland.

5 Robert Adam, "Imaginary Scene with the Pyramid of Cestius," Sir John Soane's Museum, SM 67.7.24.

6 Doreen Yarwood, *Robert Adam* (London: Dent, 1970), pp. 56-59.

7 For the best account of this fraught period in the Adam family, see Sanderson, pp. 99-107.

8 Alistair Rowan, Designs for Castles and Country Villas by Robert and James Adam (New York: Rizzoli, 1985), p. 17. See also Marrikka Trotter, "Temporal Sublime: Robert Adam and Geology in the Scottish Enlightenment," in ed. Colin Thom, *Robert Adam and His Brothers: New Light on Britain's Leading Architectural Family* (London: Historic England, forthcoming early 2019).

9 E. P. Thomson, "Time, Work-Discipline, and Industrial Capitalism," *Past and Present*, vol. 38 (December 1967), pp. 56–97.

10 David Hume, "Letter to William Strahan," 1770, in *The Letters of David Hume*, ed. J. Y. T. Greig, (Oxford: Clarendon Press, 1932), vol. 2, p. 230.

11 For a concise review of Hutton's theory and its context within the Scottish Enlightenment see Dennis R. Dean, *James Hutton and the History of Geology*, (Ithaca: Cornell University Press, 1992), pp. 2-30.

12 James Hutton, *Theory of the Earth, with Proofs and Illustrations*, (London and Edinburgh: Messrs Cadell junior and Messrs Creech, 1795), vol. 1, p. 223.

13 Stephen Jay Gould, Time's Arrow, Time's Cycle: Myth and Metaphor in the Discovery of Geological Time, (Cambridge: Harvard University Press, 1987), pp. 61-96.

14 Martin J. S. Rudwick, Bursting the Limits of Time: The Reconstruction of Geohistory in the Age of Revolution, (Chicago: University of Chicago Press, 2005), pp. 168–70.

15 Noah Heringman, *Romantic Rocks, Aesthetic Geology*, (Ithaca: Cornell University Press, 2004), p. 1.

16 Hutton, *Theory of the Earth*, vol. 1, pp. 16-17.

17 John Playfair, "Biographical Account of the late James Hutton, M.D.," reprinted in *The Works of John Playfair*, Esq., (Edinburgh: Archibald Constable & Co, 1822), vol. 4, pp. 80-81.

18 Hutton, *Theory of the Earth*, vol. 2, p. 469.

19 Longinus, *On the Sublime*, sec. 34, p. 277. Discussed in Emily Brady, *The Sublime in Modern Philosophy: Aesthetics, Ethics, and Nature*, (Cambridge: Cambridge University Press, 2013), p. 13.

20 David Hume, *A Treatise on Human Nature*, (Edinburgh, 1738), p. 279.

21 Ibid., p. 286.

22 Henry Home, Lord Kames, *Elements of Criticism* [1785] (London: Routledge / Thoemmes Press, 1993), vol. 1, p. 212. Lord Kames was one of the central figures of the Scottish Enlightenment. He was the recipient in 1763 of a much-quoted letter from Robert Adam explaining his views on the use of the Classical orders—one of the rare surviving examples of Adam's own writing on architectural theory and practice (it is transcribed in Arthur T. Bolton, *The Architecture of Robert and James Adam* (1758–1974), (Antique Book Collector's Club reprint [1984] of London: Country Life, 1922), vol. 1, pp. 50-54. Kames was also a member of the Edinburgh Council committee that in the 1760s reviewed and advised on James Craig's plans for Edinburgh New Town, as was Robert's brother John Adam. For a discussion of Kames' influence of the Adam brothers see John Fleming, *Robert Adam and his Circle in Edinburgh and Rome* (Cambridge: Harvard University Press, 1962), pp. 307-311.

23 Ibid., p. 286.

24 Ibid., p. 8.

25 Kames, *Elements of Criticism*, vol. 1, pp. 446-447.

26 Playfair, "Biographical Account," p. 115. Clerk of Eldin's illustrations were lost after his death and rediscovered in the Clerk family archives at Penicuik House in 1968. See G. Y. Craig, D. B. McIntyre, and C. D. Waterston, *James Hutton's Theory of the Earth: The Lost Drawings* (Edinburgh: Scottish Academic Press, 1978), pp. 6-9.

27 Richard Emerson has revealed the significant extent to which Clerk of Eldin was involved in architectural experimentation, adding weight to this possibility. See his "Robert Adam and John Clerk of Eldin: From Primitive Hut to Temple of Religion," in *Scottish Country Houses*, ed. Ian Gow and Alistair Rowan, (Edinburgh: Edinburgh University Press, 1995). I am grateful to Ian Gow for first drawing my attention to Richard Emerson's scholarship and to Richard himself for his very helpful remarks and suggestions. Adam and Clerk of Eldin seem to have made a practice both of sketching together and of producing drawings based on each other's compositions or a shared point of reference. Emerson, pp. 170-171, and Sanderson, p. 116. In addition to the examples Emerson mentions, the Hunterian Art Gallery at the University of Glasgow owns a "View of Crossaguel Abbey" by Adam after Clerk of Eldin's own etching, "Abbey of Crossraguel" (del. 1762; reprinted in *A series of etchings chiefly of views in Scotland*, Edinburgh: Bannatyne Club, 1855). Clerk of Eldin also accompanied Robert Adam on various site visits and to client meetings during Adam's castle period. See Sanderson, p. 116.

T
torture
form
its crim

secretly

esses

# NEGOTIATING, SUBVERTING, RECONFIGURING BORDERS IN THE ENGLISH-SPEAKING WORLD

198

PHILIP URSPRUNG

ANTHROPOPHOBIA

…I think the major issue now in art is what are the boundaries.

—Allan Kaprow, *Robert Smithson and the Art of their Time*, 1979.

Wolfgang Tillmans' *Empire US / Mexican Border* (2005) depicts a border fence reminiscent of a bolt of lightning running like a fissure across the composition.[1] The cast shadow of its grill parallels and complements this jarring, vertical movement. A sign reading "Declaration Line" confirms the politically tense location, yet the spaces intertwine in a labyrinthian manner as though inviting misinterpretation. People are captured from behind, faces angled away from the shot as though to eliminate the possibility of empathy. The clothing of the male figure in the center indicates cool weather, but alludes to prison garb. The chaos composed around the fence obscures the immediate situation.

Locating the vantage point of the camera proves to be a difficult task—normal circumstances forbid photography. The tips of the metal fencing undoubtedly point towards Mexico to impede climbing. From this, we infer the American territory is on the left and Mexican territory on the right, with the view oriented towards the south during the evening hours. Perhaps this picture shows a border crossing in Arizona or New Mexico as commuters return home from work.

I have only crossed this American border condition twice. Once in the spring of 2018 with students on a trip to Texas, between El Paso and Juarez, and once in Tijuana, in the late 1990s, with Allan Kaprow who was living in San Diego at the time. On our return trip, the officer asked him, "Citizen?" without glancing at the presented documents. Kaprow abruptly declared, "*American citizen!*" with a tone still tolerable in a time before (conspicuous) socio-political consciousness and the establishment of the United States Department of Homeland Security. Though significantly before September 11th, 2001 and the massive increases in security, defense, and societal paranoia, the authoritarian resemblance to Ancient Rome (the assumption that only Roman citizens were citizens) was all too evident.

*Empire (US/Mexico border)* references both Wolfgang Tillman's work of art as well as the concept described by Michael Hardt and Antonio Negri in their book *Empire*.[2] Their concept of empire builds upon notions of late capitalism by encompassing a larger trend of industrialized expansion. Still a valid model of understanding the current situation, the book addresses archetypal border conflicts. Fleeing from war, economic misery, and environmental devastation due to climate change, displaced people and refugees seek asylum in the fortresses of Europe and North America. If we speak of borders, we cannot ignore

Previous: Allan Kaprow, *Sweet Wall*, 1970. Photo by Dick Higgins. Los Angeles, Getty Research Institute. Opposite: Wolfgang Tillman, *Empire (US/Mexico border)*, 2005. Galerie Buchholz.

CARRIL PARA DECLARAR
DECLARATION LANE
BIENVENIDOS
A TIJUANA
CUSTOMS
INSPECTION
NO

the current political situation and prevalence of walls such as those erected between Israel and the occupied Palestinian Territories or the United States and Mexico.

Moving back in time to the late 1960s and 1970s, the work of Allan Kaprow resonates with the current discussion of borders, specifically his piece addressing the division between East and West Berlin during the Cold War. Even in 1970, twenty-five years after the end of World War II, traces of destruction remained omnipresent in the *Frontstadt*. The very epicenter of the Cold War, Berlin initially split in 1961 and was subject to further subdivisions west of the wall into American, French, and British sectors until Berlin was pockmarked by border controls and checkpoints. Only a handful of artists and dealers dared to stretch out their feelers in this rugged terrain such as René Block, a contemporary who invited Allan Kaprow for *Sweet Wall* in November 1970 on an empty lot near Potsdamer Platz. The score for *Sweet Wall* goes as follows:

> Berlin / empty lot / near the Wall
> building a wall / (cement blocks)/(ca. 30 m × 1.5 m)
> cementing blocks / with bread and jam
> toppling wall
> removing material / empty lot[3]

Allan Kaprow, *Sweet Wall*, 1970. Los Angeles, Getty Research Institute.

Like with most Happenings and Activities by Kaprow, there was no audience, but the activity was recorded through photographs and film. In 1976, Block published a booklet documenting the Activity with Kaprow offering an interpretation:

> Some art containing political references attempts to affect social change as directly and quickly as possible. Its themes are blunt and moral choices are clear. In other cases, the art's political content is a metaphor intended to play upon an already awakened consciousness… Yet this art also presumes to have some positive effect upon society; it simply doesn't specify how and when.[4]

*Sweet Wall* belongs to the latter sort of art. Kaprow was obviously aware of the significance of the wall, yet withheld explicit criticism of those either directly or indirectly responsible, be it the regime of the German Democratic Republic, the regime of Nazi Germany, or the American and Soviet governments for conducting the Cold War. In his words:

> *Sweet Wall*, looking back six years, contains ironic politics… It is for those who cannot rest politically indifferent, but who know that for every political solution there [are] at least ten new problems. As a parody, *Sweet Wall* was about an idea of a wall. The Berlin Wall was an idea, too: it summed up in one medieval image the ideological division of Europe. But it also directly affected the lives of more than three million residents, at least six governments, as well as countless non-Berliners.[5]

By performing the construction and destruction of a wall, Kaprow neither illustrated a political event nor claimed art as a symbolic problem solver. Rather, I would argue that he depicted a different kind of wall: one of connection instead of separation, even including a pleasurable component through its material choice. He offered an alternative way of seeing, experiencing, and shaping reality. In his words:

> *Sweet Wall* was free-standing. It enclosed nothing, separated no one…The Berlin Wall…will stand until either a war or a political act by a later generation removes it. The blocks of the *Sweet Wall* were bound together by fresh

> bread and jam (...), while those of the Berlin Wall were joined by cement... *Sweet Wall* could be played in the mind without serious consequence at the time. Like the wall with its bread and jam, symbols could be produced and erased at will. The participants could speculate on the practical value of such freedom, to themselves and to others. That was its sweetness and its irony.[6]

When Kaprow talks about "parody" with regard to *Sweet Wall*, this suggests that the Cold War itself was perceived, to some extent, as fictional and theatrical. Perhaps one of the most infamous examples of this occurred between American Vice President Richard Nixon and Soviet Prime Minister Nikita Khrushchev. During the summer of 1959, the *Kitchen Debate* was a televised exhibition of consumer goods. In front of an American kitchen, the two superpowers discuss the advantages and disadvantages of their respective domestic technologies.

From Kaprow's point of view, the "sweet wall" was also analogous to the "sweet home" because of its positioning within a familiar set of values. Western media and propaganda depicted the Wall as emblematic of the inhuman regime of the East, a counterpoint to the presumed moral superiority of the West. In a kind of political figure-ground play, the so-called "Free World" relied on the contrasting image of the Wall for vindication of their domestic affairs. The existence of the Berlin Wall and the Iron Curtain served as spectacular backdrop for an ideology of freedom and moral superiority to the "East." Yet it also eclipsed injustice within the capitalist societies, namely the "color curtain" of racial discrimination and the "glass ceiling" of gender discrimination.

As the very act of planning imposes limits, language and thought also inscribe borderlines. In *Sweet Wall*, there is no floor plan, elevation, or abstraction, yet every moment in the Activity remains contingent. Kaprow reflected on the potential danger of ideas and consequently, the authority of design. Aware of the colonizing potential of concepts, he states that the wall (also) embodies an idea, which manifests in his continuous critique of the claim for normative authority by his contemporaries. The following quote is Kaprow's critique of Robert Morris' essay "Anti-Form," published in *Artforum* in 1968:

> Most humans, it seems, still put up fences around their acts and thoughts—even when these are piles of shit—for they

> have no other way of delimiting them…When some of us have worked in natural settings, say in a meadow, woods, or mountain range, our cultural training has been so deeply ingrained that we have simply carried a mental rectangle with us to drop around whatever we were doing. This made us feel at home…It may be proposed that the social context and surrounding of art are more potent, more meaningful, more demanding of an artist's attention than the art itself! Put differently, it's not what artists touch that counts most. It's what they don't touch.[7]

Not only do we draw and control borders in space, we also draw, negotiate, and control borders in time. This leads to the following questions: Where is the limit between contemporaneity and history? When does an art work stop being relevant for the present and turn into a historical case?

Moving forward to the year 2013, my students and I travelled to Greece (prior to the refugee influx, but in the full throes of the financial crisis) to visit Athens and Olympia. The trip not only intended to study the ruins of the antique site, but to reenact Kaprow's Activity *Echo-Logy*, originally performed on May 3-4, 1975 by Kaprow and a group of participants in the New Jersey countryside. Like with *Sweet Wall*, there was no audience, but a booklet documents the event.[8]

> **1 carrying some downstream water**
> a distance upstream
> bucket-by-bucket
> pouring it into stream
> transferring a mouthful of upstream water
> a distance downstream
> mouth-to-mouth
> spitting it into the stream
>
> **2 sending a mouthed silent word**
> a distance upstream
> person-by-person
> saying it aloud to the trees
> propelling a shouted word
> a distance downstream
> person-by-person
> mouthing it to the sky

Top: Allan Kaprow, *Echo-Logy*, 1975. Los Angeles, Getty Research Institute. Bottom: Allan Kaprow, *Echo-Logy*, 1975. Ibid.

**3 transporting a gas-soaked cloth**
a distance upstream
(waving it gently in the air)
person-to-person
waving it gently until dry
carrying a bagged breath
a distance downstream
each adding a breath
opening the bag to the wind

As the title *Echo-Logy* points at the relation between the past and present, I wanted to discover if this piece still played a role in our present. Just outside the ancient site of Olympia, our reenactment took place in a small creek, over the course of an hour, and allowed for reflection of the trip until that point. The metaphor of an echo demonstrated curiosity in the resonance of the past in the present. This exercise also referenced the legend of Echo and Narcissus. After being rejected by Narcissus, the water nymph Echo dissolves into a voice without a body.

Can one compare Europe to the self-absorbed Narcissus and Greece to the rejected Echo, left to her destiny? Would such a metaphor help us locate our position within the field trip and help us see the change more clearly? The cup transporting upstream water arrived and I handed it to the next member of the group, downstream, careful not to spill any. Soon it would be poured out, dissolved, gone. The notion of entropy came to my mind as I recalled what we had witnessed the other day in Athens, namely the loss of confidence in the future. Did our performance of standing gingerly in the cold water, transporting a tiny quantity of it, reflect what was happening in the country on a much larger scale? Did our actions help to focus our view in order to lead to action, or would it remain symbolic?

The next cup approached, delivered between the teeth, and it became impossible to speak. Echo came to my mind, the poor water nymph, who could only mumble and mimic the sounds of what others said. Whose voices had we heard during the trip? Was it observers from the North—including ourselves—speaking *about* Greece and inadvertently telling the Greek how to act? Were we not echoing, mindlessly reiterating, what politicians and newspapers in the North reported, namely that it was Greece's fault? Where were the voices of the Greeks amid all this? While the group sent the whispered word from one to the next, I remembered the muffled voices of the people in the streets, mere shadows of the past, echoes of better days.

**Top:** Philip Ursprung, Reenactment of *Eco-Logy*, 2013. **Bottom:** Robert Smithson, *Glue Pour*, 1969, Vancouver, Canada. © Holt/Smithson Foundation/VAGA at Artists Rights Society (ARS), NY.

Finally, the plastic bag arrived, inflated breath by breath, passed down with the tender fear of collapse. Headlines once again came to mind, talking about deflation, stagflation, withdrawn capital and the fate of the Euro. Next to symbolizing the economy, the plastic bag containing our breath—*psyche* in Greek—also represented students and teachers momentarily uniting into a community.

Were we, in the otherwise hierarchic realm of academia, acting as equal participants? Were we historians caring about the legacy of a canonical artist? Were we producers or consumers; actors or observers? Were we affirming the current economic regime or subverting it? Were we the border control of the discipline, or trespassers and smugglers?

Although the answer remains evasive, I would argue, that *Echo-Logy* and *Sweet Wall* are part of our present time. Kaprow's art represents how limits and borders, whether physical or imaginary, are defined, negotiated, and challenged. Contesting means of regulating in a deregulated context is a motif present throughout his entire oeuvre.

Artist Robert Smithson expressed interest in Kaprow's Fluids, likely due to his contemporary work on Non-Sites. The similarities between Kaprow and Smithson lie in their critique of the artistic mainstream and the ideology of linear progress that reigned in the 1960s. In an interview conducted in 1969 with *Art News*, Smithson states:

> ...I think the major issue now in art is [defining] what are the boundaries...There's no exit, no road to utopia, no great beyond in terms of exhibition space. I see it as an inevitability; of going toward the fringes, towards the broken, the entropic. But even that has limits. Every single perception is essentially determinate. It isn't a question of form or anti-form. It's a limitation. I'm not at all interested in the problems of form and anti-form, but in limits and how these limits destroy themselves and disappear... There are strict limits, but they never stop until you do.[9]

In January 1971, Smithson realized *Glue Pour* for the exhibition *955000* at the Vancouver Art Gallery, curated by Lucy Lippard. A barrel of (water-based) red glue was poured down the slope of a garbage dump before shortly seeping into the ground. The connection to work produced by the painters of the New York School, specifically Jackson Pollock's technique of "drippings," is evident. Besides connecting with the recent past, these works also relate to the immediate present, namely some of the floor sculptures made around the same time. Lynda Benglis spilled colored latex directly onto her studio floor, as seen in her floor sculpture *Bounce* (1969). Similarly, Richard Serra flung hot lead onto the ground for *Casting* (1969). In these floor pieces, the focus surrounded either the production process itself or the formal outcome due to the material properties. Uniquely among his contemporaries, Smithson specifically did not want to constrain or control the formation of the work, but rather, let it run its course.

In 1972, Smithson boycotted *Documenta 5* in Kassel. While a number of artists protested what they regarded as high-handedness from the curator, Harald Szeemann, their objections did not exceed written word. Contemporaries such as Sol LeWitt, Hans Haacke, and Daniel Buren still participated in the exhibition while Smithson, along with Carl Andre, Donald Judd, Robert Morris, and Fred Sandback, withdrew entirely. Smithson's stance, and in particular his essay "Cultural Confinement," published in the *Documenta* catalogue, is a diatribe against the attempts of cultural institutions to control art. It goes far beyond the ideological disagreements between American and European artists to vehemently oppose the notion of a "warden-curator"—simultaneously a flagrant lunge at the exhibitions-maker Szeemann and a bid to promote his own idea of Land Reclamation.

A radical critique of the art museum as an institution, Smithson's text compares it to a "cultural prison." With pieces locked in and "looked upon as so many inanimate invalids, [they] wait for critics to pronounce them curable or incurable... neutralized, ineffective, abstracted, safe, and politically lobotomized [for consumption] by society."[10] The "warden-curators," as he saw them, were separating art from the rest of society.[11]

Smithson was critical of what he saw as a curator imposing restrictions on an art exhibition, rather than leaving it to the artists to set their own boundaries. At *Documenta*, he exhibited sculptural works in the open air stating, "when a finished work of twentieth-century sculpture is placed in an eighteenth-century garden, it is absorbed by the ideal representation of the past, thus reinforcing political and social values that are no longer with us."[12]

Walls, enclosures, fortifications are among the most obvious signs of architecture in times of fear. They make visible latent forms of anxiety and manifest the will to impose fear on others. From the history of art one can learn a lot, perhaps more than from a specific history of architecture, about the role of boundaries both literal and virtual. Art has changed in the last fifty years, but negotiating the place of art within society remains as vibrant as half a century ago. In connecting works of art by Tillmans, Kaprow, and Smithson, I have attempted to show connections over fifty years. Their oeuvre is a critique of boundaries that defined, colonized, and excluded. It is a plea for the constant analysis and renegotiation of boundaries. Their enduring stance on unsolved issues pertaining to the distribution and representation of art elicits emotion through its relevant message, haunting us like an undying echo.

1 This essay goes back to a lecture presented at the conference "Negotiating, subverting, reconfiguring borders in the English-speaking world" at University of Strasbourg, France, October 5, 2018. It is based on the book *Philip Ursprung, Allan Kaprow, Robert Smithson, and the Limits to Art*, translated from German by Fiona Elliott, Berkeley, Univesity of California Press, 2013.

2 Michael Hardt, Antonio Negri, Empire, Cambridge, Mass., Harvard University Press, 2000.

3 Allan Kaprow, *Sweet Wall*, Testimonials, Berlin: Edition René Block, 1976, n.p.

4 Ibid.

5 Ibid.

6 Ibid.

7 Allan Kaprow, "The shape of the art environments, How anti-form is 'anti-form'?," in *Artforum*, vol. 6, no. 10, Summer 1968, pp. 32–33, reprinted in Allan Kaprow, *Essays on the Blurring of Art and Life*, Jeff Kelley (ed.), Berkeley: University of California Press, 1993, pp. 90–94, quote pp. 93-94.

8 Allan Kaprow, *Echo-Logy*, New York, D'Arc Press, 1975, n.p.

9 Robert Smithson, "Fragments of a Conversation. Edited by William C. Lipke (1969)," in *Robert Smithson, Collected Writings* (Jack (ed.)., Berkeley, University of California Press, 1996, pp. 188–191, here pp. 190-191.)

10 Robert Smithson, "Kulturbeschränkung," in exh. cat. *Documenta 5*, 1972, unpaginated, reprinted as "Cultural Confinement" in the section "Documenta: A Portfolio," in *Artforum*, vol. 11, no. 2, October 1972, p. 39, reprinted in Smithson 1996, pp. 154-156.

11 Ibid.

12 Ibid.

# THE INSTRUMENTALITY OF FEAR

212

ERIN
PELLEGRINO

ANTHROPOPHOBIA

Co-taught with Visiting
Critics Derek Dellekamp
& Rozana Montiel

The following projects are from a spring 2018 option studio, *Fly on the Wall*, taught by Derek Dellekamp & Rozana Montiel, with Erin Pellegrino The Studio invited students to reimagine, elaborate distort, exaggerate, and dramatize the wall and cross-border territories, by observing the effects performance, and meaning of the wall in urban space, in particular the space between San Diego and Tijuana. Parting from a purely utopian stance the studio was intended as a field of experimentation from which to reflect on, debate, and question the notion of a border. Utopia, dystopia, and heterotopia, as radical provocations to wall discourse and practice, would allow the language of design to promote thought experiments that address with humor or inventiveness the pre-established limits of a border barrier.

Fear is a tool. It is the instrument by which our body senses danger and forces our vital response to physical and emotional danger. Without its presence, we could not protect ourselves from legitimate threats. Fear triggers change in our metabolic and organic functions and ultimately induces reactionary behavioral changes. It is an instinctual animal response to the unknown—a vestige of the primitive human. Today, this immediate response to difference—the new unknown—manifests itself as fear. We call this an *ignorant fear*.

Ignorance coupled with fear quickly creates instability. One catalyzes the other—the response to flee bolstered by a lack of desire to understand the unfamiliar. The body tenses; erratic and hasty decisions overshadow rational thinking.

This chain reaction causes the individual to lose control and the quality of decision-making decreases while the desire to act increases. In fact the Athenians proclaimed fear as one of the three strongest motives for action, along with honor and self-interest. For the individual, fear is a tool for survival. However, when cultivated in group settings, fear distorts into a method of control. Today fearmongering ignites support for the largest and most ignorant response to international diplomacy: the U.S.-Mexico border wall.

When the Berlin Wall fell thirty years ago, sixteen border barriers stood around the world. The meredemolition of this physical divide was, in itself, an expression of peace, progress, and freedom. Today, fear has convinced many U.S. citizens that the maintenance of democracy and freedom depends upon the *construction* of a physical barrier. In an ironic twist, the destruction of a wall no longer represents freedom. At the U.S.-Mexico border, its archaic resurrection ensures longevity.

Today, sixty-five walls, either built or under-construction, exist worldwide. This attempt to reign physically in an increasingly globalized and connected world, presents a fourteenth-century solution to a vastly complex twenty-first-century problem.

President Trump's proposed wall—a built manifestation of fear and ignorance—epitomizes the reactionary, both to the problems at the border, and to the people and culture on the other side. Even worse, it expresses the insensitivity of the United States' own role in, and responsibility for, the issues plaguing the boundary. Architecturally, it is an undercooked, oversimplified response to a design problem. It is the ultimate—and perhaps most expensive—one-liner.

As designers, we know that fear, as an acute sensibility, can be used as a tool to control the experience of a space. However, it is required that we transcend our baser instinct and utilize our well-developed frontal lobe, as this is what differentiates change to us from our primal brothers and sisters.

Many architects will tell you that they embrace the unknown in the design process. In his book *Drawing to Find Out*, Louis Kahn identifies a process by which one can discover design as a relationship to be developed rather than dictated. What if one could imagine the idea of a border, not as the simple manifestation of an extruded border line, but rather as a design challenge that is perhaps as complex and nuanced as the one that the United States and Mexico now face? What would it take to convince the necessary parties not to fear a discussion, but rather to generate excitement at the possibility of a conversation?

In architectural education, we often suggest that students problematize in the process of design. However, in this scenario, can we designers take a step back from the problem as something that must be contained, and reimagine a border as a generator rather than as a divide? Can we, as designers, but also as citizens, embrace the unknown as an opportunity to discover something new? Keeping in mind the idea that one can responsibly add to the earth in a positive way—what would that wall look like?

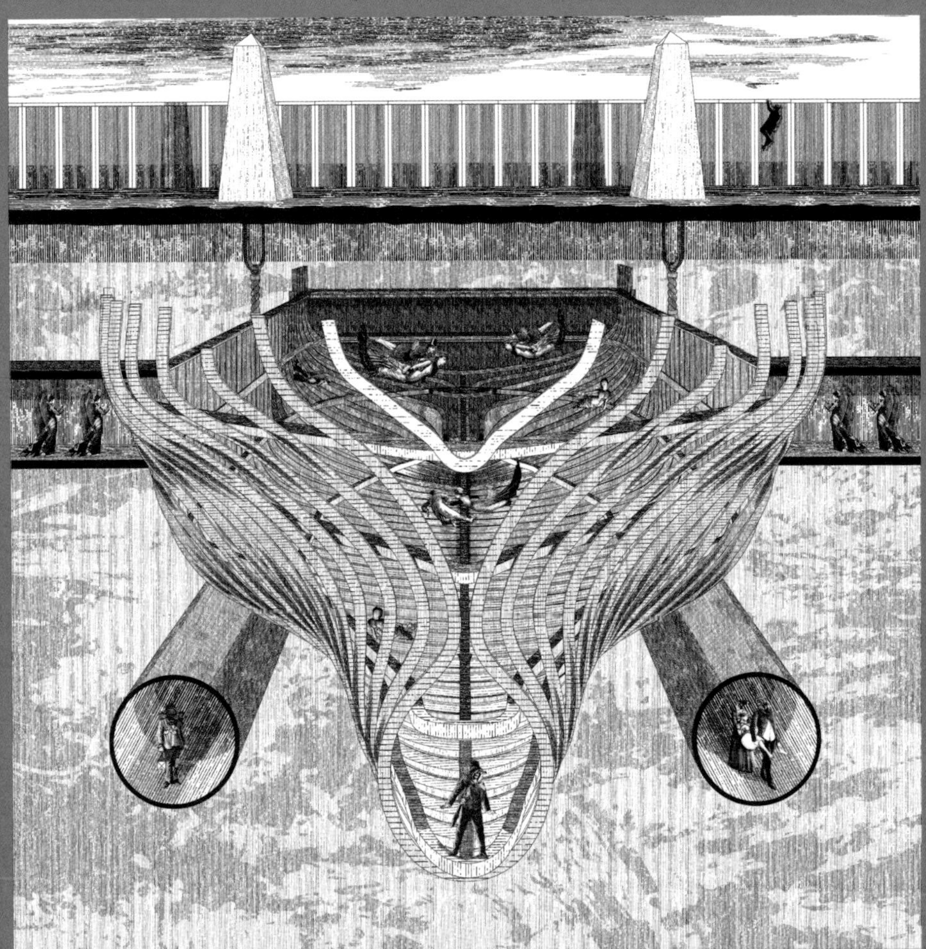

A concrete wall has been built to separate a group of people, and the primary cause of this instance is the fantasy that if you cross the wall, there will always be more profit to make on the other side. (Maria Yue Ma, *2020*, 2018.)

This page: Maria Yue Ma, *2050*, 2018. Opposite: Detail of *2050*

This page: The trip of the ark is over now, yet it has become so financially strong it is now its own nation surrounded by a wall. History is repeating. (Maria Yue Ma, 2070, 2018.); Opposite: Detail of 2070

The border's inefficiency is marred by unproductive and dangerous rhetoric. Billions of dollars flow into border protection agencies and surveillance systems to control human flow. The *100-Mile Vision* argues that those billions can be used more pragmatically and productively to control exchanges and trade surplus. The border is the final frontier—the Wild Wild West of policy prose. A new network is erected; a neighborhood of grid cities rises. (Hallie Black, *100-Mile Vision*, 2018.)

In a post-Trump future, a 30-foot Wall divides the U.S. and Mexico as a permanent reminder of a divided world, and a distant memory of what lies behind it. From its creation, the two nations' border cities developed separately, their symbiotic relationship broken as they transformed into new cities. Seen from an act of defiance, a memorial is created through an intervention at the Wall. It commemorates the past, a time in which nothing existed or happened on one side that did not affect the other. (Isabella Hübsch and Christina Zau, 2018.)

# BLOCKERS, BOLLARDS, AND BULLOCKS: PARANOID STREETSCAPES IN THE AGE OF TERRORISM

226

FRANK
WANG

ANTHROPOPHOBIA

Leading up to the New York City mayoral election, concerns surrounding terrorism prevention emerged at the forefront of campaign discussions regarding city politics and urban planning. Candidates confidently promised to reduce the incidences of terrorism through both physical protection and police surveillance. Though the focus on city and security fluctuates depending on specific occurrences and society's media-dictated attention span, paranoia has infected more and more of America's public, urban spaces since the events of 9/11. During televised debates in November 2017, incumbent Mayor Bill de Blasio said, "we can prevent terror by intelligence gathering," while his Republican opponent Nicole Malliotakis said police should have "no limits to their ability when they get their lead."[1] Nowhere was this clearer than in the public spectacle of the American political debate, where Trump used terrorism, specifically "radical Islamic terrorism," to capitalize on fear and insecurity.[1] This has resulted in the proliferation of urban paranoia, and consequently, a new generation of mobile, ad-hoc infrastructure used to commodify, intensify, and ultimately normalize public fear.

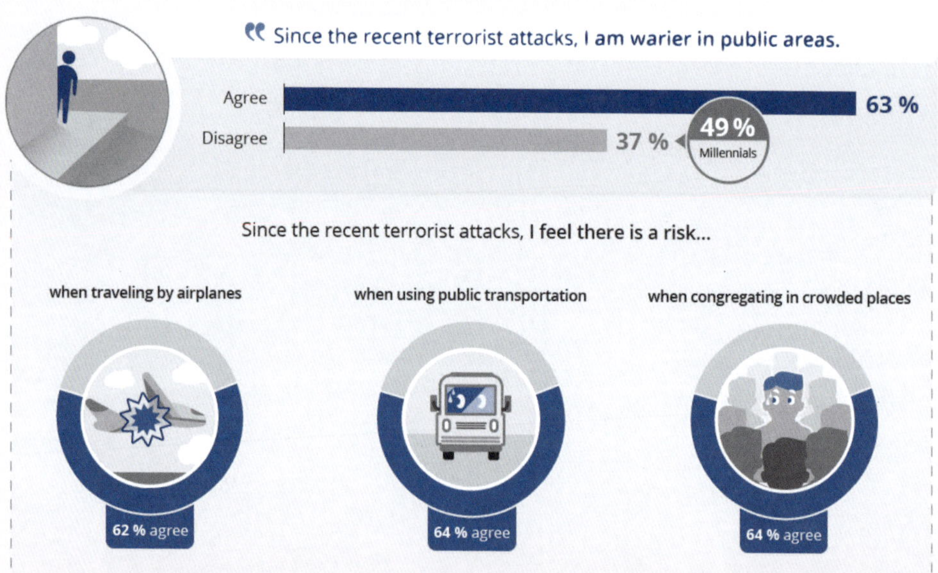
Americans are living with an increasing fear
Since the recent terrorist attacks, I am warier in public areas.
Agree
63 %
Disagree
37 %
49 %
Millennials
Since the recent terrorist attacks, I feel there is a risk...
when traveling by airplanes
62 % agree
when using public transportation
64 % agree
when congregating in crowded places
64 % agree

Anti-terrorism significantly influences urban ritual and the fortification of American cities. "If You See Something, Say Something™," Homeland Security's most famous anti-terror slogan, creates a self-surveillance atmosphere in which any person can be perpetrator, victim, or hero. Thus, the anxiety of vigilance and policing evolves from a national security matter to an individual's ethical responsibility. The media-broadcast image of terrorism exaggerates feelings of helplessness with its lack of information. Expectations rise for architecture, landscape, and urban design to mitigate terrorism as national institutions issue increasingly comprehensive counter-terrorism guidelines. Every scale of the built environment, from curb height to vegetation mass, from wall thickness to security camera sightlines, is calibrated to a scale suggesting stability and security. In the past, these considerations were made largely for explosive devices, concealed within the body. An increased threat of vehicular terrorism, however, is prompting new reactions in New York.

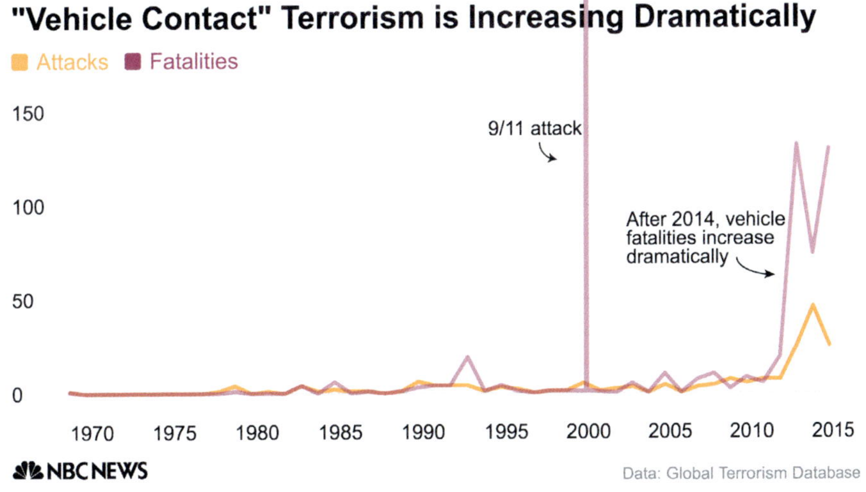


Opposite: A study by *Report Linker* showed that more than 60 percent of Americans feel there is a risk traveling by airplane, when using public transportation, or when congregating in crowded places. ("Americans are living with an increasing fear." By *Report Linker*. October 27, 2016.) This page: *NBC News* conducted a study on the recent increased prevalence of vehicular terrorism. ("Vehicles Are Becoming the Weapons of Choice for Terrorists." By Sam Petulla. For *NBC News*. June 7, 2017.)

In the last decade, vehicle-ramming attacks saw a sharp increase worldwide due to the little technical skill required compared to handling explosives. Attacks in Ohio, Charlottesville, and most recently, New York, establish the vehicle as a new terror weapon in American consciousness. Because of the private automobile's unassuming presence in dense metropolitan areas, the American city's war on terror finds a battleground on its urban streets. In the name of security, complete surveillance herds the pedestrian into protected circulation zones. Three new infrastructural objects occupy the streetscape: the mobile surveillance tower, the concrete barrier, and the bollard.

Left: The Royal Institute of British Architects published a guide for designing for counter terrorism in 2010. (Cover art by and reproduced from The Royal Institute of British Architects, *RIBA guidance on designing for counter-terrorism* (London: TPS Carillion, 2010).) Right: The United States has published counter terrorism design guidelines at nearly yearly intervals. (Cover art by Teng and Associates, Chicago. Reproduced from Federal Emergency Management Agency (FEMA), *Site and Urban Design for Security: Guidance Against Potential Terrorist Attacks* (Washington: December 2017).)

## MOBILE SURVEILLANCE TOWER

The New York Police Department purchased two varieties of mobile surveillance towers: the "SkyWatch" booth operates out of a trailer pulled by another vehicle while the "Terrahawk M.U.S.T." occupies a customized truck with the ability to transform into a tower within minutes. Both variations maneuver and overwhelm the streetscape, slowing traffic and elevating police officers to monitor and record the area from behind a blacked-out window. Verticality provides the officer protection while rendering the pedestrian subject to further exposure from a high perspective. The operational platform's conspicuous resemblance to a prison guard tower elicited complaints from the residents of various neighborhoods. As the pedestrian plays the inmate and the street poses as the prison yard, the potential for violence warrants constant surveillance.

Left: A prison guard tower at Alcatraz Island. (*On the Rock*. Photograph by David Terrenoire. For "A Dark Planet" (blog), June 2008.) Right: A "Skywatch" booth operated by New York police. (*The "SkyWatch" in Tompkins Square Park*. Photograph by William Farrington. Reproduced from Frank Rosario and Bruce Golding, "Residents blast NYPD guard tower: 'Bums are still here'." For *New York Post*, July 28, 2015.)

## CONCRETE BARRIER

The most common concrete barrier, the Jersey barrier, was developed in the 1960s to divide highway lanes. Scattered around New York City, these barriers occupy streets, bike lanes, and sidewalks in short segments. In response to the truck attack on October 31, 2017, concrete barriers were installed at fifty-seven places along the Hudson River Park bike path. These placements bottleneck the northbound and southbound lanes into a single lane, causing cyclist collisions and reinforcing notions of constant danger. Paul White, executive director of Transportation Alternatives, commented, "by installing these brutal barriers, Govenor [Andrew] Cuomo is creating another safety hazard and actively discouraging bikers, walkers, and commuters from using one of the country's vibrant public spaces."[2] While the barriers present themselves as temporary solutions according to city officials, the irony lies in the unlikelihood of a terror attack occurring in the same place by the same method (something that has never happened before in American history). A permanent solution addresses the same illogical problem: the mass, reactionary installation of bollards.

A New Jersey barrier 2000, manufactured by Cape Concrete. (*New Jersey Barrier 2000*. Reproduced from Cape Concrete Works (PTY) Ltd.)

Bollards are short, vertical posts used to control traffic and protect against vehicle-ramming attacks. Initially used to defend important political buildings, these blocks were rarely present in commercial areas. Undergoing liberal installation in Manhattan, some even appear on sidewalks narrower than ten feet. The day after the Hudson River Park attack, Senator Kirsten Gillibrand introduced the STOP Act, allotting fifty million dollars of public funds to purchase and install bollards over the next decade. The bill neglects to specify the placement of these bollards, only that they are "designed to protect pedestrians and cyclists."[3] The installation of thousands of bollards in American cities creates new borders in the streetscape while increasing public paranoia and an urban aesthetic of fear, fortification, and militarization.

As design exercises in and of themselves, architects such as Rogers Marvel conceive of bollards with street furniture functionality, while Stefano Boeri imagines large tree planter-barriers in Florence and engineers at Safetyflex create anti-terrorist tank-stopper bollards anticipating a continual escalation in vehicular attacks. These developments suggest societal tolerance of the infrastructural security measures, now presented as design challenges, to be normalized elements of cities seeking aesthetic or functional improvement. This acceptance reflects its widespread use as a political tool and as a form of urban memorialization.

Left: Bollards as part of Snøhetta's design of Times Square. (Snøhetta, *Bollards*, Times Square, New York, 2016. Reproduced from Calpipe Security Bollards.) Right: Marvel Rogers's bollard design for New York Stock Exchange. (Rogers Partners Architects + Urban Designers, NYSE: *Financial District Streetscapes*, New York, New York. Photo by Paul Warchol and Rogers Marvel.)

## BARRIER & BOLLARD AS POLITICAL TOOL

In *Indefensible Space: The Architecture of the National Insecurity State*, Michael Sorkin comments that, "for every bomb that falls on Iraq, it seems 20 bollards (generally with little actual defensive value) are added in front of yet another high value target at home."[4] The fundamental quality of the barriers resides in their ability to subdue emotional turmoil rather than protect citizens from potential threats; their presence subconsciously arouses feelings of security and comfort, reinforcing notions that elected officials prioritize safety. Layered throughout this reassurance, distraction and confusion subliminally flourish. Terrorist attacks represent only one symptom in a complex, global system of fear, violence, and inequality. To suggest that we can seriously deter terrorism at the scale of the street is a continually utilized fallacy. Furthermore, seeing as there were over 50,000 traffic collisions that resulted in injury or death last year in New York, terrorism is far from being the most dangerous threat to pedestrians. After the October 31 attack in New York,[5] City Council transportation chair Ydanis Rodriguez said, "we cannot wait for another terrorist attack when a vehicle is used as a weapon of mass destruction. The only tool that we have in our hands are pedestrian bollards." Matthew Leggatt addresses statements like these, commenting that "the securitization of architecture after September 11th was far more about manipulating emotions than it was about offering any concrete conceptualization of the present moment."[6] The spectacle of terrorist attacks and their visceral image serves as the basis for fear rhetoric allowing for politicians to use these barriers as tools to reinforce an atmosphere of stability and security, all the while highlighting their own contributions to anti-terrorism.

Next spread: A cyclist pauses by the concrete barriers placed in the bike line. (*A man pauses at a barricade*. Photograph by Eduardo Munoz Alvarez/Getty Images. Reproduced from Dan Rivoli, "Cyclists complain about concrete barriers installed on Hudson River bike path after terror attack that killed 8." For *NY Daily News*. November 3, 2017.)

The installation of militarized police units, barriers, and bollards following terrorist attacks has evolved into an urban ritual of memorialization. After the wreckage is cleared, the concrete blocks are installed, along with flowers, flags, and photos of the deceased. The placement indicates the location of the attack, the police tell us how recent, and the number of blocks correlate to the severity of the tragedy. A few weeks later, the media's gaze and local political discourse drifts elsewhere, and the barriers, or tombstones, are removed. Use of the sidewalk continues as it once did with the integration of thinner bollards serving as both memorial and reminder in an acceptably aesthetic way.

Once few in number and limited to protecting select buildings or important gathering spaces, the defensive objects of protection and surveillance proliferate in viral fashion. Rather than protect us, they make pedestrian spaces harder to navigate and create atmospheres of paranoia, what Stephen Graham notes as "the production of permanent anxiety around everyday urban spaces, systems, and events that previously tended to be banalized."[7] An image of bold indifference and transparency generates an aesthetic of insecurity and distrust in response. These objects—blockers, bollards, and bullocks—are evidence of an American urban space heavily influenced by an agenda built around public control and manipulation. They are signs of losing the war on terror.

1 *Terrorism Prevention Dominates NYC Mayoral Debate One Day after Attack*, CBS News, November 2, 2017.

2 Vincent Barone and Lauren Cook, "Manhattan Attack Prompts Concrete Barriers to Be Installed along Bike Path.," *amNY*, November 3, 2017.

3 Maya Rhodan, "Kirsten Gillibrand Has a Simple Idea to Stop the Next Terror Attack," *Time Inc.*, November 1, 2017.

4 Michael Sorkin, *Indefensible Space: The Architecture of the National Insecurity State* (New York: Routledge, 2008).

5 Auto Insurance Center. "Traffic Accidents in New York City." May 7, 2014.

6 Matthew Leggatt, *Cultural and Political Nostalgia in the Age of Terror: The Melancholic Sublime* (New York: Routledge Taylor & Francis Group, 2018).

7 Stephen Graham, "Homeland/Target: Cities and the 'War on Terror'," *International Journal of Urban and Regional Research*, vol. 30, no. 2 (June 2006).

ONE NATION UNDER GOD
WE ARE

ACCOR
europcar.com

# RACIALIZING PUBLIC SPACE: MONUMENTS TO RACISM AS OBSTRUCTIONS TO FREEDOM



TESS
CLANCY

M. Arch. Thesis
Advisors: Val Warke
& Sasa Zivkovic

There are currently close to one thousand physical Confederate monuments scattered across the United States.[1] The majority of these monuments were dedicated during the post-Reconstruction Jim Crow era—a period defined by Southern white-supremacist rule and terrorism against African Americans. The monuments fed the fire of the "Lost Cause" myth that was conjured by ex-Confederates and perpetuated, to no end, in Southern culture and "history" books. The drawings shown in the following essay are part of the design thesis *Eroding the Confederacy: Revealing and dismantling white supremacy on Richmond's Monument Ave*. The project consists of two parts: First, a "Counter-Catalog" of methods (Fig. 2–8) of architectural intervention, designed to deconstruct the intended power of the mass-produced Confederate soldier monument (Which itself could be purchased from a catalog [Fig. 1]).., and second, the application of these methods—in combination with urban planning and landscaping strategies—to Richmond's Monument Avenue, revealing the structures of racism and white supremacy embedded in the wealth of Monument Avenue and Richmond as a whole (Fig. 9–13). This essay is part of ongoing research and was written as a corollary to the project.

In an essay titled "Making History: African American Commemorative Celebrations in Augusta, Georgia, 1865–1913,"[2] Kathleen Clark argues that erecting a Confederate monument in the middle of an avenue—along which celebrations for Emancipation took place—expressed the unabashed desire to halt the jubilant commemoration of this unquestionably celebratory turning point in the history of Black America. Although it is difficult to uncover documentation confirming the broader applicability of this claim, the similarities between Augusta and the hundreds of other Southern cities and towns that collectively experienced the Confederate monument-building craze are not difficult to imagine. These urban districts express typological patterns and consistencies: the town center, courthouse square, and broad avenue leading to the courthouse or town hall. It follows, then, that Augusta cannot be unique in erecting a Confederate monument with the aim to intimidate and obstruct the celebration of Emancipation by the African American public.

The act of parading became prominant in nineteenth-century America as a method of demonstrating civic engagement and pride. In her essay "The American Parade: Representations of Nineteenth Century Social Order," Mary Ryan writes, "The parade stands out in the chronicles of American public life as the characteristic genre of nineteenth-century civic ceremony…Despite evidence of contention at some of these (planning) meetings and repeated incidents of conflict along the line of the march, antebellum political institutions both tolerated and actively promoted this democratic procedure for creating public culture."[3]

The planning of American towns and cities anticipated—or perhaps developed concurrently with—the socio-cultural significance of parading, often featuring broad boulevards leading to the town hall, courthouse, or capitol building. Throughout the South, these wide streets, often appropriately named "Broad," were frequently punctuated with monuments to Revolutionary War heroes. They established natural parade routes that were used for commemorating American Independence and subsequently for Emancipation celebrations. Following the end of the Civil War in 1865, the Fourth of July itself became a day for newly freed slaves to celebrate their freedom. As noted by Ethan J. Kytle and Blain Roberts (authors of the 2018 book *Denmark Vesey's Garden: Slavery and Memory in the Cradle of the Confederacy*), "The Fourth became an almost exclusively African American holiday in the states of the former Confederacy—until white Southerners, after

Opposite, left, Fig.1: The catalog of the Monumental Bronze Co., one of the companies that capitalized on the Confederate monument craze by providing less expensive, massproducible monuments. (Monumental Bronze Co, *White bronze monuments, statuary, portrait medallions, busts, statues, and ornamental art work*, 1882. Washington DC, Smithsonian Libraries.)
Right, Fig.2: the "counter catalog"of methods for dealing with the mass-produced monuments. (Tess Clancy, 2018.)

# AUGMENTING MONUMENTS

A [counter] catalog of architectural interventions for delegitimizing Confederate monuments

Tess Clancy

CATALOGUE OF
THE MONUMENTAL BRONZE CO.
BRIDGEPORT, CONNECTICUT, U. S. A.
OCTOBER, 1882.

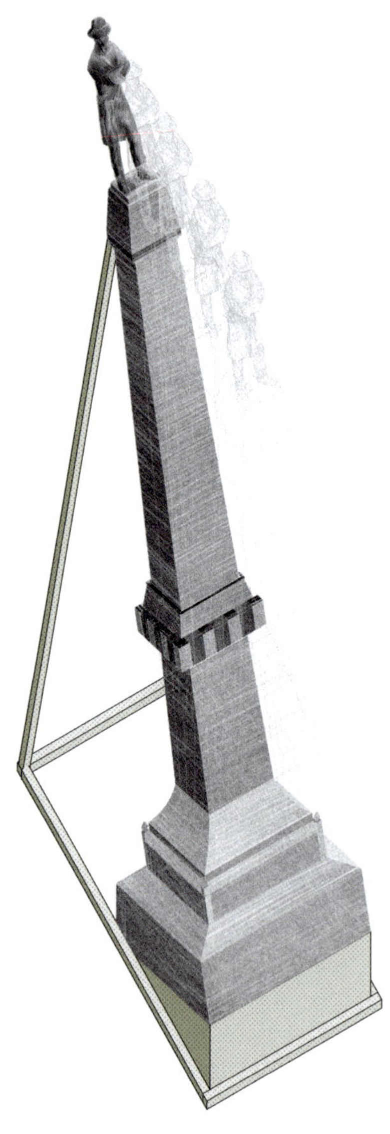

Fig. 3–4: Drawings from *Augmenting Monuments: A [Counter]Catalog of Architectural Interventions for Delegitimizing Confederate Monuments*. (Tess Clancy, 2018.) The design makes use of the story of Henry "Box" Brown, a Richmond man who escaped slavery by mailing himself in a shipping crate of dimensions 3 feet, by 2 feet 8 inches, by 2 feet—the scale for the gridded structures in the drawings.

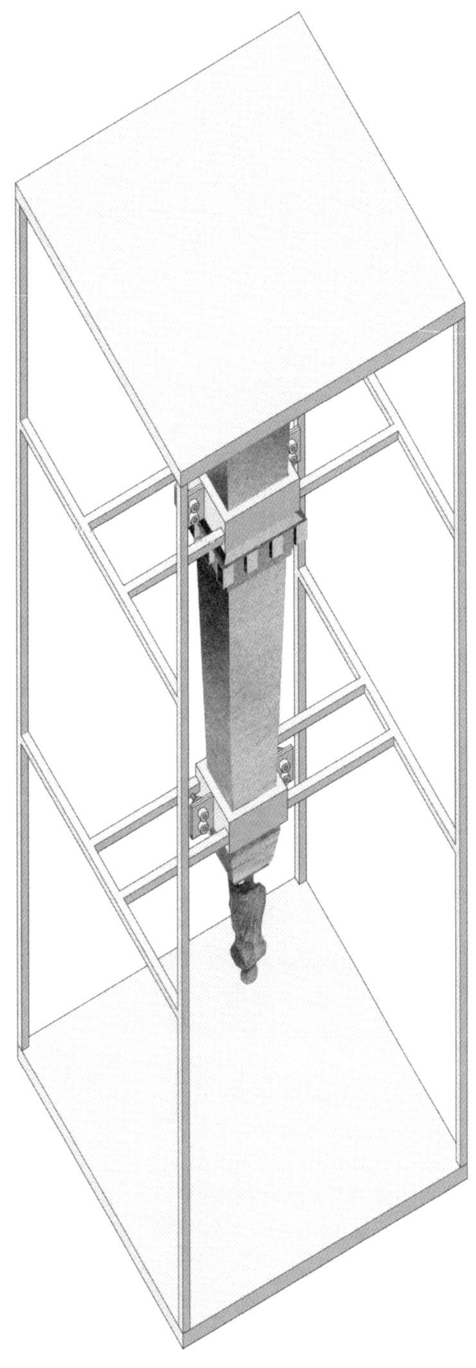

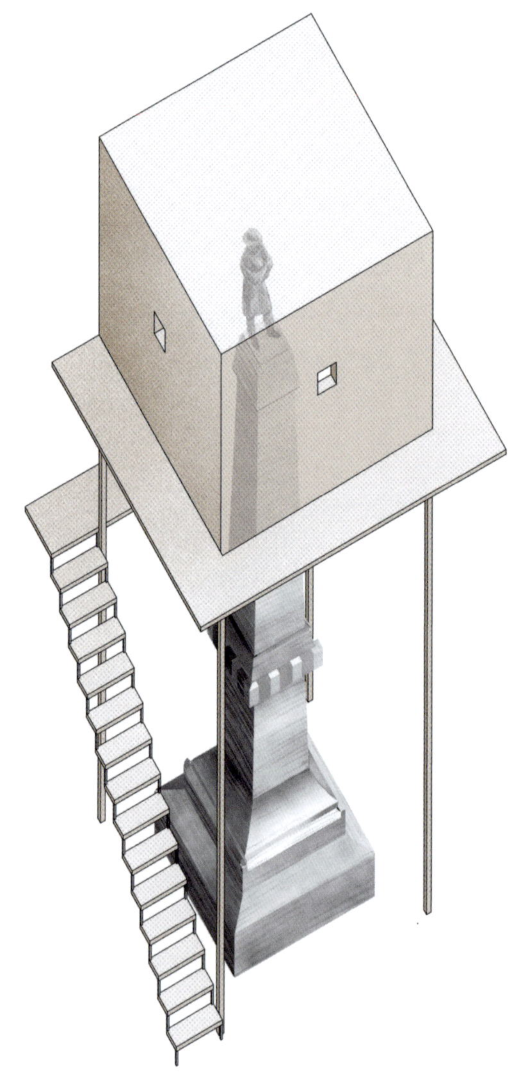

Fig. 5–6: Drawings from *Augmenting Monuments: A [Counter]Catalog of Architectural Interventions for Delegitimizing Confederate Monuments*

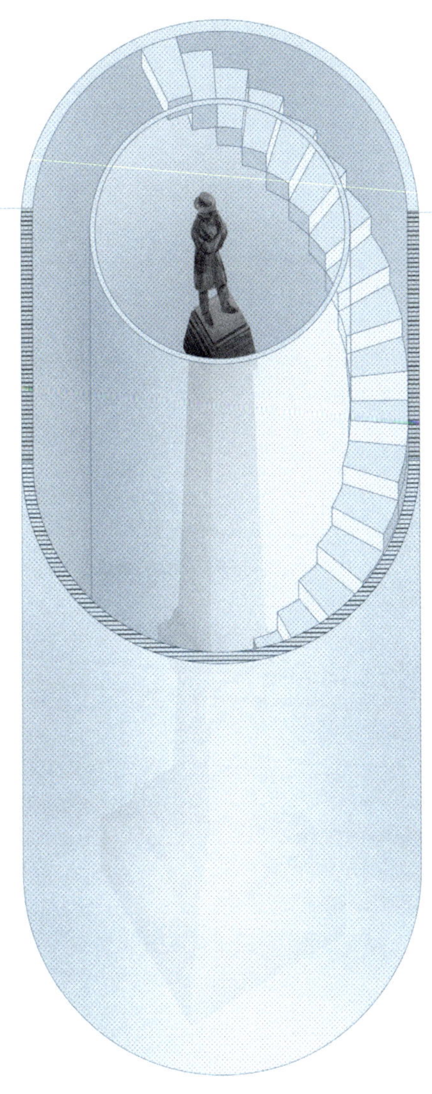

violently reasserting their dominance of the region, snuffed these black commemorations out."[4] Although the fourth holds particular significance, these celebrations unnerved white citizens—regardless of the date on which they occurred—and triggered backlash rooted in the fear of what Carol Anderson calls "blackness with ambition."[5] Of the Emancipation parades in Augusta and Richmond, VA, Kathleen Clark writes,

> ...elaborate parades demonstrated African Americans' determination to claim important public spaces as their own. Significantly, parade routes nearly always encompassed a march up Broad Street, Augusta's busiest thoroughfare and the very 'soul' of the city...their appropriation of Revolutionary icons was not lost on white observers; after black celebrants in Richmond decorated the sculpture with evergreens and flags, angry whites brooded over the matchless 'liberty' that freed people had taken with 'Virginia's great work of art.'[6]

The perception of disrespect felt by white observers can be understood in direct correlation to the seemingly perverse drive to install Confederate monuments along central avenues and in public parks and squares. Rather than private, historic, or funerary memorials, these were intended to be highly visible, triumphant assertions of power that, in effect, racialized town centers all over the South and sent the message "white men are in charge."[7] Toward the end of Reconstruction, in response to African Americans' desire for equal citizenship and "claim [of] important public spaces as their own," Southern whites shifted their tactics from outright aggression—ranging from spraying water at African American paraders to violent mob attacks—to the realm of literature, legislation, media, and monument building. Through this systematic cultural and political intervention, it was their aim, not only to suppress the enthusiasm of the African American public, but to essentially rewrite the historical narrative of the Civil War in public memory as the "Lost Cause of the Confederacy," a galant fight for states, rights, entirely divorced from the "peculiar institution" of slavery.

One might wonder how so many of these monuments were erected in such a short period of time, nearly three-quarters of a century after the end of the war. Part of the answer to that question is through behind-the-scenes efforts, through what Carol Anderson calls "working the halls of power"—that is, through nepotism, through connections to municipal governments and people in power, and through fund raising boards. As noted by Kirk Savage in *Standing Soldiers, Kneeling Slaves: Race, War and Monument in Nineteenth-Century America*, "The Ritual of Fund raising was crucial because on it turned the whole question of what public the monument stood for, whose collective memory was represented there."[8] The practice of fund raising for monument building even infiltrated the public schools, getting single-penny donations from schoolchildren.

In Augusta, members of the Ladies' Memorial Association undertook efforts to erect a Confederate Monument in the middle of Broad Street—the parade route traditionally used for Emancipation celebrations. When one considers the erection of this monument as both an intentional obstruction to African American celebration, and a method of intimidation—in essence as an attempt to racialize an otherwise neutral public space—it is difficult to see other Confederate Monuments as anything but the same. Of the monument in Augusta, Clark writes:

> It was unveiled with great fanfare before an estimated crowd of ten thousand in 1878. From that point onward, marchers occupying Broad Street on days of black celebration would have to thread their way around the soaring monument. The imposition of a Confederate monument onto the path of black commemorations stood as indelible evidence of white residents' determination—and capacity—to shape the historical landscape of the city with substantial, not to mention costly, physical markers.[9]

In Richmond, VA—the former capitol of the Confederacy described by Prof. Charles Reagan Wilson as "the Mecca of the Lost Cause"[10]—an 1890 Emancipation parade followed a route that circumvented the Capitol building (the site of the obligatory Revolutionary Washington monument) and eventually culminated at the exposition grounds in the northwest portion of the city, off of Broad Street and parallel to what would shortly thereafter become Monument Avenue. A large portion of the line of march took place on Broad Street itself.[11] Between 1890 and 1920, four of the largest and most prominent statues on Monument Avenue were erected—Robert E. Lee in 1890, J.E.B. Stuart and Jefferson Davis in 1907, and Stonewall Jackson in 1919. Considering the similarities between Richmond and Augusta, one could infer that

Next spread, Fig. 7–8: Drawings from *Augmenting Monuments: A [Counter]Catalog of Architectural Interventions for Delegitimizing Confederate Monuments*

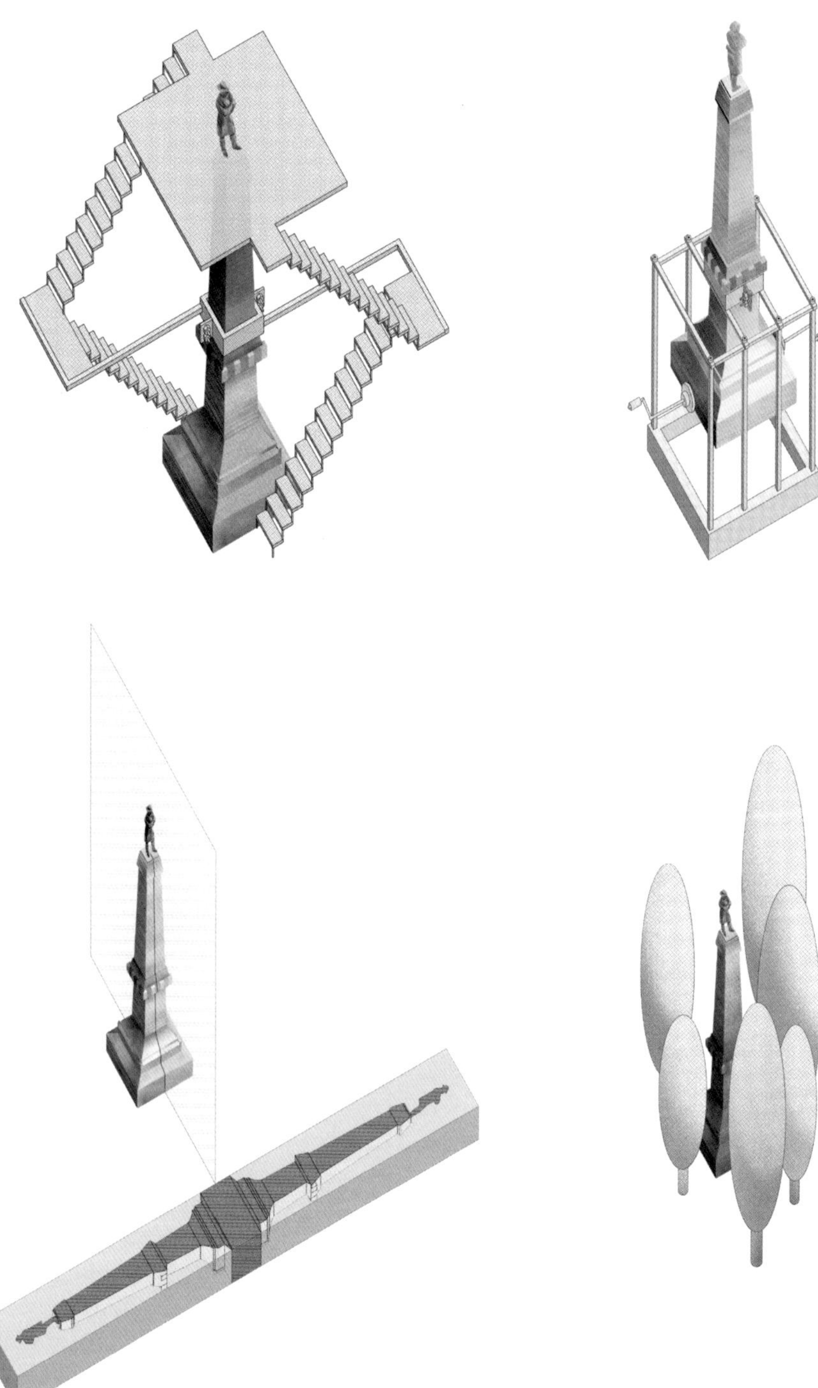

2.

Previous spread, Fig. 9: Planometric drawing showing intervention at Stonewall Jackson monument, Richmond, VA; This page, Fig. 10–11: Planometric drawing (top) and perspective drawing (bottom) showing intervention at J.E.B. Stuart monument, Richmond, VA; Opposite, Fig. 12: Planometric drawing showing intervention at Robert E. Lee monument, Richmond, VA

the line of march of the Emancipation parade in 1905 was altered in response to the placement of the statues, from being primarily in the northwest portion of the city (near the exposition grounds) to the southeast, still circumventing the Capitol building, but culminating in the traditionally African American neighborhood near the river.[12] Looking at a demographic map of Richmond from 1923,[13] it is difficult to ignore the all-white zone buffering Monument Avenue in a Northwestern trajectory out of the city—a visual manifestation of the segregation enforced by the monuments and a foreshadowing of white flight that began in the fifties and sixties.

The parade route in 1890 connected the Capitol Square to the exposition grounds and required traversing what was slated to become Monument Avenue. Was the continued erection of looming Lost Cause monuments on the avenue an indirect method of discouraging African Americans' use of this route? Because the entire Lost Cause effort aimed to erase the history of slavery from the language of the Civil War, it is difficult to uncover textual evidence of true intent, however, one possibly revealing factor in this investigation revolves around the discussion and controversy leading up to the construction of the monument to Jefferson Davis. Though it was ultimately sited on Monument Avenue, the initial two proposals sought to construct a giant memorial chapel in Monroe Park (the city's first parade grounds), or to build a triumphal arch dedicated to Davis over Broad Street, in close proximity to the culmination of the Emancipation parade.[14] If Monument Avenue had already been established as the site of other grand Lost Cause monuments, why would memorial associations have any desire to construct the monument—to the president of the Confederacy , no less—on any other street?

By its very name, the "Lost Cause" directly contradicted the decidedly victorious, albeit fleeting, moment in African American history, as celebrated and memorialized by Emancipation parades. In fabricating their self-aggrandizing mythology, white Southerners tried to permanently change the historical narrative of the Civil War. The monuments played an essential role in this endeavor by redefining public space and memory. During Reconstruction, there was a brief period of hopefulness among African Americans—a belief in the democratic process and the power of voting. In the post-Reconstruction or "Redemption" era, Southern Democrats poured resources into extinguishing this enthusiasm through the suppression of the black vote, and mass reclaiming of democratic government buildings, such as the

Fig. 13: Perspective of intervention at Jefferson Davis monument, Richmond, VA

courthouse and town hall. This was achieved by *branding* them with large and imposing Confederate monuments that exuded an aura of grandeur, power and—most importantly—permanence of that power. Parade routes (and parks, town squares, etc.), like government buildings, required the visual association of Confederate symbolism to reinforce this process of reclamation, resulting in not only an emblem of control over public space, but control of civic and democratic activity. When considering the sociopolitical intent behind the campaign to erect the statues—that is, to racialize public space through tactics of intimidation—any contemporary argument that towns should preserve their Confederate monuments as "historic" appears bankrupt at best—especially when that "history" is a blatant fabrication.

The word "monument" originates from the Greek *mnemosynon* and the Latin *moneo* or *monere*, meaning "to remind," "to advise," or "to warn." This definition suggests that a monument allows us the opportunity to both learn from the past and anticipate the future. In the specific context of the Confederate monuments, it is important to question what they serve as a reminder of, and who is being warned or advised.

There is a long history in the United States of erecting monuments to racist white men. The Southern Poverty Law Center keeps a meticulous, growing list of public symbols of the Confederacy, including physical monuments. But this list leaves out the countless other monuments to white-supremacist politicians that came after the Civil War, men who fought passionately for the preservation of segregation, against Civil Rights legislation, and some who were rumored, or even known to be members of the Ku Klux Klan. One of these stands in our nation's capitol—in Judiciary Square.[15] Today, these dark reminders extend beyond the realm of Confederates, or even racist politicians. In Montgomery, AL, just outside of the Capitol building, stands a towering fifteen-foot tall bronze statue of a white police officer. Dedicated to the Fraternal Order of Police, it was installed and publically inducted in 1983. During the Redemption era and beyond (one could argue still today), police acted as agents of the white power structure. In a city with a history of racially-biased police brutality, what is the message behind this statue? Why was it erected, outside of the Alabama state capitol building, at a time following political clashes over police-force integration, on the heels of national news stories of police violence in Montgomery,[16] and during the height of the crack epidemic?

In towns all over the South, one cannot march down Broad Street, or even enter a government building without encountering one of these monuments—whether of a Confederate, a Redemption-era politician or a police officer. As designers, we have the potential to think beyond the debate for simply keeping or removing the monuments, and instead confront these symbols of white-supremacy and violence with tangible alternatives that refute historical inaccuracy and inform, or even heal our purported democratic spaces.

**1** This number based on the Southern Poverty Law Center's growing catalog of Confederate monuments and memorials published with the study *Whose Heritage? Public Symbols of the Confederacy*, originally published 2016, updated February 1, 2019. https://www.splcenter.org/20190201/whose-heritage-public-symbols-confederacy.

**2** Kathleen Clark, "Making History: African American Commemorative Celebrations in Augusta, Georgia, 1865–1913," in *Monuments to the Lost Cause: Women, Art, and the Landscapes of Southern Memory*, ed. Cynthia Mills, Pamela Hemenway Simpson (University of Tennessee Press, 2003), pp. 46-63.

**3** Mary Ryan, "The American Parade: Representations of Nineteenth Century Social Order," in *The New Cultural History*, ed. Lynn Hunt (University of California Press, 1989), p. 138.

**4** Ethan J. Kytle, Blain Roberts, "When the Fourth of July Was a Black Holiday," *The Atlantic*, July 3, 2018, https://www.theatlantic.com/ideas/archive/2018/07/fourth-of-july-black-holiday/564320/.

**5** Carol Anderson, *White Rage: The Unspoken Truth of Our Racial Divide* (New York: Bloomsbury, 2016), p. 3. In a paragraph that begins, "The Trigger for white rage, inevitably, is black advancement."

**6** Kathleen Clark, "Making History: African American Commemorative Celebrations in Augusta, Georgia, 1865–1913," in *Monuments to the Lost Cause: Women, Art, and the Landscapes of Southern Memory*, ed. Cynthia Mills, Pamela Hemenway Simpson (University of Tennessee Press, 2003), pp. 51-52.

**7** John Kruzel, "Did Confederate symbols gain prominence in the civil rights era?," August 15, 2017 from Politifact.com, https://www.politifact.com/punditfact/statements/2017/.

**8** Kirk Savage, *Standing Soldiers, Kneeling Slaves: Race, War, and Monument In Nineteenth-Century America* (Princeton, NJ: Princeton University Press, 2018), pp. 136-137.

**9** Clark, "Making History: African American Commemorative Celebrations in Augusta, Georgia, 1865–1913," p. 55.

**10** Charles Reagan Wilson, *Baptized in Blood: The Religion of the Lost Cause, 1865-1920*, (Athens, Georgia: The University of Georgia Press, 1980, 2009), p. 29.

**11** Richmond planet (Richmond, Va.), 11 Oct. 1890. Chronicling America: Historic American Newspapers. Lib. of Congress. Accessed at https://chroniclingamerica.loc.gov/lccn/sn84025841/1890-10-11/ed-1/seq-1/.

**12** Richmond planet (Richmond, Va.), 8 Apr. 1905. Chronicling America: Historic American Newspapers. Lib. of Congress. Accessed at https://chroniclingamerica.loc.gov/lccn/sn84025841/1905-04-08/ed-1/seq-1/.

**13** "1923 Public Works map of Richmond showing black neighborhoods", accessed from the University of Virginia's Demographic's Research Group, April 7, 2015, http://statchatva.org/2015/04/07/richmonds-quiet-transformation/.

**14** "Richmond's Confederates Honor Their President," from "Said and Unsaid on Monument Ave." https://acwm.org/blog/monument-avenue-richmonds-confederates-honor-their-president.

**15** John Kelly, "Why is Confederate general Albert Pike memorialized at Judiciary Square?," Washington Post, October 22, 2016, https://www.washingtonpost.com/local/why-is-confederate-general-albert-pike-memorialized-at-judiciary-square/2016/10/22/ 9d69f26c-96ed-11e6-bc79-af1cd3d2984b_story.html.

**16** Specifically the high profile "Todd Road Incident", a violent clash that revolved around police forcefully entering the home of a black family hosting a post-funeral ceremony on Todd Road.

# POTENTIALS FOR SURGICAL URBANISM: OVERCOMING FEAR OF OBSOLESCENCE IN DOWNTOWN SÃO PAULO

258

HELENA
RONG

ANTHROPOPHOBIA

B. Arch. Thesis
Advisors: Julian Palacio
& Andrea Simitch

H
CRIAR
FLM

## I. INTRODUCTION

### Brazilian Modern Architectural Heritage and Cultural Attitudes

The robustness and immense international influence of Brazilian architecture designed and built between the 1920s and 1970s distinguishes Brazilian modernism from its European ancestor. Described as "both Brazilian and universal" by Lauro Cavalcanti in his book *When Brazil Was Modern*, Brazilian modernist architectural heritage is a summation of the country's economic might and prosperity at the time and the prolific contribution of a "brilliant generation of architects and intellectuals with ties to the cultural apparatus of the state, [which] transformed the style into a new language."[1] The modernists exerted their voice and dominance by undertaking control of the Portuguese architectural legacy of the past and by directing design of public housing and planning of the burgeoning urban centers in Brazil, providing functional solutions to social problems in addition to inventing revolutionary architectural languages and forms. The heroic inheritance of this period produced a unique cultural attitude towards architecture and the concept of newness—there can be no such thing as "new Brazilian architecture" because all Brazilian architecture since 1936 is "new."[2] Categorizing works after this period inevitably places the triumphant eras of the 1940s and '50s into the chasm of obsolescence and "oldness" since oldness is not distinguished from derelict or obsolete. This attitude is a double-edged sword: while buildings designed by famed masters rest in everlasting newness and celebration, works born out of more humble and anonymous roots tumble into deterioration by default.

### Urban Development of São Paulo

In the case of São Paulo, the city is a local metropolis in a global world characterized by continuous fluctuations and constant reconstruction through "a painful process of historical negation," a territorial and polynucleated palimpsest where the new overrides the already existing in a tireless manner.[3] Such cycles of renewal and rebuilding propitiated the expansion of the city from a small, modest Jesuit mission to the second largest metropolis in the world with a population of around twenty million.[4] Yet the absence of traces of the past sets up a scenario of premature aging described by French anthropologist Claude Lévi-Strauss as "[passing]

Previous: *Starting a Protest* visionary scenario after 10 years of development (Helena Rong, 2017.)

from freshness to decay without simply being old."[5] The urban development of São Paulo is thus entangled in an unresolved paradox: while the metropolis continues to sprawl uncontrollably onto non-structured peripheral lands through informal settlements, the built historical center undergoes severe degradation and is left with an overabundance of infrastructure and underutilized buildings awaiting reimagination. This process of simultaneous growth and contraction engenders vicious cycles of migration of people to favelas and relocation of businesses and commerce from downtown areas to new districts far removed from the city center. Within the urban context, the relentless process of verticalization requires a reexamination of its morphological and social effects, including shortage of low-income housing yet high vacancy in existing buildings, social segregation, excessive privatization of open public space and severe environmental damage.[6]

Among the biggest contradictions of the city, the Greater Metropolitan area of São Paulo generates more than 25 percent of the country's gross national product, yet few efforts have been put into regenerating deteriorated downtown urban spaces.[7] São Paulo is by no means a city for pedestrians; the clogging of traffic, heavy weaving of highways and freeways through its center, as well as dearth of public transport and impossible distances between points of interest render poor mobility to be one of the most crucial civic concerns. Characterized by vacant lots, urban dysfunctions, and concerns of safety, the deteriorating downtown of São Paulo is troubled by low-quality public spaces and an overall lack of urban consciousness.

## Research Questions

This investigation aims to tackle problematic and contradictory urban issues in São Paulo, through designing interventions, or surgical acupunctures at both an architectural and urban scale, in order to recuperate the value of vacated urban areas in the old city center and to critically reflect on the preservation, reuse, and restoration in architectural and urban sites in São Paulo's historic downtown. The proposal speculates on a new city manifesto that employs adaptive reuse as an opportunity to initiate a bottom-up, participatory development of the urban context. The following questions will be addressed: In a broader framework, what happens to architecture when it has fallen into disuse and irrelevance? Can abandoned architectural and infrastructural sites be rescued from neglect and

*Sé/República Districts Building Vacancy* (Helena Rong, 2017.)

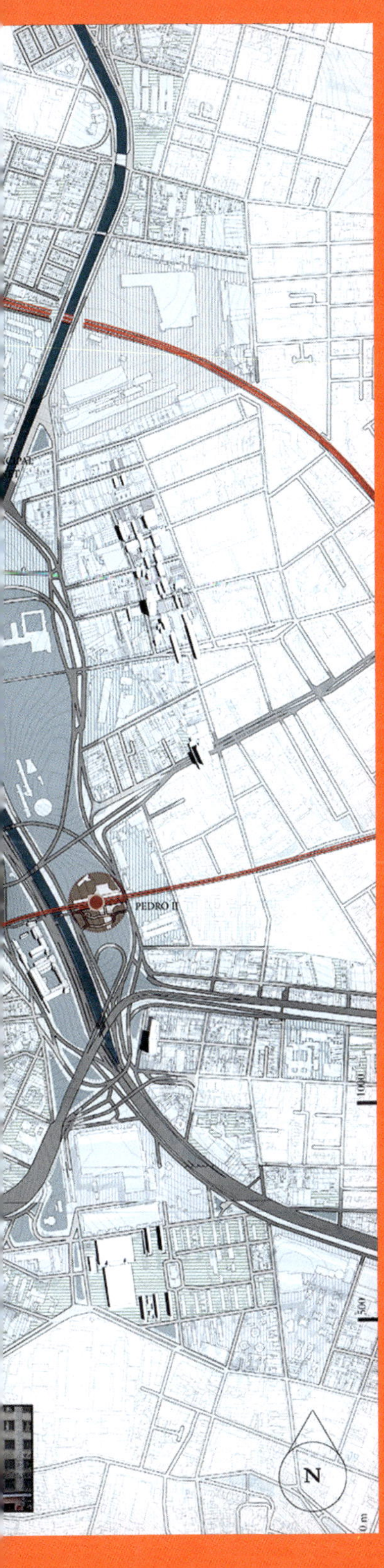
PEDRO II
N

have the potential to be preserved, repurposed, celebrated and eventually beneficial to their surrounding urban fabric? Can design at the architectural scale have a greater impact at the urban scale in order to resist simulacra and homogenization? How does urbanism—without simply becoming prescriptive ordering and an instrument of repression—confront rearticulation of a fragmented urban territory and embrace an alternative, participatory model of development rooted in change, uncertainty, and incompleteness?

## II. BUILDING VACANCY AND ABANDONMENT IN HISTORICAL DOWNTOWN OF SÃO PAULO

### The Phenomenon of a Shrinking Center and the Southwest Vector of Development

The deterioration of the inner city is largely due to the frontier mentality of land consumption. Old centers are vacated when new ones are built. They become increasingly plagued by rising security and safety concerns as well as corrosion of desirable public spaces. In a phenomenon known as the "Southwest Vector of Development," São Paulo's urban expansion experiences a fast-paced, relocation of prestigious office spaces and upper-class residential buildings from downtown to the southwestern region along *Marginal Pinheiros*.[8] As businesses constantly seek out "new investment opportunities made available by existence of cheap land and sustained by regulations favorable to redevelopment at high densities,"[9] creation of new city centers (such as the Paulista Avenue area in the 1950s to later the Higienópolis) marks the transference of interest away from the historical downtown. Yet these new commercial cores lack in historical and cultural relevance and exclude a large portion of the population.

This research focuses on opportunities of reoccupying vacant structures in the historical districts of Sé and República, mostly constructed between the 1920s and 1970s. Mainly administrative and commercial, Sé and República remain the central financial districts of the city despite their deteriorated physical conditions. Collapse of the public transport system, while partially attributable to the influence of the automobile industry, also stems from the cultural mentality of the Paulistas. They aligned their aspirations with the American consumerist way of life. The use of the car became a crucial necessity for both status and mobility,[10] and a context without car-parking was no longer acceptable.

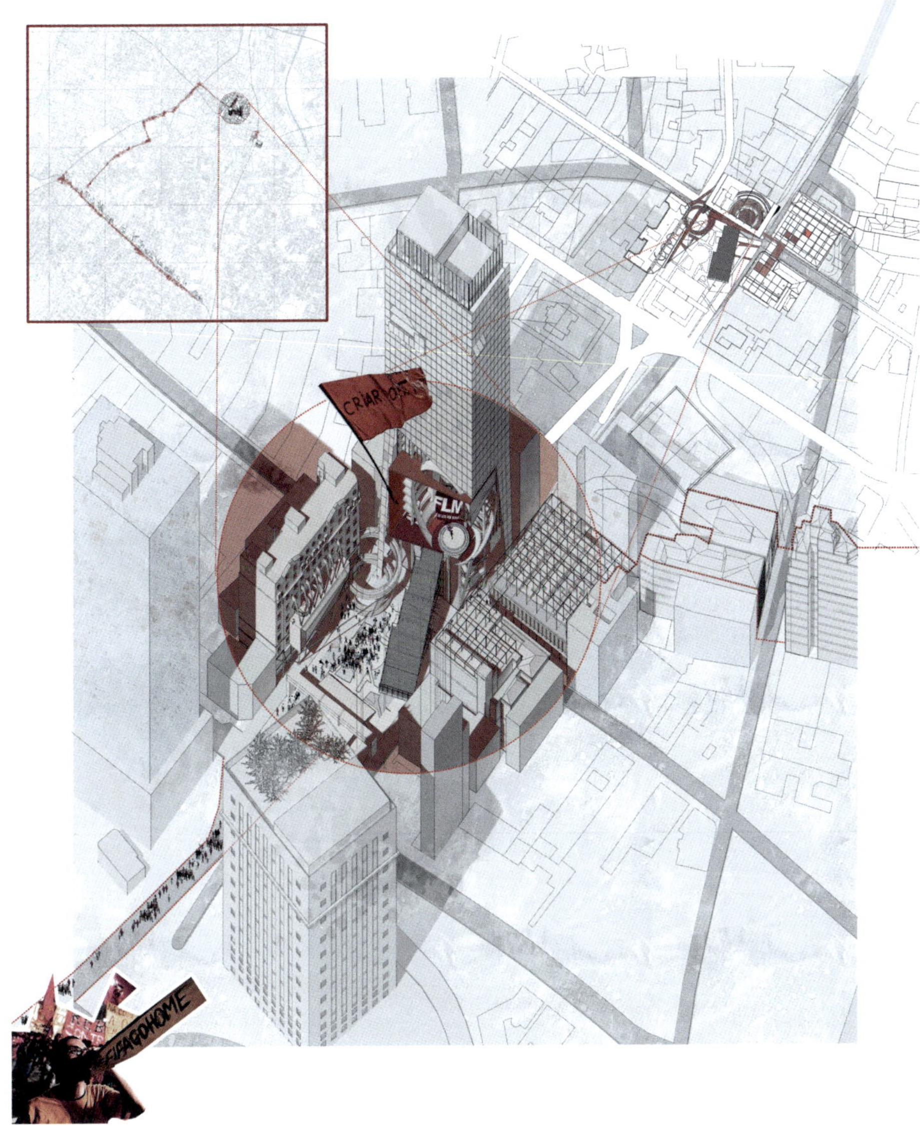

This page and pp. 268–269: Temporary development includes *Starting a Protest, Where Everyone Comes from Somewhere Else, Close to Water, More Than an Oasis, For Catching a Scent,* and *An Endless Loop.*

In her book *Brazil's Modern Architecture*, author Elisabetta Andreoli criticizes the public domain built by the Paulista bourgeoisie as "one that is badly designed, [exploiting] occupation to the [fullest] and is the result of altering legislation to obtain bigger profits… [and] meanwhile, increasing violence, the result of a massive degree of social exclusion, [pushing] the wealthy inside their homes, where they are protected by alarms, electric fences, surveillance systems and armies of security guards."[11] More than ever, rethinking urbanism and the creation of productive public space marks a new fundamental praxis in the rehabilitation of the central city.

### Facts and Figures

According to The Brazilian Institute of Geography and Statistics (IGBE) Census 2010, despite having a broad range of infrastructure, public facilities and jobs, the Sé subprefecture is the least populated administrative region in the city, covering an area of 26.2 km2 and having merely 41,106 inhabitants.[12] As of 2005, there are recorded 402,807 vacant houses and flats in São Paulo[13], and the amount of vacant properties in downtown, including both lots and buildings, numbers at 523.[14] Half of the vacant properties remain unidentified while commercial, residential, and car parking comprise the other half.

What emerges from this empirical analysis is that the enormous use of the street level for commercial activity and car parking reflects an urban liveliness and an opportunity for significant redevelopment. While the street level activities ensure an economic viability of the area, high-rise buildings with 85-90 percent of vacancy remains an untapped potential to reverse the physical depreciation of the property and to reinject possibilities into an enervating urban body.

## III. CURRENT TRENDS OF REOCCUPATION

### Problems of Housing Deficit and Illegal Squatter Settlements

A contradiction born out of São Paulo's simultaneous urban contraction and peripheral expansion is the lack of low-income housing amid vacancy and abandonment. The downtown area is characterized by infrastructural abundancy and a scarcity of housing, the latter contributing to a growing gap in social inequality and wealth distribution.

The percent urban terrain becomes a space for informal colonization. Since the 1970s, the old city has observed widespread informal economies.[15] Underprivileged groups found ways to inhabit existing architecture and infrastructure and exert their rights to basic needs for shelter and freedom of expression. Self-construction becomes the key method for addressing the immediate need for housing in the city center.

### Current Scenario: Reoccupation for Low-Income Housing Purposes

In recent years, municipal authorities and banks have initiated endeavors to reverse the decline of the city center as a strategy to contain informal urban sprawl. In an attempt to lure investors back into central areas, disused industrial buildings are converted for cultural uses and historic buildings undergo renovation.[16] The modernist tabula rasa approach to urban design no longer provides solutions to contemporary urban problems. The challenge lies in confronting the existing city rather than creating brand new infrastructures. Rather than constructing new buildings in peripheral territories, conversion of existing buildings in the city center could aid in revitalization by providing housing and filling vacancies.

We inhabit a moment in time where there is little room in urban design for "experimentation or for post-modernization of historic façades, fake place-making, and irresponsible gentrification."[17] Rather than superfluous expressions, urbanism ought to be steered by essential needs of the community and the people. Parallel to the shift in planning direction undertaken by the government, grassroots and nongovernmental organizations systematically reoccupied abandoned structures as sites for housing. Housing movements organized by special-interest groups such as Frente da Luta por Moradia (FLM), or "Front of the Line Housing Struggle," worked to convert otherwise abandoned structures into affordable housing.[18]

## IV. A SPECULATIVE ARCHITECTURAL MANIFESTO

### Spatial Agency, Terrain Vague and Indeterminate Design

In our current discourse, architecture and urbanism experience a slow shift from a model of timelessness to a model of timeliness. Emergent topics such as "ecological urbanism," "landscape urbanism,"

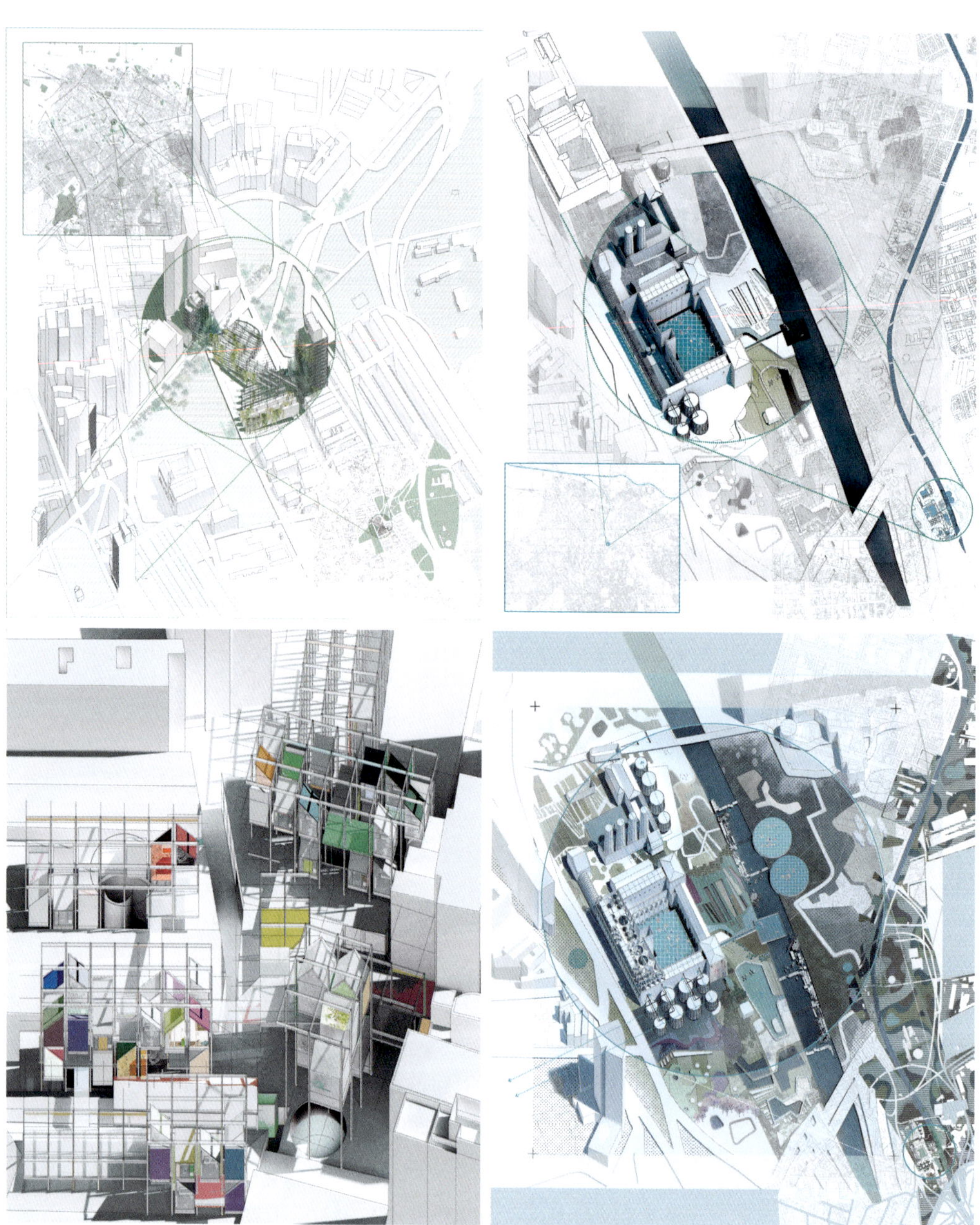

and "infrastructural urbanism" suggest a transition in operating strategies from deterministic and inflexible systems at the scale of self-referential buildings to adaptable models at the scale of cities. Participatory planning and grassroots politics that develop outside of conventional regulatory frameworks impart insightful and ingenious solutions to urban problems. In his research on the developments of African cities such as Lagos, Rem Koolhaas describes their working mechanisms as "mutating operations and adopting agents that would be considered 'marginal, liminal, informal or illegal.'"[19] In between the rigidity of the utterly prescribed planning reflecting the status quo of São Paulo's formal city, and the anarchistic, self-constructed development mirroring the city's outskirts lies a balance that embodies the benefits of both. Flexibility in urban design is achieved by negotiating imposed limits of top-down planning and simultaneous permissions for bottom-up, circumstantial adaptations that respond to unexpected change.

In his book, *Spatial Agency: Other Ways of Doing Architecture*, Jeremy Till quotes Henri Lefebvre's ideas about social space: "Social space is a social product."[20] A different understanding of space arises out of Lefebvre's redefinition: social production is a "shared enterprise," and social space is a "dynamic space... [whose] production continues overtime and is not fixed to a single moment of completion."[21] Till argues in the spirit of Cedric Price that building is not necessarily the best and only solution to a spatial problem. An alternative way of seeing architecture is one that removes the architect as the individual hero and replaces him with collaborating agents who act with, and on behalf of, others.

### Surgical Acupunctures as Constructed Narratives

The design focuses on acupunctural insertions that begin with a seeded action at the scale of architecture that would then catalyze a series of temporally successive events involving active participation by the occupants. In addition to the already-existing housing and reoccupation movements, this design proposes expanding preservation and reoccupation to greater boundaries by establishing an urban framework for bottom-up, grassroots development in site-specific, programmatically unique, yet flexible contexts. Eight narratives, each extracting a theme from existing cultural and infrastructural contexts, are sited in vacant buildings across the downtown to form a network of spaces rooted in adaptive and participatory urbanism.

Exploring concepts of spatial agency and indeterminate design, each intervention is initially composed of a "half-design" that allows room for future adaptive additions or subtractions related to topics such as community-building, living, food production, mobility, health, and water purification. In each scenario, architecture extends beyond its immediate site and relates to a broader context of existing infrastructures such as highways, roads, public plazas, or green spaces in the city. These projects are imagined to be developed in parallel with current housing movements such as FLM.

## V. CONCLUSION

São Paulo's modernist legacy immensely influenced the rapid development of the city. However, philosophies and methods of urban design from the past eras are no longer applicable in solving contemporary issues.

São Paulo's contradictory scenario of a shrinking center and an expanding periphery invites reimagination of architecture's role in supporting grassroots movements to give the city back to its citizens.

**1** Cavalcanti, Lauro, *When Brazil Was Modern: Guide to Architecture*, 1928-1960, (New York: Princeton Architectural Press, 2003), p. 13.

**2** Andreoli, Elisabetta, and Adrian Forty. *Brazil's Modern Architecture* (London: Phaidon, 2004), p. 14.

**3** Rio, *Contemporary Urbanism in Brazil: Beyond Brasilia*, p. 248.

**4** United Nations Population Division. World Urbanization Prospects: The 2001 Revision, p. 11.

**5** Andreoli, *Brazil's Modern Architecture*, p. 12.

**6** Rio, *Contemporary Urbanism in Brazil: Beyond Brasilia*, p. 102.

**7** Rio, *Contemporary Urbanism in Brazil: Beyond Brasilia*, p. 246.

**8** Shieh, Leonardo. *Urban Acupunctures as a strategy for São Paulo*, (Cambridge: Massachusetts Institute of Technology, Department of Architecture, 2006), p. 38.

**9** Andreoli, *Brazil's Modern Architecture*, p. 136.

**10** Ibid., p. 27.

**11** Andreoli, *Brazil's Modern Architecture*, p. 136.

**12** IGBE Census 2010, http://censo2010.ibge.gov.br/.

**13** Raquel Rolnik, "São Paulo zwischen Wachstum und Schrumpfung. Eine chronologische Stadtgeschichte," Arch+, iss. 190, 2008.

**14** Monfregola, Alessandro. "Vacant buildings for housing in São Paulo: How to attract inhabitants and investors in the districts of Se and Republica," p. 40.

**15** Rio, *Contemporary Urbanism in Brazil: Beyond Brasilia*, p. 252.

**16** Andreoli, Elisabetta, and Adrian Forty. *Brazil's Modern Architecture*, (London: Phaidon, 2004), p. 137.

**17** Rio, *Contemporary Urbanism in Brazil: Beyond Brasilia*, p. 252.

**18** Frente de Luta por Moradia. Princípios.

**19** Akcan, Esra. "Reading the Generic City: Retroactive Manifestos for Global Cities of the Twenty-first Century." *Perspecta: Yale Architectural Journal*, no. 41, 2008, pp. 144-152.

**20** Awan, Nishat, Tatjana Schneider, and Jeremy Till. *Spatial Agency: Other Ways of Doing Architecture*, (Abingdon,Oxon [England]: Routledge, 2011), p. 29.

**21** Ibid., p. 29.

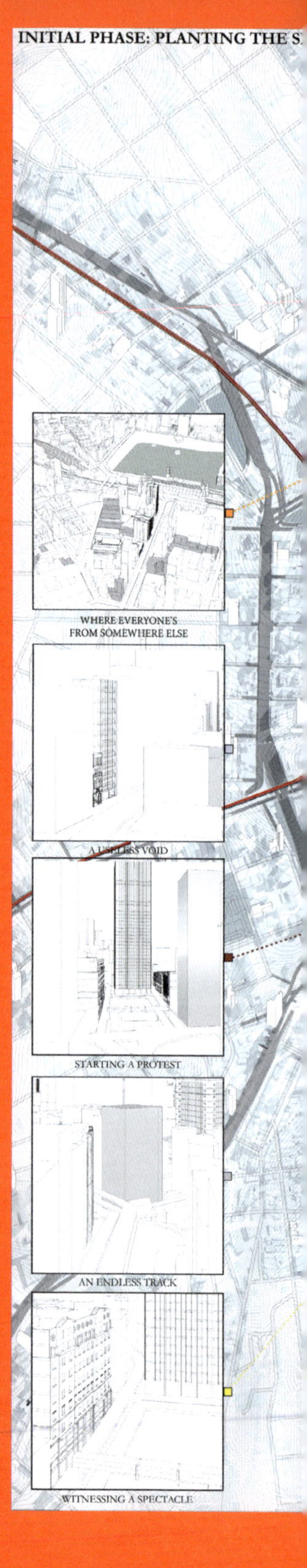


*Narrative Seeded Events*

TO CATCH A SCENT
WHERE EVERYONE'S FROM SOMEWHERE ELSE
TO CATCH A SCENT
MORE THAN AN OASIS
A USELESS VOID
MORE THAN AN OASIS
STARTING A PROTEST
WITNESSING A SPECTACLE
AN ENDLESS TRACK
SHOWING OFF A TALENT
CLOSE TO WATER
THE NARRATIVE CATALYSTS: A PROGRAM INDEX
CIVIC CLUSTERS:
protests, freedom of speech, NGO's, special interest groups
WORK/LIFE:
incubators, co-working, networking, living units, collaborating, start-up culture, accommodating
ARTISTIC:
young artists, artist studio, small galleries, musicians, filmmakers, painters, performance,
COMMUNITY/CULTURAL CLUSTERS:
ethno-hubs, residence, multicultural activities, plug-in units, economy of sharing
WATER PROGRAMS:
pools, cleansing, landscaping, bathhouse, water treatment, recreational/functional, riparian buffers
ECOLOGICAL PODS:
growing of food, farming, agriculture, aquaculture, ecological rooms, gardens, plants, clean air, recycling
UTILITARIAN HYBRIDS:
parking garage, running track, gym, restaurant, health/living, attaching to roads/highways
THE URBAN RELIEVERS:
"useless voids," the urban sublime, a place for meditation, light/dark, quietude, fields of columns, big empty spaces, small empty spaces, narrow spaces
SHOWING OFF A TALENT
CLOSE TO WATER

# HIKIHOUSE: TOWARDS RECLUSIVE ARCHITECTURE

274

WACHIRA
LEANGTANOM

ANTHROPOPHOBIA

M. Arch. Thesis Advisors:
Lior Galili & Val Warke

For the past twenty-five years, the inseparability of the internet from everyday life has facilitated a condition of Hikikomori in Japan. Defined by individuals who isolate themselves in their houses for over six months, this condition serves as an extreme example of a complete and total immersion in virtual life to the point of eliminating the need for environmental, social, and familial contact. Thus, the Hikikomori individuals have an intimate attachment to their houses where they identify the interior as a safe body, and the exterior as the terrifying society. This relationship questions architecture's current role in a virtually connected world where objects and communication no longer need a physical presence.

This thesis proposes a new type of domestic architecture generated by the behaviors of Hikikomori. Using the typology of a single-family house, the prototype physically transforms the relationship between the Hikikomori and their parents. It revives the exchange between parents and child through the daily cycle of domestic tasks.

go to bed 3 pm

wake up 2 am

surf the internet

read

bathroom break

play games

nap

bathroom break

surf the internet

read

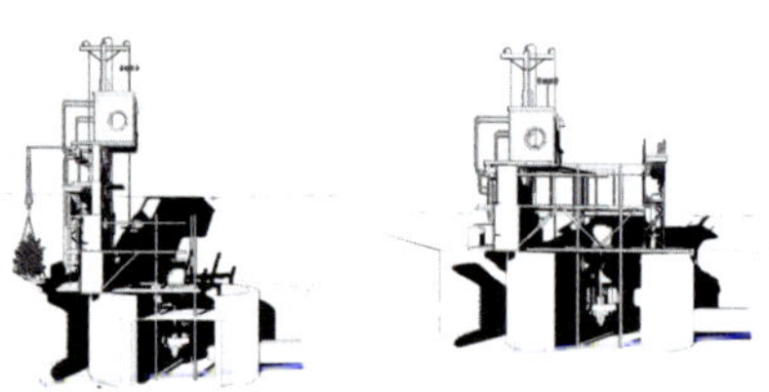

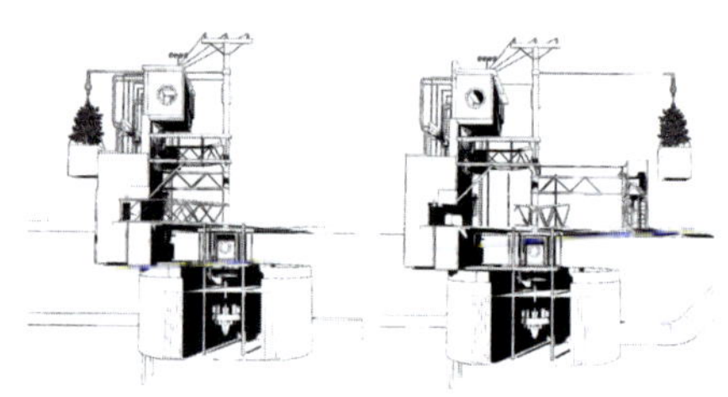

## HIKIKOMORI: DIGITAL HERMITS

The word "*hikikomori*" (引き籠り) is made from "*hiki*" (pulling) and "*komoru*" (confine). The Hikikomori condition first came to attention in the 1970s and continues to grow, typically caused by a coupling of social pressure and depression, anxiety, or in some cases, agoraphobia. The term "*hikikomori*" was first used by psychiatrist Tamaki Saito in 1998. His book *Hikikomori: Adolescence without End* explores the rising phenomenon of social withdrawal. The "shut-in"[1] condition, however, establishes a deeper connection to the notions of interiority and exteriority, rendering it a spatial matter.

According to a government survey,[2] the built environment does not have a direct effect on the Hikikomori condition since it is found in both urban and rural areas. Hikikomori individuals maintain societal ties through the internet where their anonymity allows them the freedom to indulge their interests. Japan is not isolated in this phenomenon. Studies conducted in countries such as Korea, Taiwan, Finland, and the United States have indicated similar struggles. It can be seen, then, as a global phenomenon, paralleling the development of technology.

Approximately 40 percent of the individuals stop shutting themselves in within a year, and 70 percent stop being a Hikikomori within three years. While almost everyone succeeds in getting out of this state, about 15 percent people continue beyond seven years. In 2016, the estimated number of Hikikomori was 541,000 citizens. While the majority of Hikikomori are male (about 63.3 percent), studies show that it is not because of a decrease in female Hikikomori, but because this condition sometimes disguises itself in the housewife's routine.

## SOCIAL DYNAMIC

The Hikikomori's family relates to the post-war model of the nuclear family, concerned with individual members rather than the family as a unit. The transitional period between high school and college is one of the most common scenarios that triggers the Hikikomori condition, as families place pressure on the child to pass their entrance exam. Stigma associated with the term Hikikomori blames the family for the child's behaviors, often causing families to attempt disguising the issue. There are several Hikikomori parent support groups distributed around Japan where parents can receive help and advice from ex-Hikikomori workers.

Wachira Leangtanom, 2018.

## HOUSING IN JAPAN

The Hikikomori phenomenon can be considered an indirect product of the housing boom during the post-war period. The development of mass-produced housing eliminated significant traditional spatial qualities including the richness of in-between conditions (of interior and exterior spaces) and accelerated the arrival of spatial isolation. The flexible quality of translucent, movable panels vanishes with the introduction of solid walls, allowing Hikikomori to lock themselves in. Alongside technological developments, this mass-produced housing created barriers not only between the family and society, but within the family itself.

Following the housing shortage in the post-war era, many architects attempted to resolve issues of poor standards of living through "compact" solutions prioritizing private usage. Uzou Nishiyama proposed the theory of living called 食寝分/ Shokushin Bunri,[3] separating the dining area and bedroom into its own room. At the same time,[4] many companies advertised an ideal family house with separate rooms for each child and with no communal space (unlike apartments).

## UCHI 内 / SOTO 外

家 "ie": [1] house; residence; dwelling; [2] family; household; [3] lineage; family name.

*Uchi* and *soto* are two cultural and spatial terms that describe the distinction between inside and outside. Uchi is associated with purity, cleanliness, and safety; soto is dirty, impure, dangerous, and strange. The self resides within the most inner circle and everything else is an offset from self.[5]

## WATER AS AN ENGINE

In my proposed design, the Hikikomori's house manifests around the motif of water powered by the washing machine. Deemed a hygienic monster,[6] the spread of cholera during the Meiji Era (1868–1912) changed the way people regarded their bodies and introduced the idea of home hygiene. The separation of contaminated objects from the clean ones gave structure to the bathrooms. This awareness is expressed through the separation of the bathtub from the toilet bowl as the two traditionally reside in adjacent, but distinct rooms.

Slippers designated for use in the bathroom area further exaggerate the awareness of hygiene.

There is a saying, 「汚れたら洗う」 *yogoretara arau* (if it's dirty, wash it)[7] and 「着たら洗う」 *kitara arau* (if you've worn it, wash it). The act of washing clothes is conducted as regularly as brushing teeth. A plumbing system directs the used water from the bathtub to wash the clothes so nothing goes to waste. Water is associated with guilt and shame that Hikikomori feel towards their parents. Therefore, the water element is present in all other spaces that the family members occupy.

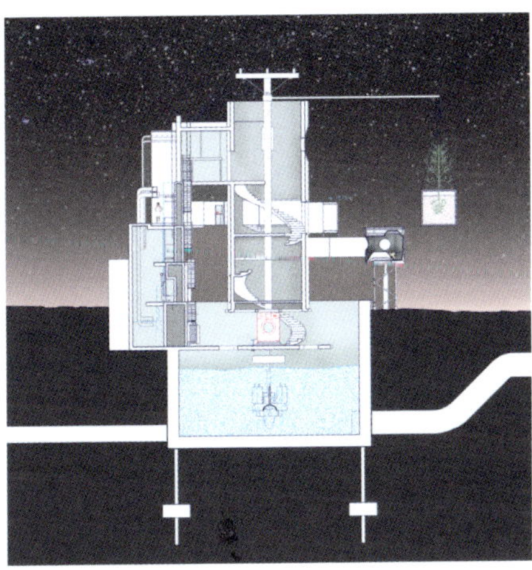

## THE ANATOMY OF HIKIKOMORI'S ROOM

While the Hikikomori's room reflects their mental condition, it also represents a miniature, ideal world filled with objects of affection. The room includes a curtain always drawn shut, with the mouse serving as a virtual hand and the keyboard as a virtual mouth. A collection of comic books, games or accumulated trash typically accompany this set-up. Everything resides within reaching distance, almost as if an extension of the body.

The nested room is slowly pulled out, finding parallels in the act of cutting the umbilical cord. Starting with the familiar post-war housing model, the structure gradually becomes estranged until the old skeleton is unrecognizable. Environmental stability becomes another concept derived from studying the Hikikomori's room. If the room itself undergoes a slight change, perhaps it can affect how the Hikikomori behaves and in turn, change their relationship with their family.

## Objects of Affection

1 The curtain is always drawn shut, the only measure of time.
2 The screen is the only external world I need: a virtual world.
3 The sound system immerses me into the virtual world.
4 The keyboard is a virtual mouth.
5 The mouse is a virtual hand.
6 The mobile phone is a portable society.
7 Food: sometimes good but only to sustain life.
8 The radio is for hobby related news.
9 Stock of beverages and food
10 The chair: an extension of my body.
11 Entertainment
12 Laptop, extra activities
13 The table: life station and support.
14 CPU: the engine of the virtual world.
15 Comic books and CDs: a treasured collection.
16 Poster: idols, hope, and fantasy.
17 The blanket: a layer of protective comfort.

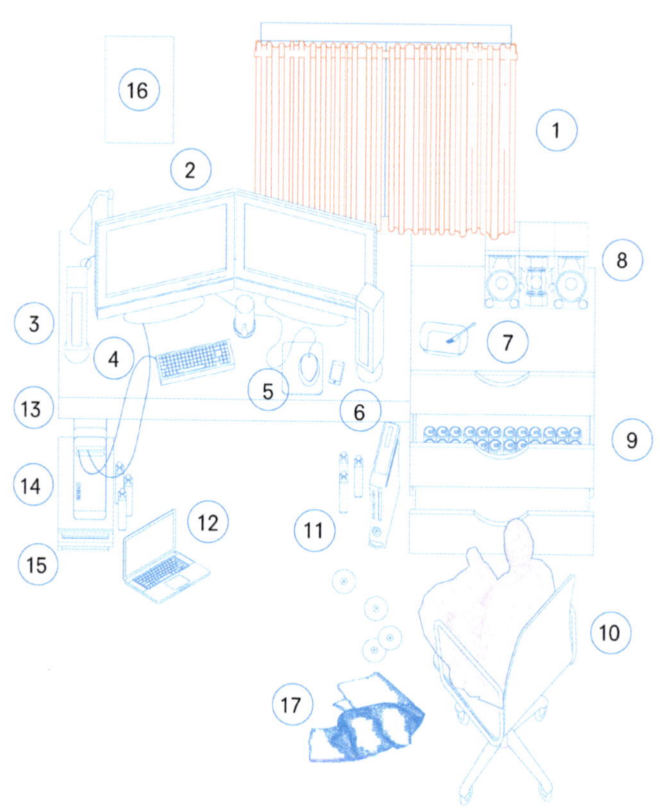

## DAILY DOMESTIC SCHEDULE

Based on the schedules of both a typical housewife and a typical Hikikomori, the mother tries to accommodate her schedule to meet the Hikikomori's needs. Although the lack of overlap in their routines permits little interaction, the cyclical activity of laundry ties both schedules together as it requires the Hikikomori to exit their room. This schedule, however, does not dictate how the Hikikomori lives.

## LEVEL UP

The rotation of each function occurs by the Hikikomori's desire to change—once they press the switch, the house begins to turn. The distribution of domestic labor encourages interaction and the Hikikomori will inherently learn survival skills for future independence. Each element in the house maintains a different level of enclosure, and each functions in relation to the human body with all spaces partially enclosed. Traversing from interior to exterior reintroduces the ambiguity of in-between spaces.

## THE LIVING MACHINE

Since the shut-in condition is considered temporary in many cases, the house changes according to the Hikikomori's current state of mind. The rooms of the Hikikomori move according to their desires. With each change, they slowly share more of the burden of domestic tasks with their mother, while gradually learning survival skills for future independence. The water basin facilitating the activities of the house creates an almost closed-loop system while the water tank supplies the hydroelectric energy to power the house. This same water also runs through the supply pipes to provide fresh water and heating. External connections are limited to air, light, and the internet. A house, completely existing in isolation, simultaneously embracing and dissuading fear, waits to once again be reconnected to the rest of the world.

1 *Shut in: Hikikomori and the Moriyama House* by Michael Wang, Idenburg, Florian, and Iwan Baan. The SANAA Studios 2006–2008: *Learning From Japan : Single Story Urbanism*. Baden: Lars Müller Publishers, 2010.

2 Nihon Naikakufu (Cabinet Office of Japan). 2010. *Wakamono no ishiki ni kansuru chōsa*—Hikikomori ni kansuru jittai chōsa. 若者の意識に関する調査・ひきこもりに関する実態調査 (Survey on youth consciousness–Surveyon*hikikomori*) (http://www8.cao.go.jp/youth/kenkyu/hikikomori/pdf_gaiyo_index.html).

3 "Postwar Residential New Towns in Japan: Constructing Modernism." PDF. Accessed September 11, 2017. http://docplayer.net/51611713-Postwar-residential-new-towns-in-japan-constructing-modernism.html.

4 Waswo, Ann. *Housing in Post-war Japan: a Social History*. New York: Routledge Curzon, 2002.

5 Ronald, Richard., and Allison. Alexy, eds. *Home and Family in Japan: Continuity and Transformation*. Milton Park, Abingdon, Oxon: Routledge, 2011.

6 Chapter 1: The Invisible Monster. Nakamura, Miri. *Monstrous Bodies: the Rise of the Uncanny in Modern Japan*. Cambridge (Massachusetts): Harvard University Asia Center, 2015.

7 "Laundry Logic." *The Japan Times*. Accessed September 11, 2017. https://www.japantimes.co.jp/news/2010/09/16/reference/laundry-logic/#.WzhAfNJKiUI.

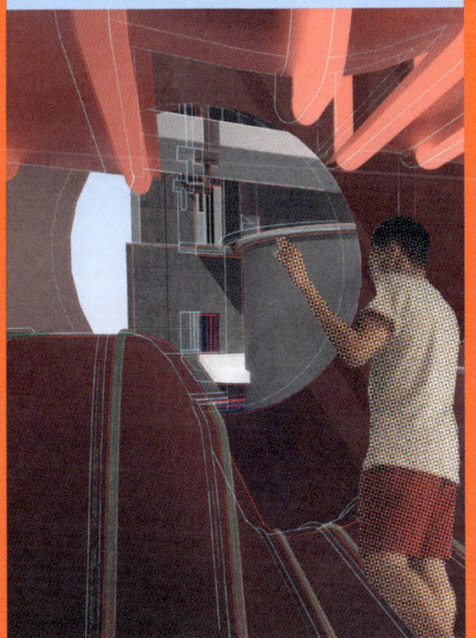

ARCHITECTURE:
THE STIMULUS OF FEAR

284

CAROLINE
O'DONNELL

ANTHROPOPHOBIA

We map the cityscapes into places I will go and places I will not, [narrating] our cartographies of avoidance, our fearing.

—Dora Epstein, "Abject Terror: A Story of Fear, Sex, and Architecture," 1997.[1]

In the pre-millenium decades, amid inner-city crises across Europe and the United States, a significant amount of energy was directed towards the impact of crime in cities and its effect on urban dwellers. As crime rates rose in certain districts, so too did the evidence of that crime. The report *Fear of Crime*[2] highlighted these so-called "incivilities" as indicators of crime in the environment and thus—in the absence of the crime itself—stimulators of the *fear* of crime. These signs, which included graffiti, trash, and broken or boarded-up windows, were frequently on the façade—coplanar with the architecture of the building. Consequently, neighborhoods became doubly consumed, first by the crime itself, and then by the trace of the crime. Significantly, the report documented that while fear increases in tandem with safety decreasing in a neighborhood, the recovery—that is, the perception of improvement once the neighborhood actually begins to recover—is not so well aligned with the reduction of crime in an area. Once the image of fear permeates the neighborhood's identity, sometimes physically grafted into the architecture of a place, it is difficult to reprogram the perception.

Today, much of the research on design and fear has been collated under the friendly title 'Crime Prevention through Environmental Design.' By now, CPTED is a mandatory part of any architect's education, featuring practical advice on street lighting, building setbacks, window openings, territory demarcation, and a host of other tips to monitor and control public space. These 'defensible space' guidelines, of course, leave some big questions unanswered, and in particular, leave the question of the surface of incivilities—the façade—unanswered.

Furthermore, the nature of fear itself has changed. In the U.S. especially, the sources of fear have shifted radically in the last five years. Previously, crime was one of the most commonly cited fears, but a recent survey shows that the American projection of fear is much larger now, encompassing a series of "hyperobjects"[3] that have pervaded society: climate change, global war, poverty, pollution, health care, and corruption are entities so large and complex that we cannot fully grasp them. Perhaps what is most striking about American fear in recent years is the uprising of environmental fears, including water pollution and drinking water quality, appearing more prominently than ever before. As Martin Heidegger noted some time ago, "place and environmentally-bound traditions [are] the only secure foundation[s] for political and social action in a manifestly troubled world."[4]

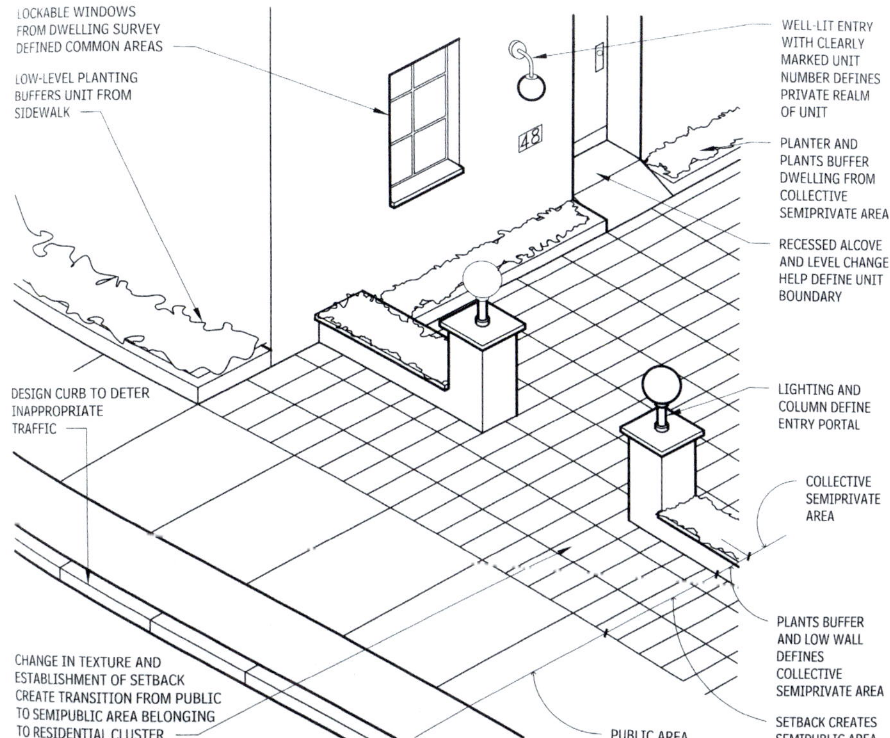


An annotated diagram from the WBDG denoting security features incorporated within building design to reduce vulnerability and opportunities for crime. This is done through both overt and subliminal security measures that instill a "sense of ownership and responsibility." (Reproduced from Whole Building Design Guide, *GSA Site Security Design Guide* (Washington DC: U.S. General Services Administration, June 2007).)

While the CPTED's principles questionably impacted architecture, the shift in fear from crime to hyperobject may provide an opportunity to return to previous studies of fear and crime, and review them in light of this shift. Ultimately, the question returns to the role of the architect. Is the issue of fear—and in particular, its potential habitation on our façades—something that the architect can and should engage with?

On the one hand, the various architects of the aforementioned inner city blocks had little control over the graffiti and broken windows that occurred as a product of time and use, and in that sense, we may conclude that this is not the territory of the architect. On the other hand, architecture as a stimulus for projections is nothing new: the temple, mosque, or church have always aimed to stimulate projections of God; the courthouse, projections of power and lawfulness; the bank, projections of stability and trust. It is worth noting that these examples are generally much more heavily ornamented than housing, and their horror vacui is perhaps what minimizes alternate projections.

The modern movement's attempt to "purify architecture by stripping off the ornament of the classical tradition to reveal the naked purity of the functional structure beneath,"[5] can be considered culpable to some extent, and countermovements, while calling for a return to expression, have headed off in two distinctly different directions. According to Nan Ellin, the "illegible" quality of postwar housing led to an effort to produce "legible" and familiar environments that often entered into the nostalgia of familiar motifs, especially notable in the New Urbanism movement.[6] This move is understandable as a reaction to the haunting muteness of late modernism.

An alternative to an architecture that appeases—whether through a return to nostalgic styles or by doubling a modernist aesthetic with copious amounts of transparency[7] that fallaciously proclaim governmental transparency—emerged in the deconstructivist movement. Here, civil instability and uncertainty were reflected in the architecture's fragmented and unbalanced forms.[8] The resultant architecture, as Mark Wigley has described it, "produces a feeling of unease, of disquiet, because it challenges the sense of stable, coherent identity, that we associate with pure form...Tortured from within, the secretly tortured form confesses its crime, its imperfection."[9]

In *The Architectural Uncanny*, Anthony Vidler suggests that the feelings of uneasiness, or the "uncanny," manifest in deconstructivist architecture.[10] Defined as an "unhomely" condition of the modern, the uncanny had already existed in short stories, exemplified by the haunting tales of Edgar Allan Poe and E.T.A. Hoffmann, which highlighted the contrast between a safe, homely place and a strange, alien one.[11] In the newly emerging urban space of the late nineteenth-century city, the uncanny reappeared in the form of agoraphobia and claustrophobia.[12] But, up until the rise of deconstructivism and the earlier Russian constructivism, with which it shared many aesthetic and revolutionary traits, the disquieting sensation of uncanniness was unintentional in architecture and in the public realm. In deconstructivist works of architects like Bernard Tschumi, Zaha Hadid, Daniel Libeskind, or Peter Eisenman, architecture was *meant* to be troubling. In the words of the collective Coop Himmelb(l)au, "[W]e don't want architecture to exclude everything that is disquieting...Architecture should be cavernous, fiery, smooth, hard, angular, brutal, round, delicate, colorful, obscene, voluptuous, dreamy, alluring, repelling, wet, dry and throbbing."[13] While these works certainly registered

*Maps.* Reproduced from Shine 5.0, *Tweak in Fear and Space: The View of Young Designers in the Netherlands* (Rotterdam: Urban Affairs, 2004).

the cultural shift, they did not act explicitly in the way that the "incivilities" did in earlier studies of fear: that is, the works gave an abstract sense of instability or anxiety, but they did not operate as a literal index, and did not openly tackle the question of fear as a projection stimulated by its environment.

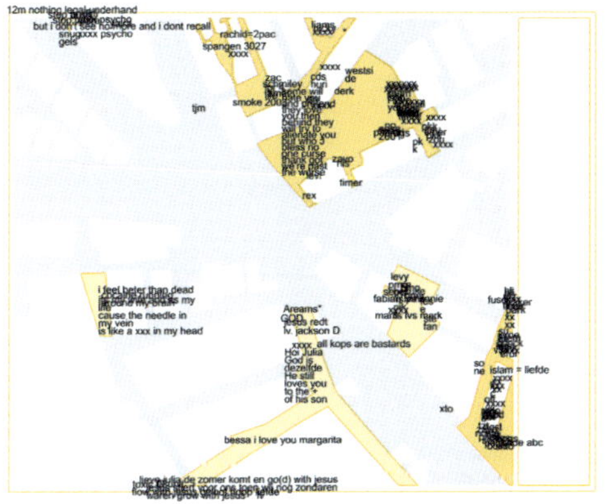

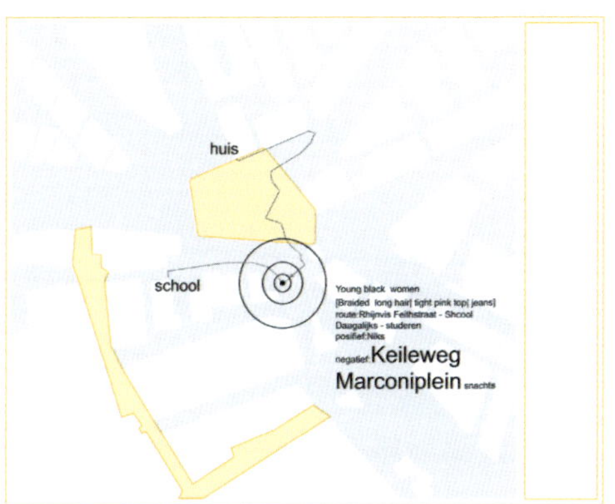


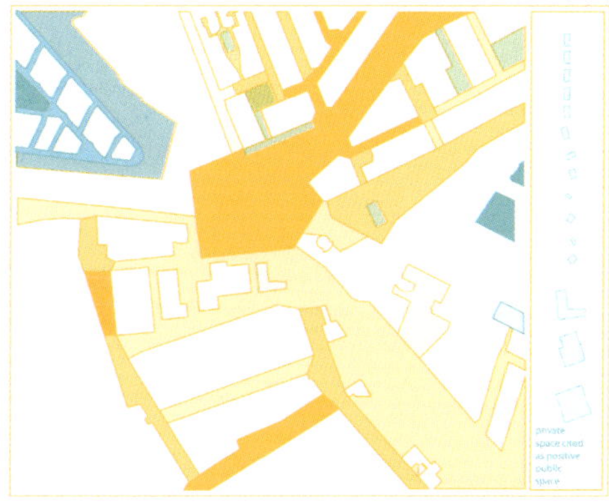


A small project in Rotterdam in the early 2000s may serve as a model for a way forward. In 2004, the group Shine 5.0[14] carried out psychogeographic research on the fear of crime in the notorious West Rotterdam borough of Delfshaven. Initially comprising an even spread of five-story red brick Rotterdamse vernacular from the turn of the century, much of the area was rebuilt in the 1950s after significant bombing in the second World War. Though varied in type, the new housing stock consisted of densely packed, low-income residential units, some of which had been designed by the most renowned Dutch architects of the twentieth century, including J.J.P. Oud, Michael Brinkman,

and Piet Buskens. Brinkman's block was one of the first implementations of novel modernist ideas such as collective space and streets-in-the-sky. Despite stylistic differences, the neighborhoods shared the unfortunate characteristics of limited outdoor space, and proximity to both Rotterdam's prostitution quarters (the 'Tolerance Zone') and a drug-dealing epicenter at Marconiplein's station. Within Delfshaven, Spangen and Bospolder were classified as "problem areas" by the municipality of Rotterdam, and Witte Dorp and Nieuwe Mathenesserweg, one step higher on the list, were earmarked as "attention areas." Between 2003 and 2004, however, all areas improved, moving up one category in the safety index.[15]

Shine 5.0's maps recorded these physical characteristics alongside interviews with local residents. In the morning, "when the junkies [were] coming home from the Tolerance Zone," Mrs. 6a would not walk the 150 feet to Marconiplein's public transport options and would limit her trajectory to the area between her front door and her car, although she did not like to drive to work. Mathenesserdijk, which ranked high on the list of incivilities, tended to be avoided in the evening. Due to the station area's closed-circuit cameras, the dealers inhabited Mathenesserdijk on the periphery of the transit hub.

As the interviews were carried out, it became clear that the fear was comprised of *imagined* scenarios; fear transformed into a paradoxical projection, simultaneously stimulated by signs in the environment and projected back into the world. In other words, as Dora Epstein-Jones put it, "city inhabitants are actively and continually produced (and reproduced) by the form of the city and the form of the city is actively and continually constructed (and deconstructed) by its *city-zens*."[16]

When asked to name a positive public space, the interviewees often did not understand the notion, and answered "my house" or "my garden." That is: they answered the question about public space with an example of private space. In her introduction to *Architecture of Fear*, Nan Ellin notes that the role of public and private space is crucial in people's understanding of safe space. "Rather than nip the sources of fear in the bud," she writes, "the more common reflex has been avoidance and self-protection…The contemporary built environment contains increasingly less meaningful public space, and existing public space is increasingly controlled by various forms of surveillance and increasingly invested with private meanings."[17]

*The Living Room Installation at Marconiplein.* Ibid.

This conflation of private and public space was the impetus for the installation *Living Room* which aimed, in some small ways, to reprogram the mindset of the community. Drawn on the ground in several locations, a series of Brinkman apartment plans formed the site for an oversized inflatable television and furniture which moved from plan to plan. The television screened the footage recorded in the previous neighborhood, depicting, for example, a woman walking home from work, or teens standing at the corner. Nothing happened, yet the film generated an expectation within the viewer, as they anticipated action. Over time, the repetition of the mundane overtook the projected mental image as the viewers waited for something to happen, became bored, and wandered away. The disconnect between the drama projected by the mind and the repetitive reality became apparent. Over time, the *Living Room* transformed "from a representation of someone's living room into a community space where identities are contributed by the collective and stereotypes can be reprogrammed."[18] Rather than countering the fears, the *Living Room* aimed to confront the viewer with their own projected preconceptions.

In Shine 5.0's research, the fears of the inhabitants were misaligned with reality: the neighborhoods were improving steadily, yet the negative images from the past lingered. When crime was at its peak, the negative images were, in fact, a sign to stay away—a useful warning, perhaps. Can architecture act as such a warning for our new fears?

Although architecture proper continues to obsess about repairing, cleaning, anodizing, sealing, painting, and generally limiting the decay of building materials, a new generation of architects have embraced the accruing dirt (Lydia Kallipoliti, R&Sie(n), Anna Heringer), rust (Herzog and de Meuron, Peter Zumthor), soot ("Shou-Sugi-Ban" techniques), weeds (David Benjamin), and water (Diller Scofidio + Renfro); as well as the eroding forces of the weather (stpmj, Emerging Objects), of pests (Nikole Bouchard, Joyce Hwang), or the generative forces of draft animals (R&Sie(n)/ François Roche), and herbivores (Ensamble Studio).

Architecture that allows itself to be open to nature, to be imperfect and degenerating, engages a new kind of ornament with the potential for new kinds of warnings. The work is, in many ways, comparable to the deconstructivist movement of the 1980s and even aligned to the so-called "uncanny" quality, "defined by indeterminacy and uncertainty," and with an intention to "make sense of and to help find our place within a newly unfamiliar world."[19]

By opening up to the environment, architecture begins to act as a societal mirror. Rather than resisting imperfection and change, it opens up to entropy, allowing nature's consumption and proliferation to stand in for graffiti and broken windows, to be a sign or a warning, and to stimulate our projections.

On February 16, 2019, an article appeared in the New York Times with the headline "Time to Panic," followed by the subtitle: "The planet is getting warmer in catastrophic ways. And fear may be the only thing that saves us."

In it, writer, David Wallace-Wells discusses the anti-alarmism and "scientific reticence" that has been part of climate change discussions, and a new turn following a 2018 United Nations report in which, "It is O.K., finally, to freak out."[20] The article notes while fear is a phenomenon previously thought best avoided, its use lies in understanding danger and taking action appropriately. Wallace gives four reasons why fear is appropriate now: First, because climate change requires worldwide, immediate action; second, because understanding the magnitude of the problem will help us better prepare; third, because Americans do not realize that by making changes, it is still possible to curb the doomsday trajectories; and fourth, because fear can actually elicit change.

In the wild, fear is an important survival mechanism. The fight-or-flight response is a legitimate reaction to a legitimate threat. Let's fight!

**1** Dora Epstein, "Abject Terror: A Story of Fear, Sex, and Architecture" in: Nan Ellin (ed.), *Architecture of Fear*, Princeton Architectural Press, New York, 1997, p. 133.

**2** *Fear of Crime*, John Howard Society of Alberta, 1999. http://www.johnhoward.ab.ca/pub/pdf/C49.pdf.

**3** Timothy Morton, *Hyperobjects* (Minneapolis: University of Minnesota Press, 2013).

**4** David Harvey, "The Condition of Post-Modernity," Oxford, Blackwell, p. 35.

**5** Philip Johnson and Mark Wigley (eds.), *Deconstructivist Architecture*, New York, The Museum of Modern Art, 1988, pp. 10-20.

**6** Nan Ellin, *Architecture of Fear*, New York: Princeton Architectural Press, 1997, p.30.

**7** See Norman Foster's Reichstag, a project purported to be "transparent" via a glass dome and concave mirrors, allowing the German people to see their politicians in action, which is, of course, symbolic rather than pragmatic. Similarly, the U.S. embassy by Kieran Timberlake in London is a wolf in sheep's clothing; fear embedded in the guise of transparency and diplomacy.

**8** See Daniel Libeskind's Jewish Museum, also in Berlin, that translates the instability of the Jewish people into a fraught and discordant architectural language.

**9** Philip Johnson and Mark Wigley (eds.), *Deconstructivist Architecture*, New York, The Museum of Modern Art, 1988, pp. 10-20.

**10** Anthony Vidler, *The Architectural Uncanny: Essays in the Modern Unhomely*, Cambridge, MA: MIT, 1992.

**11** Bart Van der Straeten, "The Uncanny and the Architecture of Deconstruction" in *Image & Narrative, Online Magazine of the Visual Narrative*, vol. 3, iss. 1. The Uncanny, ed.: Anneleen Masschelein, 2003.

**12** Anthony Vidler, *Warped Space. Art, Architecture, and Anxiety in Modern Culture*, Cambridge MA: MIT, 2000.

**13** Coop Himmelb(l)au, "Architecture must Blaze" *The Power of the City*. Ed. Robert Hahn and Doris Knecht, Darmstadt: Verlag der Georg Büchner Buchhandlung, 1997, p. 95.

**14** Shine 5.0: Ade Aboaba, Petra van Bennekum, Caroline O'Donnell, Wiebe de Ridder, Jasper Springeling.

**15** Safety Index Rotterdam, 2004, www.rotterdam.nl/veilig Retrieved July 1, 2004.

**16** Dora Epstein, "Afraid/not: Psychoanalytic directions for an insurgent planning history," In L. Sandercock (Ed.), *Making the invisible visible: A multicultural planning history*. Berkeley: University of California Press, 1998, p. 212.

**17** Nan Ellin, *Architecture of Fear*, New York: Princeton Architectural Press, 1997, p. 36.

**18** *Fear and Space: The View of Young Designers in the Netherlands*, edited by Urban Affairs, a publication by the Fonds BKVB, Nai Publishers, Rotterdam, 2004, p. 142.

**19** Introductory text from "Ambiguous Territory" exhibition: Organized and curated by Kathy Velikov, Chris Perry, Cathryn Dwyre, and David Salomon at the University of Michigan Taubman College of Architecture and Urban Planning, September 2018 and at Pratt NYC, 2019.

**20** David Wallace-Wells "Time to Panic" New York Times February 16, 2019. https://www.nytimes.com/2019/02/16/opinion/sunday/fear-panic-climate-change-warming.html.

They

our

they

feel our

reath

SASA
ZIVKOVIC

# CHRONOPHOBIA

296

# SCARY ROBOTS?!: AN OPINION

Cornell RCL. 2017–2018. Admittedly, a fifteen-year-old, scratched-up, and self-built KUKA KR200/2 industrial robot wielding a 250 pound, five-foot-tall, and five-horsepower DIY bandsaw without protective casing naturally exudes a glooming aura of scariness—or at least uncertainty. Various conflicting narratives—a mix of joyful anticipation and anxiety—converge in Dionysus, an open-source robotic platform built by the Cornell Robotic Construction Laboratory (RCL). (*Dionysus KUKA KR200/2 with DIY bandsaw end effector*. Photograph by Sasa Zivkovic.)

With the advancement of computation and robotics comes the potential for ever increasing degrees of automation in all sectors of life and economy. Developments in self-driving cars and trucks, self-aware grocery stores, self-assembling buildings, fully automated assembly lines, robotic construction, automated legal representation, automated care for the elderly, and especially artificial intelligence, have the potential to drastically impact society at a global scale. What are the opportunities and dangers of such forms of automation? What are the new economic models? What are the impacts on the city? What are the implications for jobs? What are the architectural consequences? What are the new forms of human-robot cohabitation? What are the possible political consequences?

While architecture as a discipline cannot single-handedly address any or all of the above questions—by no means a comprehensive list—they pose great concern and should be taken into account in both academic research and practice. Issues of "digital craftsmanship" and the inherent formal, material, structural, and spatial opportunities afforded by computational tools and robotic fabrication have long dominated the discussion in our field. Technological and material innovation presents an exciting opportunity to advance architecture: new spaces, forms, structures, materials, and atmospheres of robotic construction are also the focus of recent work by HANNAH and RCL.

Although these architectural opportunities are exciting, the broader societal and cultural questions are often of little consequence in these disciplinary considerations. It is our responsibility to provide bold vision, think bigger, and take into account complex issues beyond our immediate research. The production landscape is changing, especially in the construction industries, one of the last strongholds of non-automation. As companies such as Katerra vertically integrate design and fabrication at a large scale and within closed systems, negative architectural effects of automation will undoubtedly proliferate and multiply (as is already the case with Revit). Now is the time to critically discuss and investigate—from the ground up, and across disciplines—the broad and complex socio-economic, cultural, as well as architectural implications and opportunities of "scary" robots.

ANDREW
SANTA LUCIA

CHRONOPHOBIA

300

COLOR ME SAFE AND SOUND

As a historical concept, safety is complicated at best. In architecture, it conjures several legal, institutional, and practical considerations when producing a building, but what consequences await the discipline? Within safety practices, the main argument suggests that architecture should do as little harm as possible in its built form. However, this does not account for the acculturation of harm, nor the proliferation of exacerbating harm by ways of standardization and moralization within the profession. For the purposes of this research, I will identify some significant yet often overlooked factors concerning the production of safety, most specifically within the use of color as an architectural element.

I will not derive a contemporary sense of safety out of classical uses. Instead, its application in this essay will borrow some key concepts from the term *harm reduction*, as it refers to the minimizing of social and physical consequences associated with legal and illegal practices.[1] During the AIDS epidemic of the 1980s and '90s, harm reduction critiqued the abstinence-only models—of both drug use and sexual activity—associated with more conservative socio-political, homophobic, and moralistic policies.

Harm reduction is further applied in this essay through discussion of methods and modalities that Office Andorus employed in designing color and architecture around and for drug users. These include the following: First, the construction of recovery centers that use Medication Assisted Treatments (MAT) such as suboxone and methadone; second, DCR (Drug Consumption Room) exhibitions in the nature of tactical urbanism and interior objects for public educational purposes; and third, prototypes for DCR injection stalls. It is important for architects to consider harm reduction as a significant dimension of architecture, rather than merely a legal or policy practice. The hope is that color might be able to aid in harm reduction and become a powerful tool to curb fear, danger, and crisis within public opioid use in the U.S.

One possible avenue for incorporating harm reduction finds its origins in an earlier theory entitled "Strange Optimism" for architectural instrumentality outside of utopian technocracy and dystopian assemblage.[2] Borrowing from philosopher Jacques Rancière's concept of the strange, these three projects embrace the absurd, debilitating, terrifying, and potentially deadly realities that users of opioids face daily, reorganizing them around a progressive harm reduction approach to healthcare programming and design, as well as a color discourse disinterested in meaning, but invested in a constructive representation that builds collective identities through intersectional practice. These projects harness fear—of users of opioids, death, and public perception—and transform it into an applicable dimension of architecture, where color, shape, and activism are on equal ontological playing fields.

In very general terms and in the order of importance between color, shape, and activism, color is ostensibly less valued. Perhaps this is the case because it is cheap and easy to apply, or because of the limited color palette of typical construction materials. Activism or policy—its legal corollary—rank considerably higher on the spectrum of importance. The shape, or form of a structure has overarching effects on the world around it, as explained in Somol and Whiting's *Doppler Effect*.[3] To impose a hierarchy of order or even importance between these three considerations degrades the development of new protocols, applications, and adaptations of color in architecture and color in activism.

It follows that architecture helps develop new subjectivities, where people use buildings to further delineate identity—collective or otherwise. In Can Onaner's debate response during the conference *Positions on Emancipation*, they state that, "…there exists an almost ideal relation, an osmosis, between architecture and the crowd… (where this relation) will become the new architecture onto which the crowd will experience itself."[4] The crowd acts as a stand-in for a contingent public rather than the generic public. This seems to be a critique of modernism's anonymous and vast public interest. The scales of crowd onto which Onaner places architectural agency seem workable but in need of a curatorial stance, an awareness on the aesthetic realities of architecture and public interest. Regarding the architectural production of safety, the crowd and the project emerge as corroborators of many possible forms of safety; graphic representations of programming, formal manipulations of circulation, security in numbers and public ownership of aesthetic legibility all present themselves in this instance. Color falls within this spectrum of architectural participation, albeit as a few millimeters of paint that influences us in strange ways.[5] Onaner's suggestion that people identify through architecture seems to reify Graham Harman's definition of a sensual object, one that unifies a broader footprint of users and other objects that articulate it in different ways. Color accomplishes this.

Furthermore, architecture and color can be ontographically considered within the architectural history of the production of safety.[6] During the Renaissance, architecture moved away from *coloré* and towards *disegno*, when confronted with its more technically focused representation, not even making an attempt to stick with coloré's production of affect and effect.[7] This historical turning point would relegate color to the realm of meaning and application, away from the discipline's core processes. While generally accepted that architectural modernism was predominantly white in color—more purposeful than reductive—the use of color as a standardization of institutional aesthetics is very apparent in health care spaces of the era.[8]

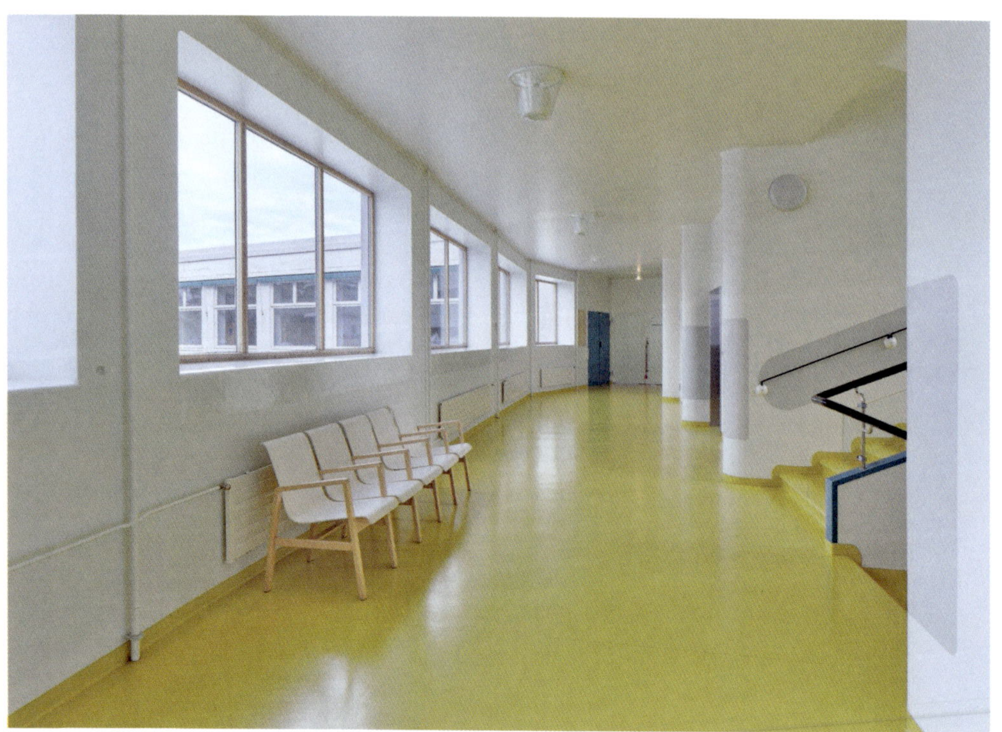

After undergoing two years of rigorous development, Alvar Aalto's sanatorium in Paimio, Finland found itself at the center of extensive, color-oriented discourse, perhaps most notably about his use of Yellow (1050-Y) tiles that seamlessly extend from the reception lobby and up the stairs into adjacent spaces. Even after renovation, the color is an indistinguishable element in both the disciplinary and public history of the space, yet there exists little latitude when describing it as an element of architecture.[9] Yellow arguably acts as a traditional means of graphic wayfinding, but since this Sanatorium is within one of the darker places on earth, the yellow in its brilliance and warmth allows residents to interiorize photons in a manner comparable to absorbing sunshine. Even within this explicit description, metaphor reigns supreme in overmining the value of color. Sans metaphor, we might only describe it as a yellow corridor or as a yellow floor plate. This undermines yellow as a sensual object and the sensual qualities it communicates, outside of the determinism of what it does or the indeterminism of what it means.

We must introduce innovative, descriptive tools to rethink the use of color. Ian Bogost's *Alien Phenomenology* discusses one possible mutation of the cataloging of things. The three projects referred to in this paper exemplify ontography, or the cataloging and coupling of objects and qualities. Bogost further states that,

> Today, photography has become so commonplace that we scarcely think about its equipment, except perhaps to compare statistics on the latest gadgets. But Shore's photography cannot be fully appreciated without an understanding of the nature of the view camera. To take a photograph with one, the photographer must set up the device and frame its image on a ground glass plate inserted in the film back. The lens projects onto the film plane upside down, requiring the photographer to compose and focus in a way that is decidedly unlike the way we normally think of photography, as an unmediated way of looking. Once composed, the photographer replaces the ground glass with emulsion and uses a wired release to trip the shutter and expose the film. The process invites the artist to see the scene to be captured separately from the way the camera will see it. It offers a phenomenal parallax that already invites curiosity toward the objects in the scene: the view through the ground glass is not only rotated but also translated from the photographer's natural vantage point.[10]

Alvar Aalto, *Paimio Sanatorium*, Paimio, Finland, 1933. Photo by Fabrice Fouillet.

Photographer Stephen Shore's viewpoint, composition, technology and focus, all constitute his photograph but ultimately escape each other as objects in and of themselves. However, their relations drive the creation of a new object and provide an interesting language to describe architecture, space, color, and the production of safety. The coupling of architecture and color in Aalto's Sanatorium lends itself to the possibility of architecture flourishing in a disciplinary lineage of complex relationships between elements, forms, cultures, and ecologies with some being more necessary than others in various engagements.

The affordance ontography gives architecture and its relation to color is paramount in reframing deterministic critiques centered on how phenomenology overuses metaphors to imbue things with more meaning than should be ascribed. It provides architects a new medium to critically discuss the architectural techniques and theories deployed in the materialization and representation of the discipline. Furthermore, borrowing Graham Harman's description of ontographic relations, specifically those between Real Objects and Sensual Objects, we have yet another framework to describe architecture, a real object (defined by space, material, form, representation) and a sensual object color (pigment, effect, material). In his text *The Quadruple Object*, Harman suggests that real and sensual objects engage in a sincerity of immediate contact.[11] Within architectural theory, these same ideas have been teased in part by Sylvia Lavin's seminal libretto *Kissing Architecture*[12] as well as John McMorrough's essay *Blowing the Lid Off Paint*,[13] both attempting to reframe how the wall interacts with other sensual and physical applications to achieve something much greater than, regardless of complexity or expense.

To introduce one last term to the architectural production of safety, Andrew Atwood's book *Not Interesting: On the Limits of Criticism in Architecture* provides an art historical, cultural, and social definition of the concept of comfort, particularly its problematization as an architectural mode of production. Atwood states that,

> ...the apparent contradiction between freedom and support, pointed out by (theorist) Galen Cranz, reveals an important trend in the relationships between the different symptoms of comfort...On the one hand, we find words like soft, tolerant, and empathetic as suggesting connection, stasis, and dependability. These terms describe architecture's provision

of various systems of support. As these terms suggest, comforting architecture is architecture that feels "good" and provides a frame or basis for other things. On the other hand, we see comfort described by words like cool, relaxed, indifferent, and free—suggesting the ability for detachment, movement, and independence. These terms describe comfort as a form of relief from strictures or rules. This partial indeterminacy allows ample space for the viewer to insert her own interpretation or context, so that comforting architecture looks "good" (i.e. cool) to a relatively large audience.[14]

The theoretical relation between empathy and comfort seems clear. If comforting architecture engenders some form of empathy towards aesthetics, then their connective possibilities—socially and materially—appear plausible, reproducible, and transformative in the development of architectural safety. As a promotion of independence, relaxation and freedom might also affect more stringent programmatic qualities within comfortable architecture, rendering it safe from a social point of use. Ultimately, my hope is to engage these mechanisms of comfort to promote safety beyond its legal connotations. This might be read as a repositioning of the more pragmatic, deterministic, and policy-oriented goals of public-interest design towards a disciplinary language sympathetic towards its aesthetic implications as equal to other formal considerations.

In the following three projects, the ontographic factors of sincerity, immediacy, comfort, and contact attempt to translate the trauma associated with drug use and public perception. At points, colors become aesthetic markers in a delicate system of urinalysis. They sheath activist education in turquoise hues with abundant privacy afforded by oculi instead of windows. They separate events, objects, and sterilization during more mechanical and dexterous movements within a safe injection stall. Sometimes colors are directionally sincere and, at points, comfortably formal in how they mediate human-object relationships with public health systems and material realities. Sometimes color immediately recenters personal contact within a group therapy environment. Color can be many things at once, but it certainly does not have to escape description either in its application or its acculturation as an architectural element.

## TURQUOISE, LEAD WHITE AND SAFE SHAPES

> Yielding subdued hues, terre verte (turquoise), green earth, a natural pigment employed by antiquity's Romans, was drawn from clay coloured by, variously, iron oxide, magnesium, aluminium silicate, or potassium…Created by steeping warmed plates of brass, copper or bronze within vast vats of fermenting wine, later vinegar, the resultant copper carbonate accretions were removed from said plates and dried, to form the pigment's base. Verdigris' preparation appears within Roman naturalist philosopher Pliny the Elder's encyclopedic Naturalis Historia of 77 AD; he himself expiring alas with Mount Vesuvius' cataclysmic eruption of 79 AD.[15]

Safe Shape was designed in 2015 and constructed in 2016. Initially, Andorus was approached by Dr. Gregory Scott, Professor of Sociology and Visual Ethnography at Depaul University, Scott works in the world of drug-reform activism by filming documentaries and helping run the Chicago Recovery Alliance—one of the earliest U.S. organizations advocating for needle

exchanges and a robust harm reduction approach to public opioid use. A traveling exhibition of a mock drug consumption room, centered on public education through architectural means (programming, spatial organization, color, and aesthetic legibility), Safe Shape employs hues of turquoise or copper carbonate and lead white on its two fabric-tensioned skins meant to be adaptable for interior and exterior use. Both skins communicate, sheath, and organize key uses of Safe Shape by dividing stages of the DCR experience, protecting against rain or inclement weather if deployed outside, providing translucent surfaces for interior lighting and video projection, and performing as a starkly different object within any urban, landscape, or interior condition.

The design development of Safe Shape reified safety through a few pragmatic means including physical parameters. Pavilion structure must be easily deconstructable, be under 150lbs, fit into four check-in bags for domestic air travel, and cost less than $5,000. Its max volume was ten cubic feet, initially agreed upon with a contractor for aluminum framing and fabric tension sheathing. While lightweight and portable structures must reconcile with issues of tectonic overdesign (perceived as hardness or rigidity) in many cases, we wanted to maintain an inherent softness with Safe Shape.

The floor plan builds on existing health care models and DCRs around the world to emphasize a horizontal model producing authentic circulatory experiences. Scott states that,

> Upon entering, the visitor encounters a greeting area and supplies station. From there the visitor is routed to the injection station, where DCR clients can engage in supervised and hygienic injections of pre-obtained drugs. The final stop is the "chill room," where DCR clients can relax in a low-stress space and also access information on housing, employment, drug treatment, and so forth. This exhibit constitutes its own argument in favor of the DCR as a public health measure.[16]

The video footage playing on the tablets arrayed strategically throughout the exhibit demonstrates how a DCR can be—and has been—used by people who inject drugs. This footage is juxtaposed with the video images projected against the exhibit's exterior walls, which reveal spaces users frequent when unable

*Safe Shape 1*, 2016. Photograph by Dr. Gregory Scott.

to access a DCR. The dualities presented when contrasting these images yields an argument in favor of the DCR as a critical public health initiative. The tight and pliable nature of Safe Shape's programming lends itself to a truncated pyramidal form with one interior partition and several types of apertures that engage the history of architecture—ribbon windows, corner windows, oculi, doors, and passageways.

This page: *Safe Shape 2*, 2016. Photograph by Dr. Gregory Scott. **Opposite:** *Rehab Center, Waiting Room*, Auburn, Maine, 2018. Reproduced from RecommendedRehabs.com.

Initially, it was important to study the effects color and materiality of different fabrics had on the overall aesthetics of Safe Shape. On one end, the initial use of lead white and translucent fabric quoted modernism's use of white as material and color, but also was purposeful in being a beacon for a particular community. The duality of white and translucency played well into video projection, allowing the skin to take on multiple images and colors in motion. However, this application inadvertently limited itself to nice summer days. The powder coated white aluminum frame blended in with the pyramid shape of the skin to produce an almost seamless and volumetric form. Common associations with the color white, specifically the sterility of healthcare spaces, express how Safe Shape was responsibly designed and scientifically justified through the power of color to inform policy decisions and safety considerations.

A rain-resistant material was chosen for the high-contrast turquoise skin, in order for it to be easily deployable in bad weather. The deployment of copper carbonate or terre-verte-like hues were meant to connect Safe Shape with the tradition of landscape painting as outlined in *An Atlas of Rare and Familiar Colour*. The terrestrial associations with this softer hue of greenish-blue amplified the cultural connotations of safety in an outdoor setting, at once contributing to the rain resistance with a purely aesthetic gesture. Dr. Greg Scott states that, "Safe Shape's multimedia interactivity promotes a substantive dialogue about drug use in the community and creates a provocative rhetorical relationship with each of its visitors."[17] The explicit tasks of this mediated environment revolve around the fundamental value of education; ultimately, Safe Shape operates at the scale of a policy object, an aesthetic tool to enact legal and social changes via time-based events, turquoise, and lead white.

## NATURAL MALACHITE, REX ORANGE, IROX YELLOW AND MEDICATION ASSISTED TREATMENT

This second project was prompted by a simple question: what is the mood of safety? The first goal was to remove people from their current environments into a non-judgemental space that could challenge abstinence-only models with medication assisted treatment (MAT). Furthermore, this project encouraged clients to absorb the absurdity around the entire operation. As a form of legal healthcare covered by insurance companies, weekly or periodic drug tests were necessary to ensure that clients of this particular rehab were only taking Suboxone. In application, this absurdity was harnessed by calling it out through color, furniture and plants.

Philosopher Jacques Rancière's concept of strangeness promotes a direct relationship between aesthetics and politics. At its core, this project is an interior design strategy for progressive drug rehab that uses both MAT and group therapy together to promote a healthy transition out of harmful drug use patterns. The introduction of color, form, furnitures, patterns, art, and designed objects into one's daily realities frames the preexisting strangeness of their enterprise.

The interior uses a combination of turquoise, yellow, and orange hues, mixed with green foliage. The art uses pink, sunburst, and green fluorescents as accents. In the group therapy room, turquoise organizes the collective discussion around two canonical Eames knock-off chairs in shades of natural wood, yellow, and white. These chairs circle a series of translucent nesting tables meant to be disassembled during sessions and reassembled as a basic, collective exercise. The motion of yellow and white Eames rockers, as well as the natural wood of the Eames molded plywood lounge chair, meet clients where they are and can be easily reshuffled into new forms of collective arrangement, a stimulating, but defamiliarizing assemblage. Hanging plants and bronze light fixtures in the group therapy room further the vibrant saturation by enveloping conversation in an unsterile build up of colors with pop, historical, designed, and natural associations.

This page: *Rehab Center, Desk*, Auburn, Maine, 2018. Reproduced from RecommendedRehabs.com. Opposite: Andrew Santa Lucia, *Rehab Center*.

For individual meeting rooms, yellow serves to simulate a familiar environment with doctors and therapists. The pink impressionist paintings in these rooms, as well as the pop-art Ikea rugs, alter moods surrounding typically difficult conversations for intake patients, and stimulate more check-in driven discussion for existing ones. The pieces of lead-white plastic and faux-leather Eames office chairs reenact the classical distance between two people—one with more power than the other. Furthering this absurdity, green foliage breaks up the monotony of a black or white file cabinet, alongside a bronze or brass floor lamp, and a giant oversized metallic adjustable table lamp. Each piece was selected to critique the formal conversations happening in the room.

Finally, painted in an outlier color, a bright orange bathroom functions as a wildcard to offset the monotonous and terrifying nature of the drug-testing necessary when receiving weekly suboxone treatments. A full harm reduction approach would render drug-testing unnecessary. The orange exposes this policy measure as part of the system but also critiques it. This exalts the human condition in all of its beauty and fear by connecting it to an orange surface where ceramic planters present themselves as animal faces and warm light creates a safe space for all test-related processes.

### ULTRAMARINE, REX ORANGE, AND DCR FURNITURES

The last project is a furniture prototype intended to be placed in existing buildings, for the purpose of converting them into useable DCRs. Since creating DCRs in the United States remains illegal, our project exists only as a built prototype. The material surfaces used in the creation of these furniture objects generate the architectural relationship between space and users.

As an individual unit, the use of turquoise, rex orange, ultramarine, stainless steel, and birch plywood divide the different stalls into a series of discrete actionable surfaces—ultramarine for personal effects, stainless steel for injections, turquoise as the beginning of proximate privacy, and orange as the end. The specific sequence and pattern of orange, ultramarine, stainless steel, and turquoise is meant to reorganize the very mechanical nature of teaching someone how to inject with the intended outcome of reducing the amount of bodily harm. This includes testing the drugs for very common additives—like fentanyl

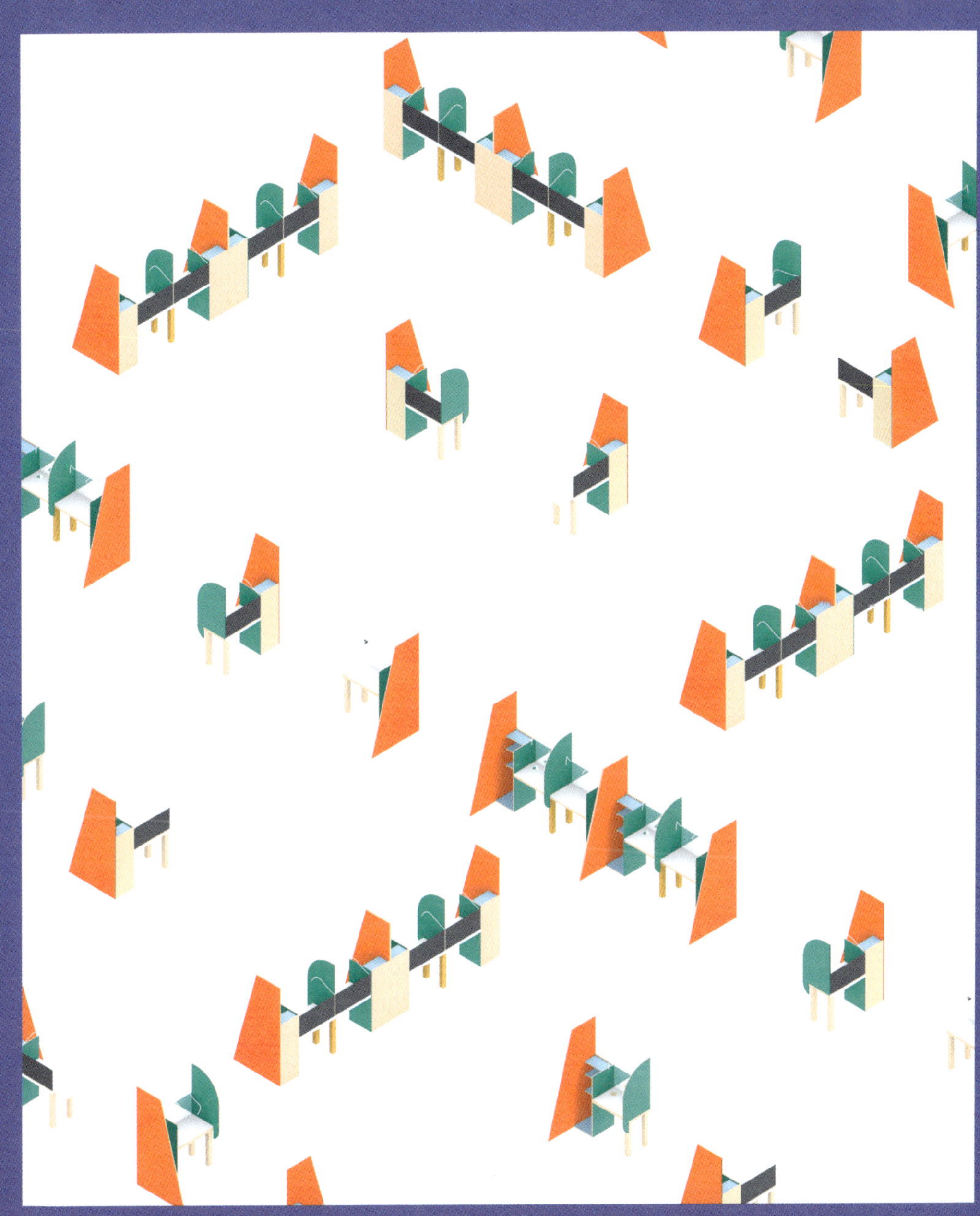

or baby laxative—and keeping Narcan preemptively nearby for administration in case of an overdose. The hopeful sequence of color is meant to provide a spatial roadmap to mechanically reproduce a safe injection every time.

*Furniture*. Photo by Andrew Santa Lucia.

## SAFETY REPRODUCED

These three applications of color encourage the architectural production of safety in a few key ways. Primarily, they function within the realms of privacy and consent, as they meet users at their own levels, abilities, usage patterns, and status imbuing a foreground for their treatment. Secondly, the colors within these design strategies intend to delineate comforting architecture, not force it to recede into the background as accent or applique. To an extent, they resist abstraction and/or reduction of the human body into a series of generalized norms—of experience, tactility, and ideals. Thirdly, these projects use color, shape, typology, and program as a form of palette cleansing. The architectural concerns are folded into specific personal iterations of drug use and drug treatment—a form of disciplinary intersectionality.

Color here amplifies the primacy of form where both formal and spatial manipulations might not be possible in favor of a progressive aesthetic palette (i.e. away from standardized health care space). The result introduces the construction of a new normal, a benchmark of architectural techniques that welcome color to reify the production of safety: a spatial corroboration of a radical social movement and an embrace of underrepresented users of architecture.

1 Pat O'Hare in their article "Merseyside, the first harm reduction conferences, and the early history of harm reduction," discusses the history of the term harm reduction and the promotion of safer drug use habits in Liverpool in the early 1980s. They state that, "The Mersey Harm Reduction Model concentrated on reducing the harms rather than, as previously was the case, trying to reduce drug use itself. This policy was given great impetus by the emergence of HIV and the danger of infection from using contaminated injection equipment. It became imperative to reduce this kind of risk behaviour by providing clean injecting equipment, prescribing methadone (and in a small percentage of cases, heroin) and by using outreach workers to go into the community and help people where they lived and to attract them into services. The police played a key role. Service uptake was rapid and included many who had never had previous contact with services. An HIV epidemic did not happen amongst injecting drug users in Mersey. In 1991, the approach was applied to the new phenomenon of the use of MDMA with the publication of the leaflet 'Chill Out'. The First International Conference on the Reduction of Drug Related Harm took place in Liverpool in 1990 as a response to the interest shown in what was happening in the region and the International Harm Reduction Association was born out of these conferences." Found in O'Hare, Pat. "Merseyside, the first harm reduction conferences, and the early history of harm reduction," in *International Journal of Drug Policy.* March 2007, vol. 8, iss. 2, pp. 141-144.

2 "Optimism is a contentious term at best, sometimes associated with concepts like hope, utopia and instrumentality. First, a key cultural difference between optimism and hope is that hope deals in particular goals/ outcomes tied to a situation, while optimism is a form of proactive engagement with the future. Second, the history of the term utopia is more closely related to the idealism of a "future without a past," which differs from the real-time agency optimism offers. In regards to both hope and utopia, Aldo Rossi's critique of naive functionalism locates the problem of idealism in the concept of function during Modernism, as a stand in or replacement to the structure and formation of architecture as a cultural, temporal and social element with a past and potentially negotiable future. It follows that architectural instrumentality is precisely the interface between discipline and culture that must be engaged when delineating a genealogy of optimism because of its ability to provide both agency to a public, as well as control of architectural effect." Found in Santa Lucia, Andrew. *Architecture's Optimism from the Critical through the Cruel to the Strange*, 2017 ACSA National Conference Proceedings. Washington: Association of Collegiate Schools of Architecture, 2017.

3 Robert Somol & Sarah Whiting, "Notes around the Doppler Effect and other Moods of Modernism," *Perspecta*, vol. 3 (2002), p. 75.

4 Onaner, Can. "Architecture as a Theater of Emancipation," in *Positions on Emancipation: Architecture between Aesthetics and Politics*. Zurich: Lars Müller Publisher, 2018.

5 Harman states that, "The sensual object is a unity over against the swirling accidents that accompany it." "The eidos is not the same as the sensual object, since different aspects of the eidos can be articulated by different statements, whereas the object itself is always unified in the manner of a rigidly designating proper name." Found in Harman, Graham. *The Quadruple Object.* Winchester: Zero Books, 2011, p. 203.

6 Ian Boghost states in Alien Phenomenology, "The practice of ontography–and it is a practice, not merely a theory–describes the many processes of accounting for the various units that strew themselves throughout the universe. To create an ontograph involves cataloging things, but also drawing attention to the couplings of and chasms between them." He writes further that Ontography is, "the study of the different possible permutations of objects and qualities." in Bogost, Ian. *Alien Phenomenology, or What It's Like to Be a Thing.* University of Minnesota Press, 2012, p. 50.

7 Sylvia Lavin states that, "The primary art historical formulations on the subject took place in the context of the debate between coloré and disegno, a conflict over whether painting should be organized around meaning or affect. This dialogue began while art theory and architecture were still intermingled and the disciplines not fully differentiated, yet architecture seems to have studiously avoided engaging the question. In fact, whether buildings have been colored or not, the discipline of architecture conceives of itself in relation to design, which is to say in relation to the logic of the drawing, of the line and of the code, all of which are historically and discursively pitted against color. Architecture so sided with disegno, so aligned its discipline with the regulations of design, that the possibilities of colore barely inflect the field, even when its buildings have been significantly colored. But the long tradition in architecture of subjugating color to meaning does not preclude the possibility of developing for architecture a less "meaningful" but more effective sense of what it can do in and through color. It only makes the embrace of the sensibility of color more new." Found in Lavin, Sylvia. "What Color Is It Now?" in *Perspecta*, vol. 35, "Building Codes," 2004, pp. 98-111.

8 The use of color in the institutionalization of modernist architectural typologies was meant to produce certain standards or normalize the experience of an institution, by highlighting the experience of modern space. Influenced by famed painter Amédé Ozenfant, Post-War architects David Medd and Olivier Cox popularized the use of architectural color, particularly Ozenfant's ideas about: the standardization of national color; how form and color were totally inseparable; and that color should be rationalized. By using the available color systems, Ostwald & Munsell, Medd and Cox developed their proprietary Archrome Range, later adopted in the 1950s by schools and universities in Great Britain. Found in Baty, Patrick. *The Anatomy of Color: The Story of Heritage Paints and Pigments.* New York: Thames & Hudson, 2017, pp. 318-330.

9 Riksman, Elina, *Paimio Color Research* 2015-Part 1 of 2. Alvar Aalto Foundation and Getty Foundation, 2015–2016. Accessed online on December 21, 2018. https://issuu.com/alvaraaltopublications/docs/appendices_cmp___colour_research_pa.

10 Bogost, Ian. Alien *Phenomenology, or What It's Like to Be a Thing.* University of Minnesota Press, 2012.

11 Harman, Graham. *The Quadruple Object.* Winchester: Zero Books, 2011.

12 Lavin, Sylvia. *Kissing Architecture.* Princeton, NJ: Princeton University Press, 2011.

13 McMorrough states that, "Paint is usually seen as a passive ground, complimenting a room's furnishings but never overpowering them." found in McMourrough, John. *"Blowing the Lid Off Paint"* Hunch 11. Rotterdam: Berlage, 2007.

14 Atwood, Andrew. *Not Interesting: On the Limits of Criticismin Architecture.* Novato, CA: Applied Research and Design Publishing, 2018.

15 Khandekar, Narayan. *Atlas Of Rare And Familiar Colour.* S.L.: Atelier Editions, 2019. Khandekar's description of turquoise coupled with the life and death of Pliny the Elder (the seeming alchemy of its steeping process and its direct geologic pigmentation being tied to painterly figuration and coloration in *An Atlas of rare Familiar Colour*) captures the difficulties of categorizing color as an orthographic exercise.

16 Safe Shape SIF." Safe Shape: A Traveling Drug Consumption Room Exhibition. Accessed December 12, 2018. http://safeshapesif.com/.

17 Ibid. (www.safeshapesif.com)

PETER
STEC

CHRONOPHOBIA



# DOM-BOTS: GHOSTED HOMES

The speed at which our environments dematerialize, at which value shifts from substance to data, is frightening.[1] The architect's definition of architecture is hollowing out, taken over by its meaning of abstract organization, as in computer architecture, or "architecting." Previously aligned with the industrial revolution of concrete and steel,[2] its inertia leaves it on the periphery of an industry shifting to mine structures of pure data.

The houses we remember, mineral and quiet, are archetypes of stasis. The solid walls isolate, dampen thermal fluctuations, and stop intrusions. The glass in the windows floats imperceptibly down, a liquid on the time scale of architecture. Structures reconfigure slowly, creakingly, to invisible forces. These houses are sinking, the difference too minute to be noticed but for the cracks in the walls.

Their advanced equipment is expected to keep our environment stable: temperature optimal, lighting compensated, fridge content constant. "The house is a machine for living in,"[3] mechanically supporting our needs. But those spaces privy to our inner secrets can pamper us and—judging from Bastide's fictional Little House[4] or Gray's Villa E.1027—even seduce us:[5] "A house is not a machine to live in, it is the shell of man, his extension, his release, his spiritual emanation."[6] The quiet spaces and inert furniture arrangements form a trusted shell that cuts our personality in half: on the outside, our public face is a collection of curated moments, patterns to be referenced socially, mediated through soundbites and works. It is a series of discrete images remixed and spun to different audiences.

Inside, the home envelops a self unswayed by vectors of public expectations. It consists of habits so ingrained they drive our routines without submitting them to memory: how to recall the breakfast from a week ago, or Monday's bedtime? This time, spent to support our deliberate actions, is dissipating without trace. These are almost perfectly black holes where little information filters across the shell: people live inside, unguarded in their actions, uncritical of their behavior, uncoached in their character.

If only those houses could remember us. They could recover the time spent sauntering. They could use our traces and make sense of our shadows on their walls. All the elements composing our domesticity, obfuscated by habit, would suddenly reappear and steer this aimless wandering.[7] They could learn our habits to assist us throughout the day, creating a gold mine of time—a data mine for architecture to regain some ground, albeit virtual.

Increasingly, those shells start to be inhabited by ghosts. Composed of mineral, and thus expected to be stable, they instead become slowly animated.[8] They sense our presence. They feel our breath.[9] They evaluate the load of visitors, register the paths of movement. Components of architecture familiar to us through a long history of iterations now start to conceal new faculties.[10] Interconnected among each other and to us, these elements embed a bargain of new material and conceptual possibilities exchanged for gathered data. Endowed with senses and language, they are, for now, welcome intruders into our sheltered domesticity. Observing everything, they learn to anticipate our wishes.[11]

Walls, doors, windows emanate an aura[12] modulating spatial properties beyond their physical presence. Air heats up locally; glass drifts in and out of transparency. The boundary of architectural components extends beyond solids to reach us through thermal radiation, sensor-triggered lighting, or scents. Programmed in a mindset reminiscent of hygienic modernism,[13] they are poised to challenge our habits towards healthier lifestyles. Between the large urban scale[14] and small personal devices, they insert the scale of interior wandering. Progressively, our spaces learn. They go beyond adjusting the tiny details of daily routines. By now, they can guess our anger or melancholy.[15] They can respond by modulating the inner atmosphere, with blazing daylight or brooding grayness, not for physical comfort but for empathy. They set a stage and are the protagonists. Gradually, they turn domesticity into a spectacle. The stage set of homeliness can be alluring: the effortless readjustment of spatial configurations to the circadian rhythm, a careful and accommodating environment, an instant transfer of preferences to dispersed living pods.

The house becomes a live assistant. It predicts our wishes and constructs our personality. *Rossum's Universal Robots* introduced the corvée, labor owed to feudal lords, into domestic spaces. Some Slavic languages designate this public work—in contrast with private pursuits—as "robota." We now introduce ghosts—to coach and entertain us—into the shells and cocoons of our private spaces. With dom-being the Indo-European root of domesticity, these could be called Dom-Bots.

Their capabilities emerge by learning from any data. They shadow each inhabitant. They're structured from daily patterns, computed in the clouds, and become increasingly efficient over time. For instance, upon visiting, or upon relocation, a parent's house may exude a strange behavior, a trace of a long symbiosis, a memory of habits indexed within the walls and floors. Gradually perhaps, that distant parent comes alive through the shell, impressing on the current inhabitants behaviors appearing as if from nowhere—perhaps they moved in to feel the waning presence of a hidden genius.

Uncovering, understanding and supporting our secret behaviors, these embedded ghosts have nevertheless an uncanny capacity to undo the homely comforts we expected them to support if, for example, a security breach forces them to flip into spying or oppressing agents.[16] But there is an ordinary threat perhaps more insidious than houses heating up malevolently or refusing to open. Once they know too much, they fulfill all our wishes instantly, without friction. We don't have the time to think of the next step and those ghosts present it without asking. Lovingly, they envelop us in their gracious cocoon, reinforcing our behavior. Nonjudgmental, they strangle us through our own bad habits.

## EVENTS AND ELEMENTS

Will spaces behave, on a scale from symbiosis to malice? Isn't the future of architecture about designing their performance in addition to form? A network of whispering architectural elements can give life to excessive spatial behaviors. The houses can turn gloomy or mischievous, extrapolate the moods of visitors, seducing them with a spatial personality. With an intensifying capacity to feel, remember, and learn, our environments will become surprising and unpredictable.

This performance is embodied, but its body is blurred. The boundlessness of effects propagating in space, attenuating or modulated, easily evades grasp. Aesthetically related to the sublime,[17] their fluctuations have to be represented as varying gradually in space and time. They must be designed and controlled as multiplicities of vectors, clouds of intensities, similar to a composition consisting of sound clouds rather than melodies.[18] In drawings, isolines emerge to denote propagating effects. Series and storyboards convey the varying phases and configurations.

But conceptually, the temporal organization of domestic events and responses remains a tabula rasa to be explored with bespoke representations.[19] Will architecture stay true to its traditional medium of space, if design, as a function of time, hints at the rich aesthetics emerging from crossbreeding with performative disciplines? Beyond mechanical responses, such an orchestration of architectural components uses temporal tropes like feedback loops and recursions, on par with spatial effects of repetition, symmetry, or embedding. It now demands an elegance of algorithmic design that is precise and deliberate.[20]

Peter Stec, *Digital collage*, 2018.

## UNIVERSAL FEELING SPACE

1. Sights, scents and sounds: Ghosts in the gallery;
2. Material weather;
3. Transient noise-cancelling wall;
4. Whispering bricks;
5. Display/view combination on demand

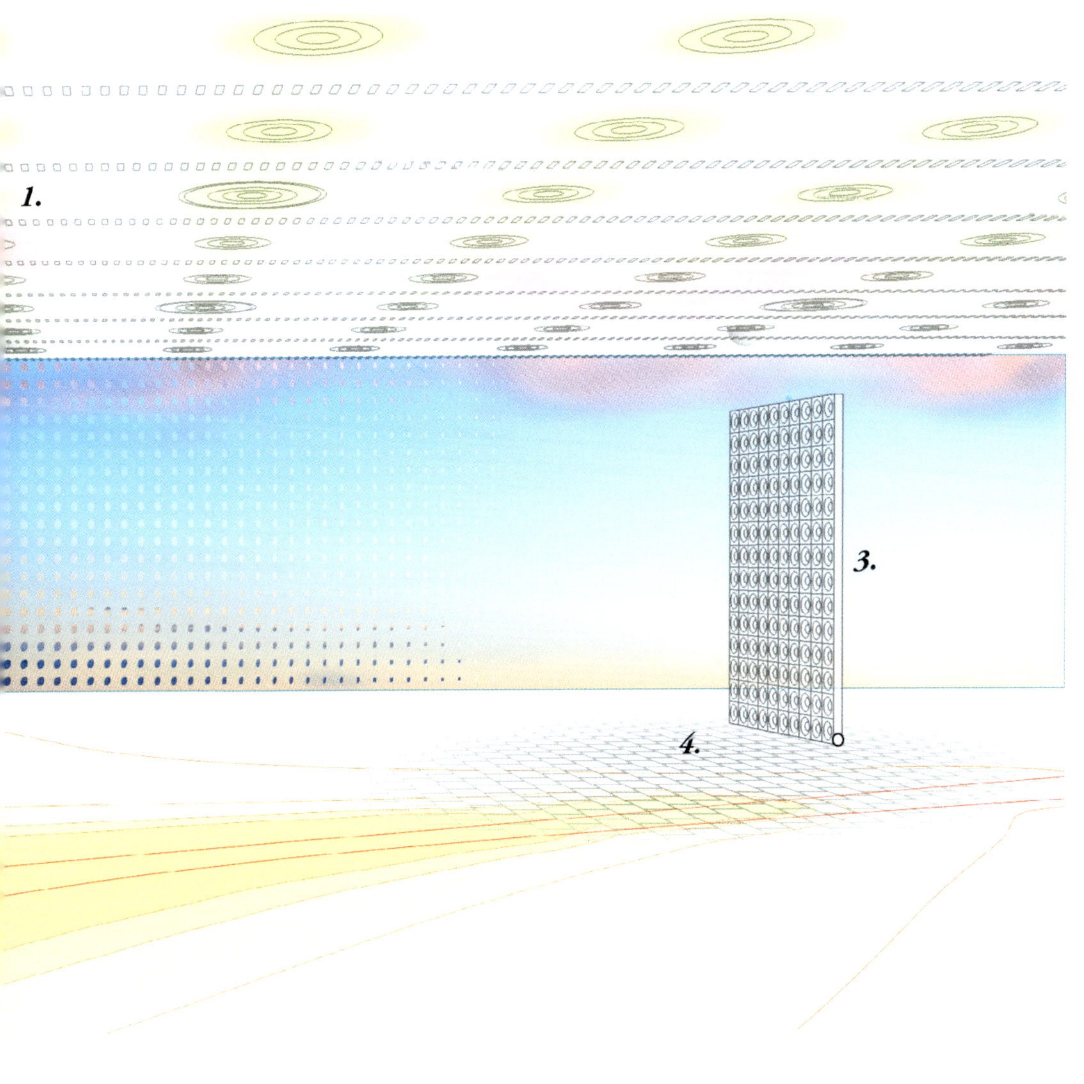

## 1. FAKE EVENT

We enter the room without noticing the inconspicuous sensors on the walls. Cupcake scent fills the air and we start to hear wine glasses rattling. Synthetic sounds of an imagined event attract everyone to an otherwise empty vortex of activity. Congregating visitors amass in increasing numbers…

While the event is fictional, the interactions of visitors are not: gradually, they frame and compare their perceptions to isolate the illusion. Suspicions of gaslighting[21] are confirmed, but the denial of psychological conclusions only heightens the sense of manipulation.

Even if uncovered, the illusion nevertheless changes the appearance of the event space. The injected smells and sounds, perceived in a state of distraction, influence by cross-modal perception[22] the impression left by the visit.

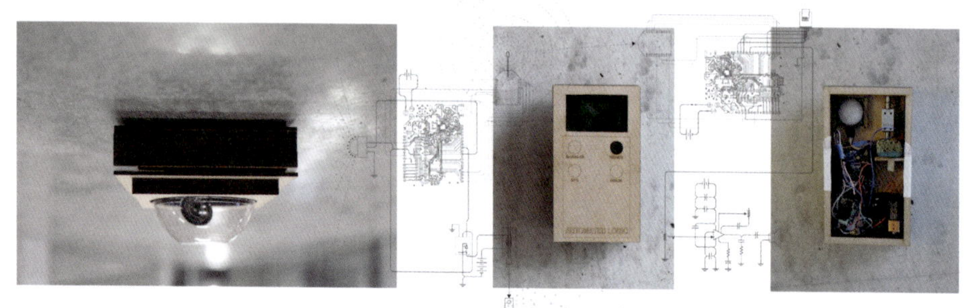

This page: Emma Boudreau and Maureen O'Brien, *Ghosts in the Gallery*, 2017. Reproduced from "Haunted Houses" seminar at Cornell AAP. Opposite and next spread: Han Zhang, *Architecture's Timelessness and Responsiveness in the Changing Seasons*, 2015. Reproduced from "In & Out" seminar at Cornell AAP.

## 2. MATERIAL WEATHER

Glass can be more than a reflected or refracted reality. Looking out, it overlays patterns of weather to come, or conditions observed across time zones. But it can also actively exploit connections between weather and moods to theatrically stage preferred weathers, or even read individual emotions and adjust the interior weather accordingly.

Having broken the need for a direct link to the building's exterior, the weather now wanders towards the entrails of spaces. In the deepest interiors, its patterns are no mere representation; acting on a large set of environmental variables, the weather elements create a daily cycle of varying humidity and temperature, controlling the dew point and injecting artificial cloud formations to create hyper-local weather conditions radically different from just a few steps beyond.

In fact, this weather is performative, supporting the emergence of a fully artificial interior landscape with specifically adjusted conditions; the plants cultivated inside, real for now, only need blue and red light. Magenta thus bathes space full of growing seedlings appearing black, only occasionally complemented by green and yellow spots appearing for the enjoyment of human passers by.

## 3. TRANSIENT WALL

To paraphrase Dalí, the least we can expect of a wall is that it should keep still.[23] But under the constant pressure of dematerialization, spatial boundaries leave the solid state behind with the invention of the air curtain or radar.[24] Through a combination of mass and nimbleness, partitions sensing our proximity may reconfigure spaces imperceptibly and gradually. Less material, they start partitioning space on demand through control of airflow, temperature gradients or active noise cancelling.

Changing their location, these itinerant walls modify the proportions and comprehension of spaces by denying those inside a fixed frame of reference.[25] Stealthy, they can cause psychological effects akin to *Zersetzung*—tactics of psychological manipulation expanded by the Stasi in East Germany to destabilize opponents by breaking into their private spaces to manipulate furniture, stocks or decorations surreptitiously.

Wachira Leangtanom, Alexander Terry, and Christopher Yi, *Movement Sensing Mobile Partition*, 2017. Reproduced from "Haunted Houses" seminar at Cornell AAP.

## 4. WHISPERING BRICKS

Spaces come alive through minute reactions to our movements—reverberating footsteps, echoing voices, and humming technology provide an ambient background situating our activities.

These tremors are perceived incidentally and add a haunting duplicity to the environment. If we are left in the dark concerning their origin,[26] the space becomes populated by doppelgängers following in our tracks.

Re-taking control, we can play those fears like a musical instrument, using building elements as keys. Our steps and touches register on transducing bricks, turning entire spaces into strange scores, creating an ambient composition by adding a structured sonic layer to the white background noise.

This page: Brad Nathanson, *Feedbrick: Resonance within the Uncanny Brick*, 2017. Reproduced from "Haunted Houses" seminar at Cornell AAP. Opposite: Martin Hejl, Peter Stec, and Ján Studený with Maroš Bátora, Ethan Davis, Martin Mikovčák, and Jan Nálepa, *Competition proposal for the Pavilion of Slovakia at the Expo 2020 Dubai*, 2018.

## 5. APPENDIX: FOREST SPIRIT

To present a land keen on its natural heritage, we propose to import a fragment of it to the 2020 Dubai Expo as a representation of an atmosphere, rather than as a literal graft. The proposal samples a deep forest and distills its essence for the visitors. It shows a highly valued ecosystem often displayed in appealing bucolic images, nevertheless quickly receding due to changes to climate and economy, gradually replaced by logistic halls and infrastructure.

For the Expo, we invert the relationship and propose a robotic hall, but one that is manufacturing a substitute landscape. Populated mostly by Automated Guiding Vehicles (AGV), it now becomes accessible to visitors, many previously oblivious to how these backbone spaces of the twenty-first century function.

The AGVs operate two types of landscape elements. Horizontal crates nurture an artificial landscape of forest seedlings well adapted for distribution to stabilize encroaching sand dunes. Vertical LED columns adopt various spatial configurations.

Forests of varying densities are captured as 3D scans. The media columns assume respective positions as ersatz trunks and display a section through the forest point cloud, scanning through as they slowly drift. The ghostly atmosphere emerges through the interaction of the virtual trunks, artificial humidity, and scintillating ambient light.

This page and next: Loom on the Moon, Peter Stec Studio, and Studený Architekti with Ethan Davis and Martin Mikovčák, *Competition for the Slovak Pavilion at the Expo 2020 in Dubai*, 2018.

1 The fear now has a name, *fomo*, of missing out on excess of information.

2 "The industrialization of the building trade is a question of materials. Consequently, a call for a new building material is its first precondition." Ludwig Mies van der Rohe, "Industrial Building," in *G: An Avant-Garde Journal of Art, Architecture, Design, and Film*, 1923–1926, eds. Detlef Mertins and Michael W. Jennings (Los Angeles: Getty Publications, 2010), pp. 120-125.

3 Le Corbusier and Jean-Louis Cohen, *Toward an Architecture* (Los Angeles: Getty Research Institute, 2009), p. 87.

4 With examples summed up by Rodolphe El-Khoury, "Introduction," in Jean-Francois de Bastide, The Little House (New York: Princeton Architectural Press, 1997), p. 33. For theatrical effects, see e.g. ibid., pp. 99-100: *"Suddenly, the table dropped down into the kitchen in the cellar, and the new table descended to take its place. It promptly filled the gap left in the flooring, protected by a balustrade of gilded iron. This feat, incredible to Mélite, roused her from self-absorption and invited her to consider anew the beauty and the ornamentation of the place that was offered for her admiration."*

5 The cipher E.1027 denoting the famous house Eileen Gray built for her lover Jean Badovici is a cryptic embrace, with respective initials replaced by their position in the alphabet: E.JB.G. About the villa and the conflict stemming from a naked Le Corbusier "tattooing" it with murals, see Beatriz Colomina, "War on Architecture: E.1027," *Assemblage*, no. 20, "Violence, Space" (April 1993), pp. 28-29.

6 As cited in Peter Adam, *Eileen Gray: Architect/Designer* (New York: Harry N. Abrams, 2000), p. 309. A shell, or a mouth: "Entering a house should be like the sensation of entering a mouth which will close behind you." Ibid., p. 217.

7 A defamiliarization potentially achieved by spatial technological devices, related to literary ones as described in Victor Shklovsky, "Art as Technique," in *Twentieth-Century Literary Theory*, ed. K. M. Newton (London: Palgrave, 1997), pp. 3-4.

8 As described with cinematic examples in Spyros Papapetros, *Malicious Houses: Animation, Animism, Animosity in German Architecture and Film—From Mies to Murnau* Grey Room 20 (Summer 2005), pp. 6–37.

9 See Omar Khan and Laura Garofalo, "Open Columns," in Bradley E. Cantrell and Justine Holzman, *Responsive Landscapes: Strategies for Responsive Technologies in Landscape Architecture* (New York: Routledge, 2015), p. 250.

10 Rem Koolhaas, "The Smart Landscape: Intelligent Architecture," *Artforum.com*. Accessed April 11, 2015. *https://www.artforum.com/print/201504/the-smart-landscape-intelligent-architecture-50735.*

11 On the uncanny of the "omnipotence of thoughts," see Sigmund Freud, "The Uncanny," *The Standard Edition of the Complete Psychological Works of Sigmund Freud*, vol. 17 (1917-1919), *An Infantile Neurosis and Other Works* (London: The Hogarth Press, 1955), pp. 217-256, 240.

12 For an elaboration of auras: Sean Lally, *The Air from Other Planets: A Brief History of Architecture to Come* (Zurich: Lars Müller Publishers, 2014), pp. 98-103.

13 Beyond homeostasis, where our environment becomes just an increasingly perfect cocoon as parodied in Jacques Tati's *"Mon Oncle,"* even the modernist vision of hygienic living spaces strived for a more proactive role of architecture providing ample sunshine and aeration to support physical activity and well-being. "Today we need a house whose structure finds accord with our bodily feeling, as it has been liberated by sports, gymnastics, and our corresponding way of life—light, transparent, flexible." Sigfried Giedion, *Befreites Wohnen* (Zurich: Orell Füssli Verlag, 1929), p. 5. Cited in Harry Francis Mallgrave, *Modern Architectural Theory: A Historical Survey*, 1673–1968 (Cambridge: Cambridge University Press, 2009), p. 264.

14 Emily Badger, "Google's Founders Wanted to Shape a City. Toronto Is Their Chance," *The New York Times*, October 20, 2017, https://www.nytimes.com/2017/10/18/upshot/taxibots-sensors-and-self-driving-shuttles-a-glimpse-at-an-internet-city-in-toronto.html.

15 By sending face snapshots for AI analysis to a cloud service such as Azure: "Face API-Facial Recognition Software | Microsoft Azure," accessed July 22, 2018, *https://azure.microsoft.com/en-us/services/cognitive-services/face/*.

16 *"One woman had turned on her air-conditioner, but said it then switched off without her touching it. Another said the code numbers of the digital lock at her front door changed every day and she could not figure out why. Still another told an abuse helpline that she kept hearing the doorbell ring, but no one was there."* Nellie Bowles, "Thermostats, Locks and Lights: Digital Tools of Domestic Abuse," *The New York Times*, June 29, 2018, *https://www.nytimes.com/2018/06/23/technology/smart-home-devices-domestic-abuse.html.*

17 Anthony Vidler, "The Architecture of the Uncanny: The Unhomely Houses of the Romantic Sublime," *Assemblage*, no. 3 (July 1987), pp. 6-29.

18 Iannis Xenakis, *Formalized Music: Thought and Mathematics in Composition* (Hillsdale: Pendragon Press, 1992), pp. 12-18.

19 A direction explored in Bernard Tschumi, *The Manhattan Transcripts* (London: Academy Editions; St. Martin's Press, 1981), or later for example in his Notation for Fireworks: Bernard Tschumi, *Architecture Concepts: Red Is Not a Color* (New York: Rizzoli, 2012), pp. 170-171.

20 Architecture now incorporates tools to evolve and optimize projects in the design phase or respond to changing parameters propagating through a chain of design steps. But beyond interaction, it did not yet find a clear use case for elegant organization algorithms similar to Google's PageRank, while machine learning already appears as the new frontier.

21 Etymologically based on Patrick Hamilton's play *Gaslight* and subsequent film adaptations, the term denotes a deceptive attempt to sow doubts in the victim's perception of reality.

22 "In contrast with the modular view of perception, and the view of vision as the dominant modality, the accumulating evidence, especially over the last several years has revealed that visual perception can both quantitatively and qualitatively be modified by the input from other modalities." Ladan Shams, Robyn Kim, "Crossmodal influences on visual perception," *Phisics of Life Reviews* , vol. 7, iss. 3 (September 2010), pp. 269-284, *https://doi.org/10.1016/j.plrev.2010.04.006.*

23 Salvador Dalí upon seeing Alexander Calder's mobiles, as cited in Kari Jormakka, *Genius Locomotionis* (Vienna: Edition Selene, 2004), p. 13.

24 Manuel DeLanda, *War in the Age of Intelligent Machines* (New York: Zone Books, 1991), p. 77.

25 "He [American perceptual psychologist James Gibson] shifted the emphasis away from the retinal image as the effective stimulus for vision [...] towards the totality of the environment, what he called an 'optic array.' According to Gibson, when we move within this array, we make sense of the world by way of relating our movement to what he called 'invariant patterns in the environment,' certain constant properties, as opposed to variant patterns, or those that move as we move. Invariants are properties or patterns that remain constant when the observer, the environment, or both change their position." The arguments are developed in Hashim Sarkis, "Constants in Motion: Le Corbusier's Rule of Movement, at the Carpenter Center," in *Perspecta 33*, The Yale Architecture Journal (Cambridge, MA: MIT Press , 2002), pp. 114-125.

26 *"The walls would be subject to faint, inexplicable tremors; strange sounds would creep along the roofs and down the gutter-sounds that our human ears might register, maybe, but whose origin remained beyond our power to fathom, even had we cared to try."* Gustav Meyrink, *The Golem*. (New York: Dover Publications, 1985), p. 16.

# Designed 2 man public

to control

ipulate

emotions

**Rubén Alcolea** (p. 108) has been deeply involved in academia, editorial work, and curation, alongside his continued professional work. In 2000 he founded his own practice, alcolea+tárrago arquitectos, which has been awarded more than twenty national and international competitions, published in specialized magazines and books, and received several architecture prizes for built work. Alcolea graduated in 2000 from the School of Architecture at La Universidad de Navarra and received his Ph.D. in 2005 with a dissertation focused on Early Modernist architecture and photography. He taught at the School of Architecture at La Universidad de Navarra–Pamplona, Spain, from 2000 to 2015, where he was vice dean for research and academic programs from 2009 to 2015. He currently teaches at Cornell University.

**Elie Boutros** (p. 122) is an architectural designer at KPF and has previously worked at firms such as Olson Kundig and RCL. His thesis, featured in the *Journal*, studies the role of memorials in Beirut, Lebanon and won the Charles Goodwin Sands Memorial Award. He received his B.Arch. from Cornell University in 2018.

**Tess Clancy** (p. 238) is a 2018 graduate of the Cornell M.Arch program and a current teaching associate. Her thesis project, *Eroding the Confederacy*, was awarded the Richmond Harold Shreve thesis prize. In addition to her M.Arch degree, Clancy holds an undergraduate degree in *Growth and Structure of Cities*, from Bryn Mawr College. Her academic interests lie at the intersection of architectural/urban history and the history of race relations in the United States.

**Stephen Duncombe** (p. 042) is Professor of Media and Culture at the Gallatin School of Individualized Study and the Department of Media, Culture and Communications at the Steinhardt School of New York University. He is the author, co-author, editor, and co-editor of six books, including *Dream: Re-Imagining Progressive Politics in an Age of Fantasy; White Riot: Punk Rock and the Politics of Race*; and *(Open) Utopia*. Duncombe is also the creator of the *Open Utopia*, an open-access, open-source, web-based edition of Thomas More's *Utopia*, and co-creator of Actipedia.org, a user-generated digital database of creative activism case studies.

**Ignacio Galán** (p. 164) is a New York based architect, historian, and educator concerned with the role of architecture in the articulation of societies. His scholarship addresses the relationship between architecture, politics, and media, with a particular focus on nationalism, colonialism, and diverse forms of population transience. His research has led to the production of several publications and exhibitions including the installation *Cinecittá Occupata* for the 2014 Venice Biennale prior to joining the Department of Architecture at Barnard+Columbia Colleges in 2016. Galán taught studios and seminars at Columbia GSAPP and PennDesign and served as an assistant instructor at Harvard GSD, Princeton SOA, and ETSAM.

**Wachira Leangtanom** (p. 274) received a Master of Architecture from Cornell University in 2018 and a Bachelor of Science in Architecture from Chulalongkorn University in Bangkok. Her thesis won a Richmond Harold Shreve Thesis Award for Excellence and Originality. She is currently working as a junior designer at MdeAS Architects in New York City.

**Thom Mayne** (p. 012) is an architect and educator. In 1972 he co-founded both the interdisciplinary practice Morphosis and the architecture school SCI-Arc. He is a professor of architecture and urban design at UCLA, and has taught at Columbia, Yale, Harvard, the Berlage Institute, the Bartlett, and Cornell (in both Ithaca and New York City). For Cornell, he's designed both the Bill & Melinda Gates Hall in Ithaca and the Emma & Georgina Bloomberg Center at Cornell Tech in New York. His awards include a Rome Prize, a National Design Award from the Cooper Hewitt, the MacDowell Medal, the AIA Gold Medal, and the Pritzker Prize.

**Mark Morris** (p. 026) is currently the Head of Teaching and Learning at the Architectural Association in London, England, where he works with staff and students on diverse curricular objectives across the School and teaches within History and Theory Studies. He completed his M.Arch. at Ohio State University where he received the AIA Henry Adams medal, and took his Ph.D. at the London Consortium supported by the RIBA Research Trust. His research focuses on questions of visual representation in the context of the history of architectural education. Mark previously taught architectural theory and design at Cornell University where he served as Coordinator of Post-Professional Degree Programmes, Director of Graduate Studies, and Director of Exhibitions. He is the author of two books: *Models: Architecture and the Miniature* and *Automatic Architecture*. Mark represents the AA at the Higher Education Academy and London Higher Directors Group.

**Jonathan Ochshorn** (p. 074) is a registered architect whose teaching specialties are in the areas of construction technology and structures. Prior to joining the faculty at Cornell in 1988, he taught at City College of New York while serving as associate director of the City College Architectural Center, a research center supplying technical assistance to community groups in New York City. Since 1976, he also has practiced architecture and urban design in New York and California. Ochshorn's academic background is in structural engineering (M.I.T.) and urban design (M.U.P., City College of New York), as well as architecture (B.Arch. '75, Cornell).

**Caroline O'Donnell** (p. 284) is the Edgar A. Tafel Professor of Architecture and Director of the M.Arch. program at Cornell University. Her research and teaching areas are in ecological and contextual design, as well as in nonlinear materiality. She is a licensed architect, and sole principal of CODA, and winner of MoMA/PS1's Young Architects Program in 2013 with the project Party Wall. O'Donnell was the editor of the *Cornell Journal of Architecture* issues 8–10 and founding editor of *Pidgin magazine*. Her first book, *Niche Tactics: Generative Relationships between Architecture and Site*, was published by Routledge in April 2015. O'Donnell has previously taught at Harvard GSD and at the Irwin S. Chanin School of Architecture at The Cooper Union.

From Northern Ireland, she received her B.Arch. (specialization in bioclimatics) from the Manchester School of Architecture, England and her M.Arch.II from Princeton University.

**Erin Pelligrino** (p. 212) is a visiting critic in architecture at AAP and founder of the studio Make, Think, Design. The work focuses on small-scale design/build interventions, rich with contextual relationships and material expression. Her most recent work is a series of renovations of modernist structures on Martha's Vineyard. In 2018, NCARB named her a Scholar of Professional Practice, for professional focus on the future of the practice of architecture and design. In 2016, Pellegrino completed Alpine Shelter Skuta, a collaborative realization of a mountaineering shelter in the Alps of Slovenia. She gained experience in the offices of Tod Williams Billie Tsien Architects and Studio Gang, honing a focus on craft, rigor, and quality. She holds a B.Arch. from Cornell University, as well as an M.Arch.II and M.B.A. from Harvard University.

**Helena Rong** (p. 258) is an architectural designer whose interests include urban design, computation, and the role of technology in shaping future cities. Her numerous awards include the Charles Goodwin Sands Memorial Silver Award for her undergraduate thesis investigating a redevelopment of São Paulo, the KPF Travel Fellowship, and MIT Office of the Dean for Graduate Education Ida M. Green Fellowship. She holds a B.Arch from Cornell University ('17) and S.M.Arch.S. in Architecture and Urbanism from MIT ('19).

**Richard Rosa** (p. 086) received a Bachelor of Architecture degree from Syracuse University and a Master of Architecture from Harvard University where he was awarded the Faculty Design Award. He is a fellow of the American Academy in Rome where he was the recipient of the Katherine E. Gordon Rome Prize in Architecture in 1998. Rosa is a tenured associate professor at the Syracuse University School of Architecture where from 2012-2016 he served as Director of the Syracuse University Florence Architecture Program. He has served as the Ralf E. Hawkins Visiting Distinguished Professor at UT Arlington and has held full-time positions at the University of Virginia, Harvard University, and Cornell University where he currently serves as a Visiting Associate Professor. His current work includes *The DNA of OMA*, a book deciphering the cultural historical sources and layered trajectory of the work of OMA and Rem Koolhaas. Other works include, *Desk Crit Diaries*, a book tracing the tactics and evolution of design education drawing published in the fall of 2019 and *The F Word*, a publication extending analytical insight on the relationship between formal structure and narrative content.

**Danny Salamoun** (p. 058) is currently a Designer at Machado Silvetti. Salamoun grew up between Saudi Arabia and Lebanon, migrating to California in 2006. He received his Bachelor of Arts in Architecture from the University of California, Berkeley, and his Masters of Architecture from Cornell University. He is a recipient of the Robert James Eidlitz Travel Fellowship and the Richmond Harold Shreve award for his graduate thesis at Cornell.

**Andrew Santa Lucia** (p. 300) is a Cuban American architect, activist and critic based in Portland, Oregon, whose work engages the myriad ways that the architectural discipline mediates culture. Andrew directs Office Andorus, a practice that develops architectural research and design speculations as well as exhibition curation and installation. He is also a partner at Asquared Buildings and Objects based in Chicago and Portland. His current research, *Strange Optimism*, develops a discourse between culture and shape, linking Jacques Rancière's theories on critical art to an optimistic architectural instrumentality that affects public participation. He is currently the Assistant Professor of Practice at Portland State University.

**Peter Stec** (p. 318) founded his firm, Peter Stec Studio, in 2013. His firm recently won and completed a boarding school master plan and has placed in other urban competitions. The practice is interlaced with academic research, such as a recently completed Fulbright Advanced Research Fellowship at Rice University, and studios previously completed at the Academy of Fine Arts and Design in Slovakia. These works continually explore process as an architectural medium through interactive spatial installations, animated and evolutionary design, dynamic urban planning, and the representation of design memory. Stec holds a diploma from the University of Applied Arts in Vienna and a master's degree in architecture from Princeton University.

**Warisara Sudswong** (p.134) is an architectural designer influenced by her international experiences in Thailand, Japan, and New York City. Prior to pursuing her graduate degree at AAP, she worked at Kohn Pedersen Fox Associates in New York City, with a focus on airport design and super tower projects. She earned a bachelor of science in architecture and design degree from Chulalongkorn University in Bangkok, Thailand. She was a teaching associate for Design I + II at Cornell University and is currently practicing at Lehman Smith McLeish in Washington D.C.

**Marrikka Trotter** (p. 180) is an architectural historian and theorist whose research examines the historical intersections between geology, architecture, agriculture, and landscape in the eighteenth and nineteenth centuries. She is co-editor of the contemporary architectural theory collections *Architecture at the Edge of Everything Else* (The MIT Press: 2010) and *Architecture is All Over* (Columbia Books on Architecture and the City: 2017), and her writing has appeared in publications such as Harvard Design Magazine, Log, and AA Files. She received her PhD from Harvard University in 2017, and her work has received funding from the Paul Mellon Centre, the Graham Foundation, the Canadian Centre for Architecture, and Sir John Soane's Museum, among others. She is a full-time faculty member at SCI-Arc, where she coordinates the history and theory curriculum.

**Philip Ursprung** (p. 198) studied art history, history, and german literature in Geneva, Vienna, and Berlin and has taught at various institutions such as the Université de Genève, ETH Zürich, Universität Basel, and Columbia University. He currently teaches history of art and architecture courses at ETH Zürich where he has also been Dean of the Architecture Department since 2017 and Chair for the History of Art and Architecture. In 2013, he was awarded the Golden Owl for excellent teaching by the student association of ETH Zürich and in 2017, the Prix Meret Oppenheim by the Swiss Federal Office of Culture.

**Frank Wang** (p. 226) Earned his B. Arch. from Cornell in 2018. He works as an architectural designer at June14 Meyer-Grohbrügge in Berlin, Germany, and has recently been participating as a guest critic for graduate studios focusing on temporal synchronicity at DIA Dessau. At Cornell University, he was the recipient of the William S. Downing Prize for his undergraduate thesis project on the potential of commonality in a Nazi airport. His research gravitates toward urban rituals, landscape anomalies, and dirty things.

**Michael Young** (p. 146) is an architect and educator practicing in New York City where he is a founding partner of the architectural design studio Young & Ayata. Young & Ayata was awarded one of two first prizes in the international competition for the New Bauhaus Museum in Dessau, Germany, and received the Young Architects Prize from Architectural League of New York. Michael has taught design studios and seminars at Yale, Princeton, Columbia, Syracuse, Pratt, and Innsbruck University. In addition to practice and teaching, Michael is invested in writing and research in relation to the confluence of geometry, representation, and aesthetics. Michael earned his M.Arch. II degree from Princeton University and his B.Arch. from Cal Poly San Luis Obispo. He is a registered architect in the State of New York.

**Sasa Zivkovic** (p. 296) is an assistant professor in the Department of Architecture at Cornell University where he directs the Robotic Construction Laboratory (RCL), an interdisciplinary research group investigating robotic-based construction technologies such as additive concrete manufacturing and robotic wood construction. Zivkovic is co-principal of H.A.N.N.A.H, an experimental architecture practice based in Ithaca, New York. In December 2018, H.A.N.N.A.H was named a Next Progressive by *Architect Magazine* and recently completed a 3D-printed Guard House in Suzhou, China; a pro bono Modular Dental Clinic in Ladakh, India; and a 3D-printed Corbel Cabin in Ithaca, New York.

# IMAGE CREDITS

|  |  |
|---|---|
| Cover | Luben Dimcheff. *Untitled*. 2019. Courtesy of the artist |
| 013–19 | Courtesy of Thom Mayne |
| 028-032 | Courtesy of the Library of Congress |
| 033 | Courtesy of Val Warke |
| 034 | Courtesy of the Library of Congress |
| 036-037 | Courtesy of Sam Jacobs |
| 040 | Courtesy of Denise Nestor |
| 043 | Courtesy of © Punin Archive, St Petersburg |
| 044 | Public domain |
| 045 | Courtesy of © Punin Archive, St Petersburg |
| 049-052 | Public domain |
| 054 | Courtesy of Mark Clayton |
| 055 | Courtesy of Steve Lambert |
| 062-063 | Courtesy of Danny Salamoun |
| 066 | Public domain |
| 067 | Courtesy of Danny Salamoun |
| 068 | Courtesy of AP Photo/Spencer Platt |
| 070-072 | Courtesy of Danny Salamoun |
| 076 | Courtesy of Jonathan Ochshorn |
| 077-079 | Image courtesy of Jonathan Ochshorn |
| 084 | Courtesy of Peter Eisenman Architects, image courtesy of Jonathan Ochshorn; Courtesy of © Collection Frac Centre/ Philippe Magnon, image courtesy of Jonathan Ochshorn |
| 089 | Image courtesy of Richard Rosa; Ibid. |
| 090 | Courtesy of Rizzoli International, image courtesy of Richard Rosa; Courtesy of OMA, image courtesy of Richard Rosa |
| 092 | Image courtesy of Richard Rosa; Courtesy of © J. Paul Getty Trust.Getty Research Institute, Los Angeles (2004.R.10), image courtesy of Richard Rosa; Ibid. |
| 093 | Courtesy of *El Croquis*, image courtesy of Richard Rosa; Courtesy of Pedro Kok, image courtesy of Richard Rosa |
| 094 | Courtesy of *El Croquis*, image courtesy of Richard Rosa; image courtesy of Richard Rosa |
| 096 | Courtesy of Eugenio Aglietti, image courtesy of Richard Rosa; Image courtesy of Richard Rosa |
| 098 | Image courtesy of Richard Rosa; Courtesy of OMA, image courtesy of Richard Rosa; Courtesy of © www. aviewoncities.com, image courtesy of Richard Rosa |
| 101 | Images courtesy of Richard Rosa |
| 103 | Courtesy of Richard Rosa; Public domain; Courtesy of Menno Janssen, image courtesy of Richard Rosa |
| 105 | Courtesy of Steve Silverman, image courtesy of Richard Rosa; Courtesy of Richard Rosa |
| 109 | Courtesy of the Art Museums and Art Gallery, Birmingham, public domain |
| 110-111 | Courtesy of Photo © Tate |
| 113 | Courtesy of © Tullie House Museum, image courtesy of Rubén Alcolea; Image courtesy of Rubén Alcolea, public domain; Courtesy of The Louvre, public domain |
| 114 | Courtesy of the Metropolitan Museum of Art, public domain; Courtesy of The Louvre, public domain |
| 116 | Courtesy of the Library of Congress, image courtesy of Rubén Alcolea; Courtesy of © Edmund Teske Archives / Laurence Bump and Nils Vidstrand, 2001 |
| 119-120 | Image courtesy of Rubén Alcolea |
| 124-133 | Courtesy of Elie Boutros |
| 135-145 | Courtesy of Warisara Sudswong |
| 147 | Courtesy of © 2019 Artists Rights Society (ARS), New York/ VG Bild- Kunst, Bonn, image courtesy of Michael Young |
| 153 | Courtesy of Philipp Schaerer |
| 158 | Courtesy of Ruy/Klein |
| 164–177 | Courtesy of Jacob A. Riis / Museum of the City of New York. 90.13.4.153, image courtesy of Ignacio Galan |
| 180 | Courtesy of the National Gallery of Scotland |
| 183 | Courtesy of © Sir John Soane's Museum, London; Image courtesy of Marrikka Trotter |
| 184 | Courtesy of © Sir John Soane's Museum, London |
| 186 | Courtesy of the National Gallery of Scotland |
| 190 | Courtesy of Sir Robert Clerk Bt. of Penicuik |
| 191 | Image courtesy of Marrikka Trotter; Courtesy of the National Gallery of Scotland |
| 192 | Image courtesy of Marrikka Trotter; Courtesy of the National Gallery of Scotland; Image courtesy of Marrikka Trotter |
| 194 | Image courtesy of Marrikka Trotter |
| 199 | Courtesy of Hannah Higgins, image courtesy of Philip Ursprung |
| 201 | Courtesy of Galerie Buchholz Berlin/Cologne |
| 202-206 | Image courtesy of Philip Ursprung |
| 208 | Image courtesy of Philip Ursprung; Courtesy of © Holt/ Smithson Foundation / VAGA at Artists Rights Society (ARS), NY |
| 217-221 | Courtesy of Maria Yue Ma, image courtesy of Erin Pellegrino |
| 222-223 | Courtesy of Hallie Black, image courtesy of Erin Pellegrino |
| 224-225 | Courtesy of Isabella Hübsch and Chirstina Zau, image courtesy of Erin Pellegrino |
| 228-231 | Image courtesy of Frank Wang, public domain |
| 232 | Courtesy © Copyright 2019 Cape Concrete, image courtesy of Frank Wang |
| 233 | Image courtesy of Frank Wang, public domain; Courtesy of © 2019 Rogers Partners, image courtesy of Frank Wang |
| 236-237 | Image courtesy of Frank Wang, public domain |
| 241 | Courtesy of Smithsonian Libraries, public domain, image courtesy of Tess Clancy; Courtesy of Tess Clancy |
| 242-254 | Courtesy of Tess Clancy |
| 259-273 | Courtesy of Helena Rong |
| 276-283 | Courtesy of Wachira Leangtanom |
| 287-290 | Image courtesy of Caroline O'Donnell |
| 297 | Courtesy of Sasa Zivkovic |
| 304 | Image courtesy of Andrew Santa Lucia, public domain |
| 308-310 | Image courtesy of Andrew Santa Lucia |
| 311-312 | Image courtesy of Andrew Santa Lucia, public domain |
| 313-316 | Courtesy of Andrew Santa Lucia |
| 322-323 | Courtesy of Peter Stec |
| 324 | Courtesy of Emma Boudreau and Maureen O'Brien, image courtesy of Peter Stec |
| 325-327 | Courtesy of Han Zhang, image courtesy of Peter Stec |
| 329 | Wachira Leangtanom, Alexander Terry, and Christopher Yi, image courtesy of Peter Stec |
| 330 | Courtesy of Brad Nathanson, image courtesy of Peter Stec |
| 331-332 | Courtesy of Martin Hejl, Peter Stec, and Ján Studený, image courtesy of Peter Stec |
| 334-335 | Courtesy of Loom on the Moon, Peter Stec Studio, and Studený Architekti, image courtesy of Peter Stec |

Department of Architecture
College of Architecture, Art, and Planning
139 E. Sibley Hall
Ithaca, NY 14853
U.S.A.
Tel: (607) 255-5236
cornelljournalofarchitecture.cornell.edu
cjoa@cornell.edu

Chair, Department of Architecture
Andrea Simitch

Editor-in-Chief
Val Warke (B.Arch 1997)

Managing Editor
Hallie Black (B.Arch. '19)
Aya Mears (B.Arch. '18)

Assistant Managing Editor
Eliana Drier (M.Arch. '18)

Submission Editors
Tess Clancy (M.Arch. '18)
Shruti Shah (B.Arch. '20)

Editorial Participants
Seo Yun Bang (B.Arch. '20)
Rachael Biggane (B.Arch. '19)
Ottavia Boletto (B.Arch. '19)
Catherine Breen (M.Arch. '20)
Mwanzaa Brown (M.Arch. '19)
Zachary Calbo-Jackson (B.Arch. '19)
Samuel Capps (M.Arch. '18)
Lin Sen Chai (M.Arch. '21)
Ibrahim Desooky (B.Arch. '18)
Ouping Ding (B.Arch. '19)
Alexandra Donovan (B.Arch. '18)
Lucy Flieger (B.Arch. '19)
Brian Havener (M.Arch. '18)
Shinhyuk Kim (B.Arch. '18)
MuZe Li (B.Arch. '20)
Sibei Li (M.Arch. '18)
Sumi Li (B.Arch. '20)
Allan Mezhibovsky (B.Arch '22)
Melanie Monastirsky (M.Arch. '18)
Ellen Park (M.Arch. '19)
Ian Pica Limbaseanu (B.Arch. '19)
Jing Wei Qian (B.Arch. '20)
Sasson Rafailov (B.Arch. '18)
David Rosenwasser (B.Arch. '18)
Shovan Shah (M.Arch. '18)
Jacob Soley (B.S. URS '20)
Beth Tesfaye (B.Arch. '18)
Jiaying Wei (B.Arch. '20)
Cheryl Xu (M.Arch. '18)
Yilin Zhang (M.Arch. '18)
Anqing Zhu (M.Arch. '18)
Yuheng Zhu (B.Arch. '20)

With special contributions by
Katherine Chen (B.Arch. '18)
Luciana Ruiz (B.Arch. '19)
Lawrence Wyman (M.Arch. '18)

Design
Studio Elana Schlenker

Printing
Ofset Yapımevi, Turkey

Our appreciation to:

The special guests in the seminar "Architectural Publications: CJoA11," Julia van den Hout, Kyle May, Elana Schlenker, and Caroline O'Donnell, whose insights and perspectives were essential in the development of this journal.

The students and faculty of the Department of Architecture at Cornell and in the College of Architecture, Art, and Planning, whose advice and support motivates the substance of this effort.

All of those who contributed to this journal, for their commitment, efforts, and patience.

And especially, to the memory of Mrs. Ruth Thomas, whose belief in the importance of speaking, writing, and publishing architecture, and whose support in honor of her son, Preston Thomas, continues to provide the funding and inspiration without which this journal and its predecessors would never have been possible.

# COLOPHON